Books by Mary Van Rensselaer Thayer

Hui-Lan Koo (Madame Wellington Koo)
an Autobiography as told to Mary Van Rensselaer Thayer
Jacqueline Bouvier Kennedy
Jacqueline Kennedy: The White House Years

Arriving at Union Station to greet King Hassan of Morocco.

Jacqueline Kennedy
The White House Years

Mary Van Rensselaer Thayer

Little, Brown and Company   Boston   Toronto

LIBRARY OF CONGRESS CATALOG CARD NO. 78–121429

T04/71

Third Printing

Sections of this book first appeared in *McCall's* magazine.

Lines from "The Gift Outright" from *The Poetry of Robert Frost*, edited by Edward Connery Lathem, are reprinted by permission of Holt, Rinehart and Winston, Inc. Copyright 1942 by Robert Frost. Copyright © 1970 by Lesley Frost Ballantine.

Published simultaneously in Canada
by Little, Brown & Company (Canada) Limited

PRINTED IN THE UNITED STATES OF AMERICA

TO
JOHN FITZGERALD KENNEDY
THIRTY-FIFTH PRESIDENT OF THE UNITED STATES
AND HIS WIFE
JACQUELINE

Foreword

About a year and a half after the death of President Kennedy, an Arab ambassador who was my friend wished to make a contribution to the John Fitzgerald Kennedy Library. He had never met the widow of the President and as he was anxious to make the gift personally, in the name of the Ruler of his state, the ambassador asked if I could arrange the presentation. Mrs. Kennedy had never accepted contributions for the library directly from the donors. But because she had known me a long time and was aware of my interest in Arab countries, and perhaps because I had written the biography of her youthful years, she agreed to receive the ambassador.

The brief and mutually satisfactory ceremony took place in her New York apartment. After the ambassador had taken his leave, I remained with Mrs. Kennedy. We talked for a long time in a relaxed way, mostly about the White House and Washington. I listened delightedly as she switched casually from highlights to amusing inconsequentials. Though she had left Washington months before, obviously forever, the sharpness of her impressions had not dimmed and it seemed as though we were viewing this private drama with exceptional clarity through the small end of a telescope. I became aware that in her own way she was spinning an absorbing story of her days in the White House.

Until this pleasant meeting I had never realized or even imagined the scope and extraordinary variety of events which had crowded her brief span as First Lady. Nor had I really comprehended the skillful organizational ability and unceasing behind-the-scenes work which had made Mrs. Kennedy's White House tenure so memorable. I recalled that, of the thirty First Ladies who preceded Jacqueline Kennedy, many presided over the White House for eight years, yet few had left any lasting impression on history. And only a very few had made any notable contribution to the White House itself.

I determined that the history of Jacqueline Kennedy's White House years should be set down. It should be a sequel to *Jacqueline Bouvier Kennedy,* my earlier book which had encompassed the thirty-one years from the summer day of her birth until the wintry afternoon when she became the thirty-first First Lady of our land. This second book would pick up the thread of narrative from that gala inauguration day to the sad noon when, as widow of the thirty-fifth President of the United States, Jacqueline Kennedy left the great mansion which she had made so beautiful.

I wrote to Mrs. Kennedy to ask whether she was interested in my idea and if she would help me as she had done before. She replied she was interested and would help me.

The first book, *Jacqueline Bouvier Kennedy,* had evolved in an unusual way. When John Fitzgerald Kennedy was elected to the Presidency, the general public knew very little about his wife. As a newspaperwoman I believed that an accurate account of the future First Lady's background should be written. As a family friend I telephoned her in Hyannis Port a day or so after the election to suggest that I undertake such an assignment. Though Mrs. Kennedy deplored the idea as an intrusion on her cherished privacy, she agreed her story should be told. And when she returned from Hyannis Port she lent me, on a "for your eyes only" understanding, her scrapbooks, a wealth of delightful family letters and her personal photographs, many of which had never been published. When a Secret Service agent brought this mass of fascinating material to my house I realized, with a sense of shock, that Jackie Kennedy was no longer a private person.

I had scarcely commenced outlining what was to be a series of three articles when, unexpectedly, John Jr. was born a month early. There was so much I had to know, so many questions I needed to ask but I could not telephone to Mrs. Kennedy in the hospital. Instead, I jotted down countless questions which the Secret Service obligingly relayed to the hospital and then returned with the answers, often written in pencil and always by hand on her favorite stationery; large, blue-lined, yellow legal pads.

That winter of 1960–61, when the Kennedys retreated to Palm Beach, I airmailed questions and my finished copy was picked up, usually by Mugsie, an all-purpose family retainer, who delivered it to the daily courier plane which connected the President-elect in his Florida headquarters with his multiple Washington concerns. The manuscript had to be completed before Mrs. Kennedy assumed her White House duties. Happily, the President-elect, a successful author himself, acting as editor, made only four minor corrections. So the first of the magazine series, which was published in the *Ladies' Home Journal,* miraculously appeared on newsstands on the day of the Inauguration. The book *Jacqueline Bouvier Kennedy* was published later by Doubleday.

Obviously, chronicling Mrs. Kennedy's White House years would prove more difficult and time consuming than writing the uncomplicated story of her girlhood. I followed, in part, the same written question and answer procedure. Mrs. Kennedy, now having mastered the art of dictating, not only replied with her usual generosity but also suggested people to contact and many other less obvious sources of information.

Some of these sources proved uniquely difficult to pursue. For instance, Mrs. Kennedy gave me access to her personal files which contained her White House memoranda. They were kept in the Park Avenue office rented by the government while she was winding up her White House affairs. There was no Xerox machine and I did not dare risk duplicating any of these documents outside the office. So I sat at my typewriter for two hot summer weeks copying such papers as I believed were necessary. To find the basic facts about both the redecoration of the White House private living quarters and the initial moves in Mrs. Kennedy's White House Restoration, I needed to examine the pertinent bills and correspondence of Mrs. Henry Parish, the New York decorator primarily involved in these projects. Mrs. Parish, a very busy woman, tumbled them into paper shopping bags and allowed me to spend a Labor Day weekend in her apartment, winnowing through this special accumulation. In the Presidential Library, which is housed in the National Archives, I spent over two months reading tens of thousands of newspaper and magazine clippings from every corner of the world, all about Mrs. Kennedy.

An incredible number of people had information, of both

great and lesser importance, to contribute either about the White House itself or the activities of President Kennedy and his wife. There were distinguished gentlemen like Dr. Leonard Carmichael, then Secretary of the Smithsonian Institution, and Senator Clinton Anderson of New Mexico, a Smithsonian Regent; both of whom, in different ways, were responsible for the planning and subsequent legislation which obtained the vital museum status for the White House. There were the Park Service officials, both National and Capital, such as Conrad Wirth and Nash Castro, who offered complex budgetary details of White House management. In the White House itself, there were the three gold-aiguilletted and charming Presidential Military Aides: Ted Clifton, Godfrey McHugh and Taze (Tazewell) Shepard of the Army, Air Force and Navy respectively, who were so knowledgeable about both the President's activities and Mrs. Kennedy's social functions.

I interviewed, informally, many members of the White House working staff: from Trapes Bryant, the electrician who on his own time cosseted the Kennedy dogs; to Rusty Young, the florist who created the imaginative Flemish-type flower arrangements which Mrs. Kennedy preferred; and, in the East Wing offices, Sandy Fox, the perfectionist calligrapher who was responsible for the dignified cachet of White House social invitations. Providencia Parades, Mrs. Kennedy's personal maid, took time after office hours on her new job to come to my house to talk about her "beloved lady" and show me the large account books in which she had listed so efficiently the clothing and accessories needed by the First Lady on her various state visits.

I flew to Chicago where Tish Baldridge, always so wonderfully kind, between sessions of tape recording fed me a delicious Sunday luncheon which she had cooked herself. With my tape recorder I winged down to Palm Beach where Mrs. Charles Wrightsman, at Mrs. Kennedy's request, put me up overnight in her exquisite palace. I undertook shorter sallies to Delaware and Harry du Pont at his museum Winterthur; to Newport to talk to Mrs. George Henry Warren, who initiated the restoration of that historic old town; and to New York where I spent delightfully informative hours with Jim Fosburgh, Chairman of the former First Lady's Paintings Committee, and with Mrs. Paul Mellon, who through great affection for Mrs. Kennedy had made extraordinarily valuable contributions to the White House, both as a connoisseur of art and as a working horticulturist of great knowledge and distinction.

When I interviewed those whom I did not know personally, Pamela Turnure, Mrs. Kennedy's press secretary, made the appointments to underscore the honesty of my intent.

In Washington, intimate friends of both the President and Mrs. Kennedy were unstintingly patient with me. Charlie Bartlett, who had so much to tell, suggested that I use a tape recorder. On my first attempt at mechanization, the recording tape ran out unnoticed as I listened to Angier Biddle Duke, the Chief of Protocol in the Kennedy administration. Some of his more intriguing tales of upper strata White House social activities have therefore been lost to posterity unless he writes his own memoirs. I sat hour after hour in Bill Walton's Victorian parlor and, after years of friendship, we discovered that we had both met Jack Kennedy the same day, the same place, many, many years before. Another friend of long standing, Ed Foley, who had been Chairman of the Kennedy Inaugural Committee, made available to me delightful anecdotes about the Inauguration to which Senator Sparkman, Chairman of the Joint Congressional Inaugural Committee, and his wife, also made a notable contribution. Rowland Evans, the political columnist, though he may write a book of his own about the Kennedy era, generously shared with me his remembrances of luncheon with the President-elect at Bill Walton's house on the day before the Inauguration.

There were four people without whose untiring assistance I could never have completed my difficult, though self-imposed, assignment. The Chief Usher of the White House, J. Bernard West, was the tower of strength on which I far too often depended. I not only badgered him during office hours but also telephoned him at home, spoiling his evening leisure and interrupting his weekends at every conceivable time. He knew everything, knew everybody, and never once lost his humorous cool with me. His wife, Zella, also put up with me far beyond the demands of normal friendship. James Rowe Ketchum, the young, able and brilliantly knowledgeable White House Curator, answered every one of an astronomical number of questions. He also escorted me on personal tours, provided me with photographs and checked, over and over, the numberless facts with which I had to cope.

Nancy Tuckerman and Pamela Turnure backed me at every turn. There was nothing I needed that they did not find. There was no one I wanted to see that they did not persuade to see me. They were the liaison between Mrs. Kennedy and my requests for information, both minor and major. They were always calm, unruffled and amazingly affectionate.

Then there was Jackie Kennedy. There were so many hours of her busy life which she could have filled more enjoyably than in answering my unceasing questions. But she never failed to answer a single one. She made so much of hers that was personal and private available to me. She offered me every opportunity, then let me go my own way.

Mary Van Rensselaer Thayer
Washington, D.C.

Contents

Contents

Contents

Illustrations

List of Illustrations

Prologue

"Which do you like best?" asked Jacqueline Kennedy. Smiling, she held out two supple bands of diamonds toward the men waiting in the hall below. Then she walked down the stairs of the little Georgetown house; the necklaces swayed and sparkled as she moved. "The one with the green stones!" her husband decided instantly. Their friend Bill Walton, who stood beside him, agreed: the emerald-threaded necklace complemented her white silk gown, he thought. Neither had seen the necklaces before. An admiring jeweler had lent them to the Senator's wife to give added delight to the starry evenings ahead.

That January night the narrow hallway and steep stairs of the N Street townhouse were warm, bright and familiar; but when the front door opened, it was as if a curtain had been drawn aside upon some improbable melodrama. Huge snowflakes fluttered down, graceful but relentless. On the sidewalk huddled a knot of diehard fans, their heads and shoulders powdered with snow. At the opening of the door the fans broke into a ragged cheer; a split second later the motorcycle police escort around the Senator's waiting limousine revved their engines with a shattering roar; on the doorstep a Secret Service agent opened a giant black umbrella; and with a rush the impatient cameramen closed in.

A sudden stab of flashbulbs tipped the snowflakes with shimmering opalescence as Mrs. Kennedy stood haloed against the glowing hallway. Then the door closed behind her and under the sheltering umbrella, without wrap or fur, she moved quickly down the snowy path in her satin slippers. The two men followed close behind.

The limousine, with its escort bucking dangerously through the snow, hurried along N Street. The night journey was eerie and exciting to the three isolated inside the heated car. During the ride they looked out the blurred windows and scarcely spoke. The streetlights shone mistily on deep white drifts; Washington,

D.C., lay as silent as a deserted city. Only an occasional pedestrian braved the bitter cold; and thousands of automobiles, abandoned helter-skelter in the streets, were muffled under hillocks of snow.

Soldiers, dramatically equipped with flamethrowers and backstopped by emergency sanitation crews, had cleared a twisting route to Constitution Avenue and on to the National Guard Armory. When the Kennedys' limousine and its cavalcade dipped into Rock Creek Parkway, workmen holding dazzling pink flares lighted the underpass. They cheered and waved their torches as the long black car slid by. The limousine arrived with five minutes to spare at Constitution Hall, where the Inaugural Concert — the first of many official festivities — was scheduled to begin.

The sky had been overcast that morning but the Weather Bureau, predicting "snow mixed with rain," had added reassuringly, "with no significant accumulation." By noon, however, the storm front had made an abrupt shift and zeroed in directly on the capital, while upper air temperatures trickily dropped several degrees. In 1900, a raging blizzard had forced William Howard Taft to transfer his inaugural ceremonies inside the Capitol; understandably, the Weather Bureau oracle who had promised Taft a "fine day" was fired. The four- or five-foot drifts that piled up on the eve of the Kennedy Inauguration made it the snowiest since Taft.

1

November 7, 1960
-
January 17, 1961

"Isn't He Sweet, Jack?"

In Georgetown Hospital, at twenty-two minutes past midnight on the morning after Thanksgiving, 1960, John F. Kennedy, Jr., weighed in at six pounds and three ounces. Headlines exulted: "It's a healthy, beautiful boy — and Jackie's fine!" When Pierre Salinger, press secretary to the President-elect, was asked by newsmen what the baby looked like, he reported cautiously, "Like a baby!"

Some days later, wearing his father's long, embroidered robe, John was christened in the hospital chapel. His father pushed his mother in a wheelchair along the corridors from her room. Afterwards, asked whether the baby had cried during the ceremony, the delighted father replied, "Not a bit — he laughed!"

The only reporter permitted at the christening described John, Jr., in baffled, masculine fashion: ". . . he has lots of brown hair — and a shiny nose. I thought he was pretty cute." His mother was, quite naturally, more complimentary. "Isn't he sweet, Jack?" she asked his father. "Just look at those pretty eyes!"

Before the young man had been around very long, he started making — and breaking — records. He was the first child born to a President-elect and his wife. Almost immediately after his arrival, three thousand congratulatory telegrams threw Western Union into a tailspin. Within the week, he had rung up an all-time high in floral gifts.

When he was two weeks old, John, Jr., left the hospital. Luella Hennessy, the Kennedy family's trained nurse, carried him from the car into the Kennedys' little N Street house. He was her eighteenth Kennedy baby.

While reporters and cameramen, who had gathered to record John, Jr.'s homecoming, stood patiently outside the N Street house waiting for Mrs. Kennedy to leave for the airport, their quarry slipped away unobserved, through the back garden gate,

7

to tour the White House with Mrs. Eisenhower. That afternoon the President-elect and his wife and new son had planned to fly on the *Caroline* to Palm Beach, to stay through Christmas at the senior Kennedys' oceanside villa. But as the future First Lady would not return to Washington until just before the Inauguration, this was the only day she could accept Mrs. Eisenhower's invitation. Mrs. Kennedy's obstetrician, Dr. John W. Walsh, had given permission reluctantly and with the proviso that Mrs. Kennedy use a wheelchair for the tour. Mrs. Eisenhower was alerted and at her suggestion a wheelchair was concealed behind a door at the White House in case Mrs. Kennedy should ask for it.

When the inspection was over, the First Lady and the First Lady-to-be posed together for the press for the first time. Mamie was dressy in gray broadtail, a pillbox perched behind her famous bangs; Jackie's flyaway shoulder-length hair curled on the collar of her billowy cloth coat. The caption under the published photo read: "Less than four hours after leaving Georgetown Hospital Mrs. Kennedy went to the White House and was escorted by the present First Lady on an hour-and-ten-minute tour of some twenty rooms."

At last the *Caroline* took off from Washington, two hours and twenty minutes late. Afterwards Mrs. Kennedy described the tour to a friend: "I had come straight from the hospital. I had only walked about my room and a little bit down the hall since I had had John. I really shouldn't have gone. But what could you do? My doctor said I could go only if there was a wheelchair. I don't know if there was one — or wasn't one — but I was too embarrassed to ask. And Mrs. Eisenhower took me around three floors and showed me everything! That afternoon we took the plane for Florida." She added, "There I collapsed — I had to stay in bed five days!"

The press report of Mrs. Kennedy's White House visit had concluded: ". . . Continuing a courtesy begun by previous First Ladies, First Lady Mamie saw to it that Jacqueline Kennedy had a set of plans to take to Florida with her. Mrs. Eisenhower's thoughtfulness in arranging for the architect's scale drawings solved some of Mrs. Kennedy's problems. It was impossible for her to see all of the thirty rooms set aside for family living

November 1960: Mrs. Kennedy holds John Jr. at his christening in the chapel of Georgetown Hospital. She had been brought to the ceremony in a wheelchair pushed by her husband. Mrs. Hugh Auchincloss is seated next to her daughter; the President-elect sits beside Mrs. Charles Bartlett, the baby's godmother, and Charles Bartlett, who stood in for Prince Radziwill as godfather. Mrs. Stephen Smith and Attorney General designate Robert Kennedy are standing at the rear. Miss Louella Hennessy, who took care of all new mothers in the Kennedy family, stands at the left (John Jr. was her eighteenth Kennedy baby).

December 1960: Mrs. Kennedy makes her first visit to the White House after the election of her husband to the Presidency for a tour of the mansion with Mrs. Eisenhower acting as hostess and guide.

Letitia (Tish) Baldridge, social secretary to Mrs. Kennedy from January 1961 to June 1963.

quarters in a tour which lasted little more than an hour. So, now, she can sit in the sunshiny patio and study dimensions for closets and proximity of rooms and make plans for moving day on January 20th."

The notion that Mrs. Kennedy could be relaxing in a sunshiny patio, contemplating closet dimensions and room proximity, was delightful but improbable. Former Ambassador Joseph Kennedy's house in Palm Beach is only medium-sized, and in those hectic preinaugural days the patio was about as private as a railroad station. Here the President-elect met a constantly increasing number of people, some who came seeking appointments, others whom he had summoned from all over the country. There were patronage seekers, potential appointees, advisers, staff members. The Kennedy clan drifted through. A Kennedy roommate from Choate School days sunned himself by the hour, relishing the mob scenes. Distinguished guests joined the future President at the ever-ready news microphone. Squads of reporters hovered offstage waiting for press conferences, which were called on the spur of the moment whenever a ripple of news broke. Often patio happenings overflowed into any conveniently empty room.

"It was so crowded," laughed Jackie, "that I could be in the bathroom, in the tub, and then find that Pierre Salinger was holding a press conference in my bedroom!"

She stayed in bed most of the time, writing countless letters and memos by hand on immense pads of blue-lined yellow paper. She found it difficult to dictate then (and did not master that shortcut until long afterwards). "I suppose I was trying to organize my life while I was there —" she said reflectively. "My office side — moving my furniture —"

A Statuesque Blonde from Nebraska

Several weeks before the presidential election, Jacqueline Kennedy had made a tentative first move toward setting up a personal White House staff. Her most urgent need was for an experienced social secretary, preferably a contemporary whom she already knew. An obvious choice was Letitia Baldridge, a handsome, statuesque blonde from Nebraska who had preceded Mrs. Kennedy by two years both at Miss Porter's School at Farmington and at Vassar.

A warm, openhearted extrovert, Tish had been launched as a social secretary by Mrs. David Bruce, when Bruce was Ambassador to France. Paris had led to Rome; and during the exciting years when Clare Boothe Luce had served as Madame Ambassador, Tish had become her mainstay. She had quickly added Italian to fluent French, developed a flair for maneuvering embassy households, and kept the nuances of international protocol at her fingertips. Her energy was a legend, her recall of complex names and titles almost total; and she thoroughly enjoyed the limelight reflected from her glamorous boss.

After almost a decade of glossy embassy living, Tish began to worry about becoming an expatriate and so returned to New York. She found a public relations job at Tiffany's, the famous jeweler; but though the job was a natural, her nostalgia for Italy's *dolce vita* proved unconquerable. Tish longed to return to Rome, set up her own public relations office and finish writing a much overdue novel. She was still undecided when the future First Lady suggested a White House post.

". . . I showed your first letter to Jack," wrote Jacqueline. ". . . I should think everything would be fine. The vacation, the adequate staff definitely are — the salary, of course, is a bit steep — but I'm sure there is some sort of budget for all that — none of which I'll be able to find out until after the election. But I still definitely want you to come (if November 8th goes our way). Sorry to be so incoherent — as you can see, I am really no good at dictating letters. . . ."

After the election, there was a spate of fretful speculation in the press as to whom Mrs. Kennedy would select as her social secretary. On November 16, a feminine Washington *Post* reporter queried coyly: "Is JBK's White House Social Secretary to be Tish?" Finally, the next day, Letitia Baldridge's appointment was announced.

Tish, reached by telephone, was uncertain about her new responsibilities. Previously, she had combined social and press secretary duties, she told newswomen; but now did not know whether she would handle press conferences for Mrs. Kennedy. "I shall probably just stand in the background and hand out copies of the new baby's formulas!" she said laughingly. This remark, though obviously meant to be humorous, was a jarring note to Jacqueline Kennedy, who was fiercely determined to guard her children's privacy. Once campaigning was done, she would regard personal press conferences as unnecessary and an intrusion on her own cherished personal life.

Within the week, Tish was to learn that the Washington press would take even her most casual remark very seriously indeed. She wound up her New York commitments and moved to Washington, where she was very much at home.

In succeeding days, Tish tried to sort out the ramifications of her new job. It was incredibly frustrating at first; she knew so little about the White House. "I have never eaten a meal there," she informed reporters. But during her father's single congressional term, she had been invited to a number of receptions; and some months before, Tiffany had sent her to study the lavish collection of antique vermeil recently bequeathed to the White House by Margaret Thompson Biddle. Since being named social secretary to Jacqueline Kennedy, Tish's sole direct contact with the Executive Mansion had been a telephone conversation with Mary Jane McCaffree, her opposite number in the Eisenhower administration. But Mrs. McCaffree had not offered Tish any practical suggestions.

Nonetheless, on November 23, six days after her appointment

had been announced, Tish presided at a press conference "to discuss her job." This initial meeting with the ladies of the press had been rather casually set up at the Women's National Democratic Club and it proved an unsettling experience.

"I felt that I was some sort of sacrificial offering," she said ruefully a long time afterwards, "but it taught me not to joke with reporters."

It was less than two weeks after the election and, though Tish had met briefly, a few times, with her new boss, Mrs. Kennedy's plans were still decidedly tentative. Tish, however, interpreted them rather grandly.

"Mrs. Kennedy plans to make the White House a showcase for great American art and artists," she commenced; and encouraged by the rapt attention of her audience, continued: "Mrs. Kennedy plans to make the Executive Mansion a place of current as well as historic interest. She plans to seek out paintings by prominent artists either on a loan basis or as permanent gifts."

"Where will she hang them?" chirruped a smart reporter. "There certainly isn't much empty wall space — at least on the first floor."

"That's a problem the First Lady-designate and her staff will have to face," replied Tish with a touch of hauteur. "They won't throw out portraits of Presidents and First Ladies already on the walls, but we will find a place even if it means hanging paintings in front of other paintings!" she added.

But the newswomen did not "laugh along" with Tish. To them, the White House was, as they invariably described it, "an American shrine," and therefore not to be tampered with rashly. To them, the thought of profaning the stately walls with modern art was scandalous.

In swift succession, Tish disclosed a flurry of new plans. First, Mrs. Kennedy wished to give American performing artists an opportunity to show their talents at White House functions. Now the ladies of the press were on familiar ground. After state dinners, the Eisenhowers sometimes invited stars from musicals who performed, often to the accompaniment of Fred Waring's orchestra. Fred Waring was one of their favorite showmen.

Old entertaining patterns, Tish continued, would be revamped and Mrs. Kennedy would experiment with several new ideas. What these were, Tish adamantly refused to disclose. She did say, though, that there would be more than the usual number of ladies' luncheons; and as for women's groups and the "big, vast hordes which want to be entertained at the White House" — well, "Mrs. Kennedy was thinking what to do with them." "They should be entertained," Tish emphasized, "but how often, when and so forth is something to be decided."

Tish concluded the press conference with some concrete information. As yet, Mrs. Eisenhower had not invited Mrs. Kennedy to inspect the White House private living quarters. Nevertheless, Mrs. Kennedy was planning to do them over to suit her taste with the $75,000 Congress had appropriated for this purpose. As a final fillip, she revealed that the future First Lady had ordered clothes from Ben Zuckerman, Norman Norell and Sloat, Inc.

Thus the feminine sector of the New Frontier got off to a controversial start. The press conference and the resulting publicity greatly annoyed the President-elect. All his Cabinet appointments had not created as much journalistic fuss. Shortly after Tish's comments flashed into print, countless citizens, outraged at the idea of Mrs. Kennedy hanging modern art in the White House, bombarded newspaper editors with irate letters. Fashion reporters from all over the country telephoned Zuckerman, Norell and the Sloats for detailed reports of Mrs. Kennedy's orders. They all came up zero. The designers proved unusually wary. Only Mr. Zuckerman gave a bit at the seams. "Darling," he sighed to a local fashion editor, "I don't say anything — I just keep my eyes closed!"

Almost immediately after the press conference, Mrs. Eisenhower invited her successor to visit the White House private living rooms at her convenience. And a working session between the outgoing social secretary Mary Jane McCaffree and incoming Tish was arranged.

Shocking Facts

A few days after Jacqueline Kennedy received Mamie Eisenhower's invitation, her son was born, a month prematurely. She was unable to accept, therefore, until the day she left the hospital en route to Palm Beach. But the two social secretaries, so different in background, outlook and age, discussed their mutual problems in a cordial meeting that lasted three hours. Afterwards Tish dashed off a voluminous, uninhibited, sometimes inaccurate memorandum for Mrs. Kennedy. It was amusing, confusing, informative and terribly depressing.

"Mrs. McCaffree could NOT have been more cordial to me," Tish began, bubbling over with italics. She continued to detail her findings, commencing with how her own office should be set up — and ending with a paragraph dramatically titled SHOCK-ING FACTS. "The White House budget is TOO small," she wailed.

It cannot afford proper flowers, proper linens; proper containers for flowers and plants — and, worst of all, champagne and cocktails at big dinners and receptions.

I just couldn't believe this! When the Eisenhowers have their big musicales, for instance, NOTHING is served the guests to drink. Mrs. McCaffree said that once in a while some California or New York wine grower donates some champagne for a specific party. Otherwise, the budget won't allow. At large receptions only punch, coffee and sandwiches are served. Well, that's all right, understandable, but not to have something to drink after dinner is practically a disaster.

SOS for Kennedy and Auchincloss knick-knacks. Every nice porcelain, silver or vermeil ashtray, cigarette box, table ornament, jardinière, cachepot, will be desperately needed. Please ask all relatives and friends to rifle their attics and basements for these goodies. —

Mrs. McC. said that for dinner parties there wasn't a nice thing to put down on the table in the way of nut cups, ashtrays, etc. —

Tish was more restrained in describing her own arrangements:

1. The Social Secretary's staff is divided into a small front office which will include: L.K.B.; Pamela Turnure; and a secretary.

Plus the "Social Office" of 5 individuals who will continue on in the new administration. These are calligraphers & typists who handle the invitations, lists, menus and placecard writing, etc.

Plus the "Mail & Miscellany Department," comprising 8 people, 1 of whom is on the payroll of another office. They handle the mail, prepare answers, keep card records of every appointment & records of all gifts, outgoing letters, etc. Included in this group is a dream-boat of a man, Fred Jefferson, who runs errands and drives the office car, delivering things — all this will remain.

There will be an increase of 2 on the staff, which will require budget revision: a. Pamela Turnure, an Assistant Social Secretary and, b. hiring an excellent overall letter composer, a college graduate type, to be added to the Mail Dept.

Everyone agrees, including Mrs. McCaffree, that you will receive twice as much mail as Mrs. E. They can't handle it [Mamie Eisenhower's mail] properly. They are snowed under and have no proper direction and, as a result, the letters they prepare aren't first rate.

2. *Fan Mail* — We will have to order glossies from the Air Force of a photograph you like. Then you can sign it and we will have prints made with the facsimile of your signature. Also, the President. Also, with both your signatures on a small card with "The White House" printed on them. These will be sent to children who write in by the thousands requesting your autographs —

3. *Stationery* — We will have to order your own private stationery on the outside but all official stationery is handled by the government printing office for budget reasons. The invitations and menus all seem O.K. and we have to give an order immediately on invitations, and for form letter announcements thanking people for writing congratulations on the Inaugural etc. I have samples of the stationery to show you when you can give me five minutes.

Tish's comments on "running the house" were steeped in gloom.

4. *Running the House.* The Head [sic] Usher runs the House — the butlers, cook, waiters [all White House waiters are called by the

more dignified title of Butler], maids, laundresses, etc. However, it has been run like a military camp the past 16 years or so and the place lacks female taste (real). For example: in the State Dining Room, the only permanent plant or flower container on view for all the public, is a cheap $2.98 heavy white porcelain jardinière with 3 sick ivy plants in it, on the great marble mantelpiece —

Unless you do some work on the Private Dining Room, you won't be able to stand it. [Tish was mixed up. The "Private Dining Room" she mentions is really the Family Dining Room. Under Mrs. Kennedy's aegis, it was magnificently redecorated through the generosity of Mr. and Mrs. Charles Engelhard.] It's the room next to the big State Dining Room, which seats 14–16. You will probably want to have intimate dinners there. The rug is a heavy, awfully dark maroon, and the whole room is so dark it gives one the shudders. The wrong silver pieces sit on the sideboard. All this can be changed without spending money. It's a question of substituting and exchanging.

5. *Staff.* The White House staff is mixed racially, and the chef is a Philippino [*sic*]. The only 2 servants living *in* the White House now are Mrs. E.'s personal maid and the President's valet. You will have to pay for your own nurse out of your own salary budget. There is room on the third floor for your cook to live in and Mrs. McCaffree assures me that she can come down to the kitchen and prepare your meals anytime you want.

The Eisenhowers eat on trays in their sitting room every night. The food must be plenty cold when it reaches them since it is prepared 2 floors below in another part of the house. We are going to have to work on such problems as having the food arrive HOT whether it is for a dinner of 100 or for you and the President alone. We are going to have to work on the food, too. Anyone who knows anything about cuisine says the food at State Dinners is nothing short of *awful.* I would suggest that the President-elect either ask to have the tiny steam kitchen on the 3rd floor (where the valet, cook and maid will be living) enlarged or else install some sort of warming oven on the 2nd floor near your living quarters.

6. *Entertaining.* The 1st Lady's Social schedule is supposed to end officially for the year the last day of May and begin again October first. You can ask up to 100 for dinner and 1000 to a reception. I hope you never will — crowded — crushed — no distinction. 9 to 23 White House aides are available to help. Mrs. McC. went into detail about women's press luncheons, Congressional wives' receptions, etc. —

7. *Protocol.* Imagine being able to set a whole table incorrectly and be able to do it because "the White House cannot make a mistake." But that's it. Mrs. McC. showed her seating charts — when I spotted lots of things wrong — she said they changed it to suit — when there are language problems or when an official, due to rank, has been partnered too often with the same lady.

8. *Flowers.* The man responsible for floral arrangements has been here 38 years. He buys flowers wholesale. Last year they spent $15,000 roughly on flowers and the President was terribly shocked! Mrs. McC. said that this was the minimum of flowers, stinting all the time. When I asked if we couldn't get bids from other wholesalers and underbid the present supplier, who has supplied for many years, she replied, yes, it should be done.

9. *House Emoluments.* Swimming pool, nice little movie theatre which the Eisenhowers didn't use. Even a tennis court. 2nd floor, a tiny, sunny room off the elevator where Ike painted. At Walter Reed [hospital] Ward 8 is always at your disposal. — There is a dental chair tucked away in a cranny in the White House. A top Walter Reed dentist will always come to the White House.

Tish was almost as enthusiastic about the White House police officers as she was about Fred Jefferson, her "dreamboat" in the Mail & Miscellany Department:

10. *VIP Tours Through the White House.* 150 go through every A.M., escorted by the police. I met some of these men and they are, without doubt, such a fabulous, marvelous kind of creature, they alone are worth coming to the White House for. My office will give the list to them every A.M. of who is on the day's docket. I hear Congressmen call and want all their constituents to be included.

11. *Moving in.* All redecorating must be done after you are once in, room by room, so that you can still sleep in rooms that aren't reeking of fresh paint or whatever. It's tradition that you cannot move in until 12 noon, Jan. 20th. I asked Mrs. McCaffree if we couldn't smuggle a lot of stuff over without the E's knowing and she said, yes, the Head Usher could store cartons, suitcases, etc., out of sight and then whisk them into sight on the stroke of 12 noon. Isn't that marvelous??? Right out of Alfred Hitchcock.

And so, a-tingle at the delicious prospect ahead, Tish signed off.

The Hazy Abyss

On September 11, 1960, the usually sedate *New York Times Sunday Magazine* ran a frothy article which predicted that Mrs. Kennedy would shatter the fashion taboos ordinarily surrounding First Ladies.

The *Times* story commenced briskly. "When Jacqueline Bouvier Kennedy, five days the wife of a Presidential nominee, stepped aboard a boat at Hyannis Port wearing shocking pink Capri pants and an orange sweater, reporters knew that they were witnessing something of possibly vast political consequence." For here was the wife of a presidential candidate daring to wear what she wanted regardless of the difficult campaign looming ahead. The press was entranced: it was a unique situation and one sure to produce exciting copy.

The *New York Times* amusingly capsuled the hazards of First Ladyship:

She must tread the hazy abyss of being neither too chic, nor too plain. If too smart, she loses the common touch. If too drab, she lets down the affluent American way of life.

Millions of American women regard it as their constitutional right to know what the First Lady wears, where she bought it and, hopefully, whether it was costly or a bargain.

Thousands of designers, manufacturers and store executives keep a sharp eye on her around-the-clock. If the First Lady goes hatless, the millinery industry invades the White House. If she ignores fur, the Fur Trappers' Association lobbying act would make oil and railroad lobbyists blush. Should she evince any reluctance to wear oriental pearls, the First Lady might find herself involved in an international incident. If she indicates a preference for foreign couture, Seventh Avenue goes berserk.

Besides, she is always surrounded by pressure groups within the fashion world: designers trying to persuade her to wear their clothes;

hairdressers seeking her patronage; magazine editors asking her co-operation in fashion promotion; and industry groups angling for her endorsement to revive lagging sales.

The story was larded with quotes, sampling public reaction to young Mrs. Kennedy's personal style and her presumed attitude toward fashion should she become First Lady. Mrs. Kennedy's "devil-may-care chic" (as the *New York Times* described it) was troublesome to some women. A Manhattan housewife, undoubtedly envious, exclaimed waspishly to the inquiring reporter, "She looks too damn snappy. I just don't like women who look that snappy." Some twenty spirited housewives from the Republican-oriented state of Iowa wrote a joint letter to the *Times*: "We have better looking floor mops than the bouffant coiffure you describe on your favorite Bobby-soxer." Mrs. Lyndon B. Johnson, then wife of the vice-presidential candidate, was queried as to whether Mrs. Kennedy's hairdo might become a campaign issue. She replied with her expected down-to-earth common sense, "I would hope that what is on the inside is more important than what is on the outside!"

Finally, a close friend of Mrs. Kennedy reported a whimsical anecdote: "Jackie, you are too much of an individualist," the friend pointed out. "If you get in the White House, you'll have to make some concessions!" "Oh! I will," Jackie was said to have replied in all seriousness. "I'll wear hats!"

The *Times* story depressed the future First Lady. But it was a sensationally inaccurate reportage published in the *Women's Wear Daily,* the widely read newspaper of the clothing trade, which motivated Mrs. Kennedy to take action. This story, a climax to many other such items, purported to describe her extravagant Paris shopping habits. To prevent further ridiculous fabrications, she evolved a strategy which would also stymie pressure groups in the American fashion world.

Mrs. Kennedy decided that a single person, an American and a man whom she had known for some years, would design not only her complete wardrobe but many of her hats and accessories as well. All information about her costumes could then be controlled by a single source, thus assuring reasonable accuracy rather than journalistic guesswork.

The designer Mrs. Kennedy selected was Oleg Cassini, grandson of a former czarist minister to Washington. His brother Igor, a society columnist at the time, was married to a daughter of Charles Wrightsman, the oil multimillionaire, who was a neighbor of the senior Kennedys at Palm Beach. Jacqueline had bought Oleg Cassini dresses from time to time because she admired their sophisticated simplicity and unobtrusive use of unusual materials.

In an exchange of letters before the election, Cassini wrote:

Dear Jackie:

Thanks so much for having answered my letter so promptly. I read your letter very carefully and understand exactly what you have in mind. I think I know your style and, naturally, the dresses you would get here will be specially made for you, with your counsel and direction and in keeping with your marvelous sense of personal fashion.

. . .

Then Cassini concluded:

— Let's all keep our fingers crossed and hope for the wonderful success and, of course, I am most optimistic and I am sure you are, too. So all the good luck in the world. A bientôt, Oleg.

Nine days after the election Jacqueline Kennedy wrote to Oleg Cassini again and, in a few paragraphs, summarized her fashion philosophy for her new role as wife of the President of the United States.

Dear Oleg: —

It was lovely to hear from you.

Why don't you get started designing me something, then send me some sketches and, if I like them, I can give you credit for doing most of my Spring wardrobe as I would like to start wearing them about March.

What I need are dresses and coats for daytime; dresses suitable to wear to lunch. I don't know if you design coats, but I now see that will be one of my biggest problems as every time one goes out of the house, one is photographed in the same coat.

Then, for afternoon, cocktail dresses suitable for afternoon receptions and receiving lines — in other words, fairly covered up. Also a couple of silk coats to wear over them when I go out in the late afternoon. Any suggestions for accessories you have to wear with these would also be appreciated.

Then some pretty, long evening dresses suitable for big official dinners. You know the kind I like: Balenciaga covered-up look. Even though these clothes are for official life, please don't make them dressy as I'm sure I can continue to dress the way I like — simple and young clothes, as long as they are covered up for the occasion.

I would like to have them in some of the new Spring materials, especially the ones used by Balenciaga and Givenchy — so I will be patient and wait for your sketches until you have had a chance to see the new materials.

From Christmas to Jan. 20th I will be in Palm Beach in case you might want to send me sketches there. After that I will be — you know where.

I do look forward to hearing from you, it will be such fun to work with you.

Many thanks and best always, Jacqueline Kennedy.

Shortly after the New Year, the appointment of Cassini as sole designer to Mrs. Kennedy was announced from Palm Beach. Nevertheless Mrs. Kennedy continued to ride the eye in a cyclone of fashion gossip. To check this endless flow of misinformation, on January 9 Jacqueline Kennedy sent the rough draft of a letter to Tish Baldridge. Tish was to shorten, polish and send it out over her own name and title to the most persistent offender, the *Women's Wear Daily*. The letter was addressed to the editor. The communication commenced:

Dear Sir:

I write to you at the suggestion of Mrs. John F. Kennedy, regarding several erroneous articles about her clothes which have appeared in your publication during the past few months —

Then, after enumerating the major errors, the letter continued:

Mrs. Kennedy realizes that the clothes she wears are of interest to the public, but she is distressed by the implications of extravagance, of over-emphasis of fashion in relation to her life, and of the misuse of her name by firms from which she has not bought clothes.

For the next four years Mrs. Kennedy's clothes will be made by Oleg Cassini. They will be designed and made in America. She will buy what is necessary without extravagance. You will often see her photographed in the same outfit.

Should you want to obtain sketches of these clothes, Mr. Cassini will cooperate with you and release the sketches.

Should you receive a report that Mrs. Kennedy has ordered clothes not by Mr. Cassini, I would appreciate it if you would call me and I will give you a prompt and accurate answer."

An immediate reply was addressed directly to Mrs. Kennedy.

Dear Mrs. Kennedy:

We have been in touch with Mr. Oleg Cassini who has been most cooperative and most kind.

We are also most pleased and delighted with the beautiful clothes he is making. The whole fashion world and especially the American fashion world owes you a big debt.

The editor concluded his long letter:

I am enclosing these sketches done by our artist and I hope you will like them. By the way, the Associated Press and the United Press and every newspaper have been hounding us to death for all the sketches published in our paper and we have refused to release them to anyone. I have been in touch with Mr. Cassini on this score. Thank you.

Under his signature the unsinkable editor scribbled:

I am sure you wish you were in Palm Springs incognito instead of Palm Beach.

For a brief moment, after this exchange, Mrs. Kennedy's purchases were described with less fantasy.

But the continual, relentlessly microscopic reporting on Mrs. Kennedy's wardrobe was to become almost a press obsession. (Once, truly amazed, Mrs. Kennedy asked a friend, "What difference could it make to *anyone* whether I wore *two* or *three* strings of pearls?") The reporting, sometimes accurate, sometimes faulty, would, by its overemphasis, distress her and, by the same overemphasis, place her name year after year at the head of the "Ten Best Dressed" list, a commercial accolade which, to her, was as unwanted as it was valueless.

After, as well as before, she had emerged into national prominence, Jacqueline continued to attach little importance to clothes. She played them down and bought only what she believed becoming and suitable for the occasion. So offering information about what she was to wear soon seemed both pretentious and unnecessary. After only a few months in the White House, when the Kennedys returned from Canada, their first state visit, all releases concerning the First Lady's wardrobe were stopped.

During her White House years, except for informal sportswear and an occasional gala gown, Mrs. Kennedy purchased most of her clothes from her chosen designer. But she did buy one made-in-Paris dress. A classically beautiful white satin evening gown, with a bodice laced in palest blue and red, Givenchy created it for a most special occasion during the Kennedys' state visit to France. The First Lady wore this tricolor gown in compliment to France, to Paris and to General de Gaulle at the glittering dinner in the Salle des Glaces at Versailles, and afterwards to the ballet performance in the adjoining Louis XV theater.

When General and Mme de Gaulle and President and Mrs. Kennedy entered the exquisitely restored bandbox theater, the elegant audience rose from their seats to face the group in the loge above them. The orchestra struck up "The Star-Spangled Banner" and then the "Marseillaise." As Jacqueline stood there, young and glowing beside the aging General, every woman in the house realized that she had chosen a Paris dress emphasizing their national colors to show her delight in a city which she had lived in as a student and had grown to love.

Immediately after the election had been won almost every top designer and many leading stores had written to ask Mrs. Kennedy if they could create her inaugural gown. She herself had made some tentative sketches and, of course, knew precisely what she wanted. Eventually the lovely dress and its matching, silk-lined chiffon cape were to be custom-made at Bergdorf Goodman in New York. Meanwhile Mrs. Lyndon Johnson had alerted the First Lady-to-be that Stanley Marcus, owner of Neiman Marcus of Dallas, Texas, was sending sketches for a proposed Inaugural Ball gown. Mrs. Kennedy promptly dispatched a thank-you note to Mrs. Johnson and wrote to Mr. Marcus the same day she had communicated with Oleg Cassini.

Thank you very much, [she said to Mrs. Johnson] for telling me that Stanley Marcus will send some sketches of a possible Inaugural gown. As you probably saw in the newspapers, I have already ordered one from Bergdorf Goodman, but, of course, I'd be delighted to see the sketches Mr. Marcus sends.

Again, many thanks to you for bringing this to my attention.

The letter to Stanley Marcus, dated November 16, 1960, ran:

Dear Mr. Marcus: —

I do appreciate the interest which you have shown in my Inaugural gown.

As much as I would have loved to have Neiman Marcus, I think you can understand that it is more convenient for me to pick someone nearer home, as I will have to have it very soon after the birth of my baby. Then, there will not be much time for fittings etc.

I have already decided where I will have it made, and will soon be seeing the sketches.

Some time in the future, I would be delighted to have Neiman Marcus do an important gown for me. It is just that, this year, with everything crowding so closely — the election, the birth of my baby and the Inauguration — I have had to plan all this way ahead of time. I am sure you understand.

With many thanks, I am

Yours sincerely,
Jacqueline Kennedy

The description of the Inaugural Ball gown was released to the press on January 19, 1961. The dress and matching cape were sketched separately. The single legend read:

DESCRIPTION OF MRS. JOHN F. KENNEDY'S
INAUGURAL BALL COSTUME

The dress is a full length sheath of white silk peau d'ange veiled with white silk chiffon. The hip length bodice is richly embroidered in silver and brilliants. It is covered by a transparent overblouse of white silk-chiffon. The back of the bodice is similar to the front.

The floor length cape is made of the same white silk peau d'ange and completely veiled in silk triple chiffon. Under the ring collar, the cape is fastened with twin embroidered buttons. The shape of the cape is an arch from shoulder to hem with soft waves in back. It is also lined with white silk peau d'ange and has two arm slits.

With the ensemble Mrs. Kennedy will wear 20 button white glacé kid gloves and carry a matching white silk peau d'ange tailored clutch purse. Mrs. Kennedy's shoes will be matching white silk opera pumps with medium high heels.

A First Lady's Inaugural Ball gown always arouses tremendous interest: thousands of letters poured into congressional offices as well as the White House. Curiously, despite the explicit press release, many women believed the gown to be homemade and requested souvenir scraps of the fabric or enough for doll dresses. Four days after the Inaugural, Tish began to cope with the inundation. To a correspondent from Phoenix, Arizona, she replied with polished politeness: "It would give Mrs. Kennedy great pleasure to send you material from her Inaugural gown — She regrets, however, that she hasn't the material to send as her gown was not made at home." A constituent of Utah wrote Senator Frank Moss, asking for doll dress yardage through his office, and added: "I hope that Caroline someday will be able to visit Utah and see the doll collection."

Later, when a perfume manufacturer wanted to duplicate the costume for his firm's much publicized collection of inaugural gowns, his request was turned down.

The American Wax Museum in Philadelphia asked authorization to commission Oleg Cassini to "supply a dress for the figure depicting Mrs. Kennedy." As the costume would not be a copy of the Inaugural Ball gown, the White House permitted Cassini to accept.

At a ceremony the following November, Mrs. Kennedy's Inaugural Ball gown was presented to the Smithsonian Institution. Hers was the thirty-ninth dress and the fourteenth Inaugural Ball gown in a collection of costumes which had belonged to every First Lady from Martha Washington to Jacqueline Kennedy.

The collection had been inspired in the early 1900s by Mrs. Julian James, a distinguished Washington social leader, and Mrs. Rose Gouvenor Hoes, a direct descendant of President Monroe. Mrs. Hoes had inherited several luxurious dresses which the Monroe ladies had worn. From this acquisition, in part, stemmed the idea of assembling a collection of costumes which had belonged to succeeding First Ladies. The idea was discussed with patriotically inclined friends and, finally, in 1912 it was endorsed by the White House. Then Mrs. William Howard Taft presented to the Smithsonian Institution the gown she had worn at the 1909 Inaugural Ball.

This gift publicized the glamorous and historically valuable possibilities of a First Ladies' costume collection. And by giving the evening dress worn at her Inaugural Ball, Mrs. Taft launched a trend. The gown, an exquisite creation, hand-embroidered in Japan with an all-over motif of wheat, attracted very special feminine attention not only by its beauty but because it had been worn by a First Lady on what was presumed to be the most important evening of her life. (Today, when the Smithsonian Institution requests an addition to their now famous collection, the President's wife may of course donate her personal selection; but it is suggested discreetly that the focus of public interest is on an Inaugural Ball gown.)

The response to Mrs. Taft's endorsement was immediate. Costumes which had been treasured by the families of five former First Ladies were soon added. The collection itself was widened in scope to include outfits which had belonged to the feminine relations who had presided as hostesses for widower Presidents and for the one bachelor President, James Buchanan.

Though balls were omitted from the programs of the five Inaugurations following Taft's,* handsome gowns worn by two Mrs. Woodrow Wilsons, Mrs. Warren G. Harding, Mrs. Calvin Coolidge and Mrs. Herbert Hoover were acquired. The search for vintage costumes had been successful too, and finally every President's lady was represented.

Originally the gowns were exhibited on mannequins made to dress size but with identical, whiter-than-chalk heads. Their serenely classic features were cast from a Smithsonian-owned marble bust of Cordelia, the daughter of King Lear. Mrs. Kennedy's effigy, however, was modernized with natural face coloring, eyebrows, eyelashes and an authentically styled wig. When the costume collection was transferred to the new Museum of History and Technology in 1964 all the figures had been treated in a similar naturalistic fashion and were posed in groups of about

---

* There were no Inaugural Balls between the 1909 Inauguration of Taft and that of Franklin D. Roosevelt in 1933. Woodrow Wilson, though he enjoyed dancing in private houses, believed it undignified for a President of the United States of America to dance in public. The Harding Inauguration was too close to World War I; the Coolidges were in mourning for the death of their second son; and the Hoovers shared President Wilson's views on presidential dignity.

five, against White House backgrounds decorated appropriately to their time.

Lawrence Gouvenor Hoes, son of Rose Hoes, made the presentation of Mrs. Kennedy's gown. He entertained the select audience at the ceremony with gossip about the collection. A daughter of the first Mrs. Woodrow Wilson, he recalled, did not want her mother's gown in the same (then glassed-in) case with a dress that had belonged to the second Mrs. Wilson. Mrs. Taft had asked to have her handsome features reproduced on the mannequin, while Mrs. Harding, a fussy dresser, had insisted her own underwear be used — until she was shown how the dummy was constructed! The dress Mrs. Coolidge presented had been a special problem. The early 1920s were a difficult fashion era, and her skimpy white satin brocade frock was plain and in painful contrast to the other more elaborate costumes. Tactfully, Mrs. Hoes and several friends of Mrs. Coolidge wrote suggesting that she substitute one of her more colorful gowns. Mrs. Coolidge had left the White House and returned to Northampton before she replied. The satin brocade dress, she explained, had been made in an emergency. She had needed an unostentatious dress quickly to wear at an official function shortly after the unexpected death of Warren G. Harding, when her husband had succeeded to the Presidency. If the dress was finished in time, she had promised her saleslady in a local specialty shop, it would be donated to the Smithsonian Institution collection. Grace Coolidge kept her word. Now, at home again, she went through her still unpacked trunks and selected a coral red velvet evening gown which had been much admired.

Today, those who see this gay replacement often wrongly identify it with the deeper red dress in which Howard Chandler Christy painted her picture-postcard portrait which now hangs in the White House.

Mr. Hoes climaxed his amusing reminiscences by looking a gift horse straight in the mouth. Two dresses said to have been owned by Martha Washington had been offered to the collection. But when the venerable garments were carefully scrutinized, they were found to have been sewn with machine stitching!

"So Be Discreet"

The future First Lady's "office side" lacked one essential to her own peace of mind and to the family life she was so determined to preserve. She needed a special person to cope exclusively with the insistent press. Demands for personal interviews; pleas to photograph the children; requests for TV appearances, for speeches, for charity sponsorships, were accumulating at a frantic pace. Tentatively, in self-protection, Pierre Salinger, President Kennedy's press secretary, had suggested a competent and notably aggressive feminine reporter, but Mrs. Kennedy knew exactly how she wanted her press relations handled and soon selected the person she believed capable of carrying out her ideas.

Her choice was Pamela Turnure, a mere twenty-three-year-old, yet already a seasoned success in political diplomacy. A small, fine-boned brunette with palest complexion and blue-green eyes which gazed unswervingly when she spoke, Pam seemed to understate her prettiness deliberately. Her poise was remarkable; she never raised her voice and remained unruffled under the most exasperating circumstances. She was, her friends noted admiringly, totally unflappable.

Pam's New York background was both social and conservative. After graduating from school she shared a house in Washington with three other attractive young girls. One of her roommates was a receptionist in the office of handsome Senator George Smathers of Florida.

The roommate's tales of congressional activities were so intriguing that Pam determined to work on the Hill. She had a job as receptionist at the Belgian embassy, when her chance came. She was introduced to Senator Kennedy at the wedding of Nini Auchincloss, a stepsister of his wife. Kennedy, a close friend of Smathers, told Pam there would be an opening in his office in the autumn. A few months later she was interviewed and given a dual job, as office receptionist and secretary to Timothy J. Reardon, the Administrative Assistant to the Massachusetts Senator.

Pam's job quickly developed into a combination of secretary, receptionist and troubleshooter. She proved efficient as well as tactful. Three years later, after the election of Senator Kennedy to the Presidency, when gifts in unmanageable quantities poured in, she was placed in charge of the deluge. It had become impossible to cope with the presents at the Kennedys' N Street house so they were rerouted to the Senate office to be fluoroscoped, listed and appropriately disposed of under her supervision. She also attended to an increasing number of personal requests from Mrs. Kennedy, who soon found that to "ask Pam to do it" was a sure and agreeable way to accomplishment.

After Pam had accepted the flattering but onerous task of being what would become the first press secretary in history to a First Lady, her new boss sent her a lengthy memorandum — written by hand, and characteristically lacking any indication of date or place. It set down guidelines which Pamela Turnure was to follow faithfully throughout Mrs. Kennedy's White House years, often despite bitter criticism by newswomen. The young First Lady was sincerely averse to personal publicity. She firmly believed the spotlight should be focused on her husband alone. Therefore, she avoided press conferences, never gave "in person" interviews and discouraged stories about herself for fear it would appear that she was seeking public acclaim.

The only exceptions she made were for causes close to her heart, like the Fine Arts Restoration project, and anything the President asked her to undertake because *he* thought it important. Nevertheless, because she believed it would help her restoration project, she summoned the courage to narrate a TV tour of the White House. This was a program which had required months of study to perfect, and her knowledge, as well as her grace, was applauded by many millions. Her show was an unprecedented success.

Very few members of the press understood Mrs. Kennedy. They were accustomed to politicians' wives who scrabbled for publicity on the theory that any newspaper notice, good or bad, was better than none. They were used to a sort of falsely gay camaraderie with candidates' ladies, in which they questioned the willing victims about clothes, recipes, child care, and if their target was sufficiently young, even obstetrics. Now, however, they were faced with a very real personage who refused to play their game in disclosing intimacies. The new First Lady would do what she *had* to do, but, basically, she found both talking to the press and appearing on TV difficult and distasteful. Perhaps this was partly because she was shy and, in an exaggerated sense, a private person, and perhaps also because she had been initiated into the world of politics when her husband, who was almost thirteen years her senior, was already a senator, and had built a career in which she had made no contribution.

It is quite possible, too, that the criticism that the ladies of the press leveled at Jackie Kennedy was, perhaps subconsciously, motivated by envy. Tish Baldridge may have put her finger on it with a breezy remark: "Of course, they're all jealous of her — she's young, beautiful, intelligent and rich, and besides all this, she's married to Jack Kennedy!"

At the White House, right from the start, Pam knew that her job as press secretary had an unusual slant. "I must say I always look at my job as one to help preserve Mrs. Kennedy's privacy and not to create publicity," she observed. "After all, it was Mrs. Kennedy who hired me — not the press — and so my first obligation was to her. I am not sure that any of the reporters would appreciate this kind of thinking, but it kept the White House from becoming an open house circus. I really loved my job — the few areas that were considered legitimate news from the East Wing [Mrs. Kennedy's office] — Restoration Project, State Entertainments — I personally learned so much from — I had to research everything so thoroughly it was like taking extension courses at college."

The mere hint of a public person daring to be private served to enhance Mrs. Kennedy's mystique and inspire frenetic curiosity about her most insignificant action. Given that basic liability, however, the rules Mrs. Kennedy set down in her confidential memorandum to Pamela Turnure were both sensible and shrewd.

Dear Pam,

Just a note as heaven knows when I'll see you before all the avalanche of doing my press falls on your head.

I am *so glad* you are doing it — the more I think of it — for the very reason that you haven't had previous press experience — But you have sense and good taste enough not to panic and to say the right thing —

Pierre offered me some highpowered girl but I hate that tubthumping-everything-is-great-about-my-boss kind of press relations —

Then there was Tish who could have done it — I didn't pick her, because I wanted her phenomenal energy every place else in the White House — though I might have, if she had been 3 people — everyone is trying to get at us — but you will be there as a buffer — to shield our privacy — not get us in the papers — All your experience is perfect for this —

All this is completely confidential between you and me. I think you are rather like me & so will answer questions the way I would — which is such a great relief — I feel so strongly that publicity in this era has gotten so completely out of hand — & you must really protect the privacy of me and my children — but not offend them all —

1. You can invent some ladylike little title for yourself — or decide it with Pierre — but I don't think it should be Press Secretary as I don't think a First Lady should have a Press Secretary — maybe Assistant Social Secretary in charge of Press, etc.

2. Pierre will be your boss (I will be really — as you & I will decide everything together) — but all releases & things will come from him — But you must work in my offices — wherever they are — in the W. House.

3. I hope you will be fairly anonymous — for nothing you say is taken as Pam Turnure saying it — You are speaking for me — and one misstep & I get a million letters saying, "Don't hang modern art out all over the White House, etc." Perhaps magazines & papers will want to do interviews on you — Please check with me before you accept — if you want to do it & it looks OK — just know you can't discuss us — JFK, me & infants.

4. Also in your own private life — when you go out in NY, etc. — you just mustn't answer their questions about what it is like working for us — just smile & look evasive! As everyone exaggerates so — & some tiny insignificant thing you say goes from one person to another & ends up horribly in some gossip column a week later —

None of this is meant to sound reproachful — it is just that I have suddenly realized what it means to completely lose one's privacy — everyone is so interested in us — so be discreet.

5. My press relations will be minimum information given with maximum politeness — you are great at that anyway —

6. In the beginning when I first move in — answer all questions by saying Mrs. K's biggest desire right now is to reunite her family — bring her children back from Fla. & have everything arranged for them — She is busy moving [so busy] that I can't really give you any exact details — but will later. Then you can tell me what they ask & we'll decide what to answer.

I won't give any interviews — pose for any photographs, etc. for next four years — don't say it that categorically but check with Pierre on a policy statement — a polite way to turn down all requests for interviews — also fotos — Pierre will bring in *Life* & *Look* or Stan Tretwick a couple of times a year & we'll have an ok on it — so find out from him how to turn down everyone who wants to photograph me giving the baby a bottle, etc.

I did say I'd have a press conference but tell them it won't be for a while — until I have something to tell them — & then it won't be a press conference — just having them to tea — When they ask when is press conference say Mrs. K. looks forward to having you all to tea — once she's settled —

You're just as exhausted reading this letter as I am — take lots of vitamins, poor Pam, & I will see you Jan. 21.

Jackie

"That Marvelous Book of Pictures"

Immediately after her tour with Mrs. Eisenhower, Mr. J. Bernard West, the Chief Usher of the White House, sent Mrs. Kennedy an album of White House photographs. He had selected them personally from the official record and the pictures of the private rooms on the second and third floors had never been published.

"We try to make an album for each First Lady," wrote Mr. West, "and so you will note from personal items in some of the rooms, these photographs are copies from the Truman and Eisenhower albums. However, practically all furniture shown is White House property."

He also enclosed a plan of the White House grounds with a section outlined which he hoped Mrs. Kennedy would find suitable as a play area for her children. There had been no First Family with young children of their own since the Theodore Roosevelts, over half a century earlier. The Chief Usher and his staff were looking forward to having Caroline and her baby brother in the White House.

"A six foot high hedge can be planted to screen the area off from the Rose Garden," he explained, "and the open space would be adequate to set up swings, slides etc. Under the magnolia tree in this same area the space is already covered with flagstones which would be ideal for a sandbox. Alongside the Mansion, there is a sidewalk for tricycles etc. If you find this area not desirable — any other section can be screened off as you may wish. The Fine Arts Commission does not have to be consulted," he concluded, "and you should also feel free to make any changes desired in the area under the Commission's supervision. They do not exercise supervision over any portion of the second and third floors." (The Fine Arts Commission controls purchase of furniture and overall decoration of the State Rooms.)

Jacqueline Kennedy dashed off a note of thanks.

Dear Mr. West: I do want to thank you so very much for your great thoughtfulness in sending me that marvelous book of pictures of the White House.

Together with the plans it is a most invaluable help as I can get so much thought out beforehand and then reunite my family that much sooner — which is what I care more about than anything.

Each White House photograph was enclosed in an individual plastic folder. The future First Lady penciled her comments on scraps of paper which she tucked into the appropriate envelope. These served as reminders not only to Mr. West, who would supervise any changes she planned, but also for her decorator.

In their private living quarters Jacqueline Kennedy concentrated on making her husband comfortable and keeping her children within whispering distance. "I so badly wanted the children close to us," she said, and throughout her notes the word "cosy" recurs again and again. Her basic desire was to infuse the impersonal rooms with warmth and intimacy. At first, after studying the floor plans, she decided to settle her daughter and little son in rooms adjoining her own. But this presented problems:

"When we had lived in the White House a few days and I had seen what it was like eating off trays with four butlers hovering around — or descending to the first floor to that dark private dining room," Jacqueline wrote later to a friend. "I realized that we must have our own dining room on that floor. Since these rooms [i.e. the ones she had initially chosen for the children] were connected to lower floors by a small elevator, it was the only possible place for the dining room — The children then went into two rooms down the hall — opposite the entrance to the Oval Room — and Miss Shaw's room was the book closet between them."

"I wanted our bedroom to be the same as it was in Georgetown," Mrs. Kennedy concluded. "I had my same curtains copied for there. They had been rather country-type material, and, of course, they looked absurd as the proportions of the room were so formal. But in my bedroom, and in the West Hall which was our sitting room, I had all my Georgetown things about us, and I worked at Daddy's Empire desk." Thus surrounded by familiar possessions, she tried to re-create the happy atmosphere of their once private world.

In Palm Beach, before these decisions were reached, Mrs. Kennedy scrutinized each photograph carefully. Many of the rooms had been rephotographed several times to show different color schemes and furniture arrangements selected by the previous two First Ladies. This system of rearranging instead of outright buying pleased her ingrained sense of economy. "I think this is the Queen's Room," she penciled to Mrs. Parish, "will use it as a guest room — don't care about spending $s on it. — As you can see by the [different] beds — each new occupant moves furniture around — so can we — chandeliers — everything —"

In official records White House rooms are numbered for convenience and traditionally Room 220 is the President's bedroom. "This is Jack's bedroom adjoining mine," she scribbled, "furniture arrangement is ok, too, you just have to think of pretty color wall, chintz and rug —"

On their tour Mamie Eisenhower had pointed out the West Hall with special pleasure. Wide as a spacious room, wall-to-wall carpeted and furnished with comfortable sofas and chairs, all First Families used it as a sitting room. Here the Eisenhowers had watched television as they dined on trays. Here President Truman had kept his upright piano. On her initial tour, Jacqueline had overlooked a fact vital to her pattern of living. Now she noticed, looking at the photographs, that there were no bookshelves in the West Hall. "Here's where we would sit," she wrote her decorator, "but I was wrong. It doesn't have bookcases. Doesn't any President *ever* read? No bookcases, *anywhere*. You can see on the plans where they could go — along the walls — or high ones if you suggest —"

The Third Floor met her approval. "See how cosy this 3rd floor hall is — all the sun rooms, play rooms, bedrooms, open off it. Maybe chintz is o.k. — just a few of your touches and getting rid of plants and hotel furniture — nicer lamps & painting walls would make it ideal for children & ME!"

The six guest bedrooms opening onto this hall were photographed in uncompromising black and white which made their "Early Statler" type furnishings look even more drab. Mrs. Kennedy labeled some without comment "Grandchildren's Rooms on Third Floor" — while others, succinctly "A guest room — ok, why spend $s on it?" But in little more than a year after the Kennedys moved in, each of these rooms was rehabilitated gaily with a pleasing mixture of better White House pieces, authentic Americana and charming bibelots which Mrs. Kennedy had coaxed from her family and friends.

The Oval Room, after it was refurbished in exquisite Louis XVI style, was to become her personal favorite of the 132 White House rooms, though at this stage she visualized it only as a practical place for her husband to meet visitors. But of all the rooms, there was only one in which she truly delighted from the beginning. "Lincoln's Bedroom! The only room in the whole place I like!" Mrs. Kennedy wrote happily to her decorator.

"Can't change it — wouldn't want to." The Lincoln Room has yellow walls, tufted settees, marble-topped tables and a monstrous Victorian bed. The bed, with its nine-foot-high rosewood headboard carved in tortuous curlicues, is presumed to have been bought by Mrs. Lincoln in 1861. Then it had been even more spectacular. "Twenty feet above the floor, overspreading the whole, is a magnificent canopy," wrote an awed chronicler. "The drapery is a rich purple satin print and otherwise ornamented with finest gold lace. The carved wood is adorned with gold gilt." No one knows whether President Lincoln actually ever slept in the bed. Yet today, even stripped of its regal draperies, it is the most talked about piece of furniture in the White House.

During the Lincoln administration, this room had been used for Cabinet meetings and it was here that the Emancipation Proclamation was signed. It was after the 1948 Renovation that President Truman, a true history buff and ardent admirer of his famed predecessor, had gathered here such Lincoln furnishings as he could find in the White House and several authentic pieces obtained from outside sources. The Great Emancipator himself, however, had occupied another bedroom: the one which Jacqueline Kennedy was to make her own when the alterations were completed.

On the mantelpiece of this room had been a metal plaque bearing the inscription: "In this room Abraham Lincoln slept during his occupancy of the White House as President of the United States March 4, 1861 to April 13, 1865." The plaque had been removed while the room was being painted for Mrs. Kennedy. The following Christmas, during her absence in Palm Beach, she asked Mr. West to have the legend carved on the mantel, thus assuring its permanence. Shortly before leaving the White House, Mrs. Kennedy was to have a second inscription carved on the mantel. It read: "In this room lived John Fitzgerald Kennedy and his wife Jacqueline during the two years, ten months and two days he was President of the United States, January 20th 1961–November 22nd, 1963."

Making a dining room, kitchen and pantry right in the middle of the White House, besides revamping a book closet into a bedroom, were seemingly major alterations. Yet, surprisingly, the changes were completed in a mere two weeks after the new family had moved in. Except for the kitchen, which was bought commercially as a unit, this transformation was undertaken by the thirty-five maintenance men on the regular White House staff. Their trades included electrician, carpenter, plumber, upholsterer, painter. They were all skilled men who obligingly doubled for each other on any job to be done.

"There wasn't too much to do except painting and closing up doors," disclaimed the Chief Usher. "But we did remove a fireplace from Margaret Truman's bedroom, which we then turned into a kitchen. Margaret's bathroom became the pantry and we just left the bathtub where it was and built a cabinet over it. Then we made food storage areas by putting shelves into a clothes closet," West continued. "The new dining room had always been a living room, so we had very few problems there. And, of course, the paint was scarcely dry before the Kennedys' Georgetown furniture was put in place."

Though there were a few frills, the transformation of book closet into bedroom for Miss Shaw, the children's nurse, was even less complicated. The shelves were removed, a bed and TV set installed. There was a small table for Miss Shaw's clutter and a special scrapbasket for banana peels. Bananas were her most cherished fruit and invariable between-meals snack. Yet the simplest facet of the renovation was the most important of all to one member of the Kennedy family. A large old-fashioned radiator was removed from a window enclosure in Mrs. Kennedy's bedroom. The reason for this removal was not temperature regulation: far from it! The heating unit was taken away so that Caroline could have her very own exciting place in which to hide.

2

January 18, 1961
-
January 20, 1961

Forty-four Hours

Two days before the Inauguration, a small crowd gathered at the Palm Beach airport to wave good-bye to Jacqueline Kennedy. She had arrived at the Florida resort on December 9, two weeks after the birth of her son John. Since then, she had been recuperating at the senior Kennedys' ocean-front villa. The flight north in the Kennedy family plane took four hours, and when the *Caroline* (a twin-engine Convair, purchased jointly by the Kennedy brothers and sisters to facilitate their brother's political campaigning) set down at Washington's military terminal, she was met by a squad of photographers, the vanguard of countless cameramen who were to haunt her from then on.

The following morning, newspapers throughout the country described the future First Lady in pleasant detail.

"The slim, young Jacqueline wore a black and white plaid tweed suit for her trip," enthused a Washington fashion scribe. "It was styled with slim skirt and short, loose jacket and worn with long, black kid gloves, a shiny new black alligator bag and high-heeled alligator pumps. A red suede beret perched atop her bouffant brown hair."

Back in the charming N Street house, which her husband had bought to please her after Caroline's birth, she had just forty-four hours in which to accomplish a fantastic number of things before leaving it forever. There were myriad household details to attend to, final fittings on her inaugural gown, hairdressing appointments, and above all, the necessity for as much rest as possible to save her strength for the dramatic events in which she would be the cynosure of all eyes.

In November, shortly after her son John was born prematurely, Dr. John W. Walsh, her obstetrician, had informed the press that Mrs. Kennedy would have to "curtail her activities for about six months." Dr. Walsh explained why, succinctly: "She is a perfectly healthy, normal person trying to recuperate from a

Caesarian section." Dr. Janet Travell, who had been appointed the President-elect's physician, saw the future First Lady constantly and was amazed at her stamina. "A Caesarian is major surgery," she emphasized, "and, combined with the sheer physical drain of creating a baby, would knock out most women for a long time. But don't forget that Mrs. Kennedy also flew down to Palm Beach," she continued, "and lived in a house which was not her own, through which visitors constantly paraded. Actually, she had moved out of her own home and had very little time to plan a new and much more taxing life in the White House. . . . Added to all this," Dr. Travell concluded, "the tensions of the Presidential campaign still remained while she was faced by the burden of vast, new responsibilities. It was fantastic that she was able to accomplish what she did."

Less than two weeks after John Fitzgerald Kennedy's election, the N Street house, which Jacqueline loved, had been sold to Perry Ausbrook, a lawyer. He and his wife were the first and only prospective buyers to inspect the property. All Kennedy possessions were to be removed as soon as possible though the Ausbrooks would not take possession until March. Mrs. Adele Murphy, head of Residential Services, Inc., who had organized three previous Kennedy household *déménagements,* made a complete inventory of the contents of the house, including china and linens, while the family was in Palm Beach. Mrs. Kennedy marked the list to indicate which pieces of furniture were to be sent to the White House, which to Glen Ora, the weekend hideaway they had rented in Virginia, and which simply to the spacious White House storerooms. Mrs. Murphy then handled the tedious details of packing and moving.

"Mrs. Kennedy was always easy to work with," Mrs. Murphy commented. "She always knew exactly where she wanted everything placed, and she seldom changed her mind." In this way, the moving was accomplished with such efficiency that the galoshes Bill Walton left at N Street on Inaugural Eve were neatly ticketed and returned promptly from the White House. This last day, Jacqueline had only to decide which necessary personal effects were to be taken directly to the White House after she had left for the inaugural ceremony.

Traditionally, not a trunk, suitcase or even a package belonging to the incoming presidential family was supposed to arrive in their new home until 12:01 P.M. on Inauguration Day. But through the friendly connivance of Mr. West, the Chief Usher, and Mrs. Kennedy's new social secretary, Letitia Baldridge, all sorts of Kennedy impedimenta had been finding their way anonymously into White House storage rooms for weeks.

The N Street house had been in turmoil the last two days. Secret Service agents were posted outside; and inside they guarded the front door, scrutinizing all callers, much to the annoyance of George Thomas, the long-time Kennedy retainer who would go to the White House as valet. For privacy, shades were kept drawn day and night on the living room windows which opened scarcely a few feet above the sidewalk. The library, facing the back patio, was safe from prying eyes, but a steady stream of callers marched in and out. The postman left hundreds of letters daily, while telegrams, parcels and gifts of all kinds were delivered at the side door. The letters were tied in bundles, but sometimes the string loosened and they cascaded from the hall table onto the floor. In the kitchen Pearl brewed coffee continuously, and George was kept jumping to serve it. Mrs. Kennedy remained on the comparatively peaceful second floor. Besides her household tasks, she had planned her final fittings and hairdressing appointments well in advance.

Through the afternoon, as the tempo of the snowstorm increased, it became apparent that many of those who were helping the Kennedys through this final pre-White House travail, would be unable to return home that night. Fortunately, Caroline and John and their nurses were in Palm Beach, so the third-floor bedrooms at N Street were empty. Later that evening Mary Gallagher, who did secretarial work for Mrs. Kennedy, and Evelyn Lincoln, the Senator's personal secretary, were tucked into the upstairs rooms. On the ground floor, there was a sizable sitting room for the staff. Here Provie, Mrs. Kennedy's personal maid, with her two young sons and her mother who had come to share in the excitement, somehow managed to bed down together.

On Monday morning, after the Friday Inauguration, when Mrs. Murphy arrived to supervise the removal of Kennedy belongings, she could scarcely take a step in the downstairs hall.

Provie, who had returned from the White House to tidy up, had been stripping the beds and bathrooms, then pitching the soiled linen down from the upper floors. Every piece had been listed and assigned to a specified trunk. Provie, looking down over the banisters, caught Adele Murphy's outraged expression. "Give up, Mrs. Murphy," she shouted gleefully, "there's nothing we can do about it!"

"Such a Beloved Lady"

"Such a beloved lady!" murmured Providencia Parades of Jacqueline Kennedy, whose personal maid she had been for a decade. Provie, born in the Dominican Republic, was short, brunette and so cheerful it was always a pleasure to have her around. She was also shrewd and efficient and enjoyed her job.

After three years working for Kennedy acquaintances who lived a few blocks distant in Georgetown, Provie came to the recently married Senator and his wife as what she called "a second-floor maid." Twice in the ensuing years Provie had left the Kennedys for family reasons, but each time a telephone call from the Senator had coaxed her back. She helped them settle in the new N Street house when Jacqueline Kennedy returned from the hospital with Caroline. She stayed firm and fast with her "beloved lady" until Mrs. Kennedy left Washington for New York.

When the Kennedys moved to the White House, Provie agreed to "live in" for a month. This was the trying period when alterations were being made in the private rooms and the new upstairs kitchen and dining room were being built. Then Provie, in her own words, "worked around the clock" getting settled. She was given a third-floor bedroom and, besides sleeping there when the occasion demanded, she used it as a superwardrobe, keeping all the First Lady's clothes on long, movable racks, such as are used in stores. This made the clothes easier to see and get at than if they had been hung in closets.

During the White House years Provie was not only responsible for Mrs. Kennedy's wardrobe and its accompanying accessories but also for having the First Lady dressed and ready, with split-second punctuality, for an extravagant number of engagements. Each morning she would check everything Mrs. Kennedy had worn the previous day. She put nothing away unless it was in perfect order. She never permitted anyone else to press the First Lady's gowns. She learned innumerable small tricks about clothes care. For instance, Alexandre, the fashionable Parisian hairdresser, taught her how to make Mrs. Kennedy's almost shoulder-high twenty-button white kid gloves fit to perfection. Gloves were an integral part of the First Lady's ensembles, mornings through evenings, and the twenty-button length became a Jacqueline Kennedy trademark. Alexandre had Provie stitch a tiny hem at the top of the glove to prevent the edge from turning over and then, from elbow to top, narrow them along the seam so they clung to the upper arm without wrinkle or downward sag.

Provie was usually along when Mrs. Kennedy traveled without her husband, and accompanied the presidential couple on all their official trips except the last, fateful journey to Texas.* Sometimes, on these excursions, she helped supervise the President's clothes. She knew his ways. "He liked everything perfect," she explained. In Georgetown, she had ironed his shirts with meticulous attention, and on occasion fixed his evening ties. On a tightly scheduled trip, she saw to it that, when the President returned to his room, the bath was drawn, his clothing laid out with cufflinks and shirt studs in place. "He was a very quick dresser," Provie commented, "and very particular about his clothes."

He was "very particular" about his wife's clothes, too. He didn't like brown. He didn't like anything flowered. When he didn't like one of Jacqueline's dresses, she never wore it again.

---

* Mary Gallagher, now a secretary to the First Lady, had longed to be included on one of these glamorous journeys. As Mrs. Kennedy never traveled with a secretary, Mrs. Gallagher badgered Provie continuously to change places with her. When Provie relented and obtained Mrs. Kennedy's consent, Mary flew off to Texas to act as the First Lady's maid.

Usually, though, this dilemma was avoided. Before each important engagement Provie would hang several dresses on a rack which was placed in Mrs. Kennedy's room. Then the First Lady and the President together could choose the most appropriate and becoming creation.

He was equally critical about millinery. Provie remembers a hat which Mrs. Kennedy had planned to wear when Emperor Haile Selassie of Ethiopia, a state guest, arrived in Washington. Provie described the specially made bit of headgear as a sexy overblown beret type. When his wife entered the room, as they were about to leave for the welcoming ceremony, the President took a single startled glance. "Jackie! I don't like that hat!" he exclaimed. The First Lady promptly took it off. When they drove off together to meet the Emperor at the railroad station, Mrs. Kennedy was wearing a far less spectacular creation.

The President personally approved every item of his wife's wardrobe for the Texas trip. It was the first time that Jacqueline had accompanied him into the political hustings since the 1960 campaign. More than ever he wanted every detail, including the First Lady's appearance, to be "perfect."

The morning they were leaving, the President received reports that Texas weather was unusually warm for November. He worried about her being uncomfortable. The helicopter was waiting on the White House South Lawn to ferry them to *Air Force One* at Andrews Field. Mrs. Kennedy was standing before a mirror putting on her hat when the President called from his office. "Provie," he said, "I hear it is very hot in Texas. Are you sure Mrs. Kennedy has enough cotton clothes?" Provie reassured him. It was the last time she was to hear his voice.

The following day Provie went shopping and had returned to the White House before she heard the news. When the chief of the Secret Service detail confirmed the President's death, she could not believe it. Dazed, she hovered throughout the evening near Mrs. Kennedy's room and in the early morning hour when the new widow returned from the Bethesda Naval Hospital, Provie was still there. Almost the first thing, Mrs. Kennedy asked Provie if she "minded" spending the night at the White House, instead of going home to her family. "Such a beloved lady!" Provie murmurs when she recalls this pathetic moment.

"Interested!"

Early in the morning of the day before the Kennedy Inauguration, the eyes of the world — literally — were focused on the
young President-elect and his wife. Their red brick Federal
house on N Street had been cordoned off on the opposite curb.
TV cameras were ready to go and newsmen maintained their
chilly vigil, waiting for John Fitzgerald Kennedy to emerge, or
perhaps hoping to catch a glimpse of Mrs. Kennedy at one of the
curtained windows. Shortly after nine o'clock the Senator appeared, hurried to his car and was driven away.

His destination was the White House. Here, for the second
time since his election, he was to meet with President Eisenhower. Only now there was a difference. After the first three-hour
session on December 6, the previously doubting Eisenhower had
gone on public record as approving, if not downright admiring,
his youthful successor. "I feel much better about the future of
the nation," he stated solemnly. This day before the Inauguration, they met amiably in the President's office, which had been
almost entirely stripped of his personal possessions. They were
closeted together for almost two hours, then stepped side by side
into the Cabinet Room where both outgoing and incoming
Secretaries of State, Treasury and Defense were waiting.

When Senator Kennedy left the White House, reporters were
intrigued by his complete calmness. One ventured, "Aren't you
excited?" Kennedy, flashing his contagious grin, replied with a
single word: "Interested!"

The Senator went directly from the White House to Bill
Walton's house on P Street in Georgetown. A few days earlier, he
had mentioned casually that he "might be over." His wife had
returned from Palm Beach the afternoon before, and he knew
there were too many distracting domestic activities planned at

home. He had people to meet and serious decisions to make before tomorrow's Inauguration. His secretary had made the necessary appointments and, with scarcely a by-your-leave to his host, Jack Kennedy set up a command post which suited his purpose admirably. The ground-level entrance to the Kennedy house on N Street was inconvenient: when the front door opened, part of the first floor was exposed to the inquisitive press. But ten sandstone steps led up to the foyer of Walton's substantial corner residence. A further modicum of privacy was assured by a low iron railing which fenced the square of front lawn and barred the brick walk leading to the steps. Reporters would have to remain outside the iron gate while newsworthy guests could, if necessary, be spirited in unobserved, through a back garden door known only to Walton intimates.

Inside, the President-elect took over the front room, a high-ceilinged parlor with twin mantelpieces and appropriate Victorian furniture whose well-worn upholstery blended with the faded red wallpaper. Evelyn Lincoln, his personal secretary, guarded the hall telephone; and Ralph Dungan, a former Senate staff member who had already been appointed Special Assistant to the President in charge of personnel, stayed close to his boss.

Police had scarcely been posted around Walton's house when suddenly, like ants mysteriously attracted to some carelessly discarded tidbit, people began infiltrating P Street. Their number steadily increased until cars and buses had to be diverted through other narrower Georgetown streets. Long after tomorrow's President had left, even when the snow began to fall, many of the curious remained staring curiously at the darkened house.

To the little group within the warm red room, the surrounding atmosphere became increasingly theatrical. When the front door opened, offstage noises swelled in waves like breaking surf. Whenever the Senator, hatless and without overcoat, stepped out to make an announcement to the press, the crowd cheered wildly. When the skies darkened the drama heightened, for the TV cameramen switched on their klieg lights, flooding the scene with a ghoulish, pale-green light.

"Billy Boy"

The warm friendship between the Senator and Bill Walton, a journalist turned artist, was not based on school, college, or political association: until the presidential campaign (to which Bill made an important contribution) Kennedy intimates, perhaps enviously, insisted he was primarily Mrs. Kennedy's friend.

Walton himself was compact, with gloriously florid stick-out ears, a lock of blond hair which flipped into his left eye and a basso-profundo voice with a Middle Western twang, which emerged from a permanently sideslanted mouth. A dedicated individualist, he affected blue jeans and windbreakers a generation before hippies adopted them, yet he looked ever so smooth in a conventional dinner jacket. He was polite but sardonic; extraordinarily knowledgeable on an exciting diversity of subjects, but always comfortable to be with.

A native of Jacksonville, Illinois, he came to Washington in 1947 in a switch from being a foreign editor of *Life* to reporting for the more erudite *New Republic*. As a divorcé, then with custody of a young daughter and son, he attracted enthusiastic attention from unattached ladies who clustered around hopefully, "helping" him with suggestions on how to raise his children. During the years his children were growing up, Walton had abandoned journalism for a new career as a serious artist. By the time he had settled in the P Street house his children had left home, he was really alone, and his paintings had evolved from representational to abstract.

One evening early in 1960, when Bill was dining with the Kennedys, the Senator began thinking aloud about campaign problems. Walton joined in, batting back some sensible suggestions about the primaries. Kennedy followed up cagily. "If you're so interested, why not work for me?" Walton ignored the question, but the Senator persisted. "Why not go to Wisconsin?" he said casually; then let the matter drop.

The next morning Kennedy, in high spirits, telephoned. "Well, Billy Boy, this is the Senator. What about it?" Bill, seeking escape, countered, "What would I do?" "I haven't a clue," the Senator laughed, "just take a train to Milwaukee!"

Soon afterwards, Bill Walton did just that.

Around 3 A.M. of the morning after the Wisconsin primary was won, the Senator and his staff were relaxing on the *Caroline*. As the Kennedy plane flew them back to Washington, Bill mentioned that Bobby Kennedy had asked him to help in the approaching West Virginia primary. "Thank God!" exclaimed the candidate with a grin. "I didn't have the guts to ask you!"

After a tough battle, West Virginia followed Wisconsin to the Kennedy side. Months later, when the triumphant Democratic National Convention in Los Angeles was over, Bill ducked off alone on a painting trip, leaving behind only a general delivery address in San Francisco. On his return he found a sheaf of urgent telegrams. Over long distance Bobby persuaded Bill to hurry back to Washington. But when Walton arrived in the capital, Bobby was in Manhattan and from there began urging him to take over as coordinator of the New York campaign. No longer flattered by Kennedy pleas for assistance, and reluctant to assume new political chores, Bill replied that before accepting he would have to think it over.

Nevertheless he caught the first plane to New York and taxied directly to Kennedy headquarters in the Biltmore Hotel. There, as he stepped into the reception room, a loudspeaker blared Bobby's announcement to the press that William Walton had accepted the post of campaign coordinator. Though Bill protested vehemently, it was too late. There was nothing he could do.

Walton was not a rich man. He had worked hard for months as a volunteer paying his own living and travel expenses as well. No one had mentioned either a salary or an expense account. With costlier hotel bills and expensive restaurant charges in New York, he was going broke fast. Finally, Bill told Bobby he was quitting. Obviously distressed, Bobby asked, "Whatever for?" "No dough!" Bill replied succinctly. Then for two months and two months only of his labors, Walton was paid a salary.

The grueling struggle in the primaries and the exhausting Democratic National Convention in Los Angeles, followed by three months as New York campaign coordinator, added up to almost a year of total dedication to his friend John F. Kennedy. Walton took it in stride and did not expect to be thanked. But he was thanked once, and only once; not for all the work he had put in but for an act of kindness. He had been a guest of the Kennedys for Thanksgiving luncheon. The President-elect was to leave for Palm Beach that evening. Later, in the chilly night, Bill had opened his bedroom windows and drawn a bath and was about to step into the tub, when the telephone rang. It was a reporter friend excitedly calling to say that Mrs. Kennedy, who was not expecting her baby for a month, had been rushed to the hospital. Bill knew that the Senator's plane was scarcely halfway to its destination. So without waiting to grab even a towel, he called the West Palm Beach air terminal, persuaded a feminine employee to hold the line open while she left her counter to find someone who could get through to Pierre Salinger on the *Caroline*. Shivering, stark naked, he dared not put down the receiver until he was sure Salinger had been alerted. (Landing in West Palm Beach, the President-elect abandoned the leisurely *Caroline* and flew straight back to Washington on the chartered jet press plane.)

Still unclothed, Bill then called Mrs. Hugh D. Auchincloss, Jacqueline Kennedy's mother. It was very late on a holiday night, and, in the big house in the country, the telephone rang for a long time. At last, his teeth chattering, Walton broke the news to Janet Auchincloss. Then he jumped into bed.

The following morning Bill met his friend at the hospital. The Senator, elated that his son was safely born, turned to Walton and said with unaccustomed seriousness, "Thank you for all you did last night."

Walton's job as New York campaign coordinator encompassed many unusual facets. Perhaps one of the most pleasurable commenced as the most nervewracking. One of the rare occasions when Mrs. Kennedy was able to join her husband in active campaigning was for New York's dramatic traditional ticker-tape parade shortly before the election. She rode, perched beside the Senator on the folded-back top of their car, through the sky-scraper-lined canyons of Wall Street, where they were blizzarded with literally a ton of ticker tape and scraps of white paper, up Broadway and toward the Bronx. An estimated two million on-lookers cheered them along the route.

Though it was a thrilling occasion, it was also very risky for Jacqueline Kennedy. She was terrified that, should the crowds become uncontrollable, break through the police lines and jostle their automobile, she might lose her baby. As safeguard, Bill was planted in a bus loaded with Secret Service agents which trailed the candidate. If Mrs. Kennedy felt the slightest tremor, she was to signal and Walton would move in immediately. At one moment it was touch and go, but the surging crowds, eager to shake hands or even touch the Kennedys, were stopped just short of the car.

Near Columbus Circle she left the parade while her husband continued his politicking. Bill joined her and, as camouflage against recognition, she turned a raincoat inside out and wore it over her coat. They sauntered along Madison Avenue, stopping at the Tibor Denagy Gallery to see an exhibition of contemporary paintings, then dropped into several other art galleries before returning to the Carlyle Hotel. Curiously, though millions had watched the parade and other millions had followed it on television, Bill Walton was convinced that no one on the street or close to in the galleries identified the future First Lady. The raincoat had proved an unexpectedly effective disguise.

Walton's last day as coordinator was spent in Hyannis Port. On election night, in the Senator's house, with author Theodore White, journalist Ben Bradlee and his wife, Tony, and the Kennedys themselves, they watched the returns on television. At midnight, when the verdict was assured, the Secret Service closed in, and Bill Walton's job was done.

Later, as Walton became involved with the Kennedy artistic and architectural projects, the President appointed him chairman of the Fine Arts Commission, when the incumbent retired. President Kennedy was unaware that it was strictly a prestige job and thought he was offering his friend a most appropriate position with a pleasant salary. Again Walton was destined to work hard without compensation, but the idea tickled his sense of humor. "No one was more surprised than the President," he said, "when he found out that the job had no salary!"

A Glamorous Emergency

At his P Street house, that cold day before the Inauguration, Bill Walton functioned as staff. He welcomed visitors, either escorting them through the front hallway or along a narrow passage leading from the back garden. Those whose appointments overlapped he stacked, so to speak, in the adjoining dining room. This system broke down only once, when Ted Sorensen, Kennedy's most intimate political collaborator, arrived with a bevy of family: seven nieces and nephews and their parents. Fresh off a plane from Nebraska, they spilled along the hall, jittery with excitement at the prospect of meeting the President-elect.

First on the appointments list was stocky Army General Lyman Lemnitzer and, hurrying on his heels, came Arthur Goldberg, sparkling with euphoric energy. The General was to become chairman of the Joint Chiefs of Staff. Goldberg, already tapped as Secretary of Labor, succeeded in coaxing the Senator to pay an unscheduled call later that afternoon on a group of labor leaders who were in town for the Inauguration.

William S. White, a political writer, accompanied Newbold Noyes, executive editor of the Washington *Evening Star,* the local newspaper in which White's syndicated column was then appearing. Noyes, who had only met Senator Kennedy socially, had asked White to arrange the meeting. The three were chatting amiably when Kennedy was summoned to a nearby telephone. Dean Rusk, whom he had appointed Secretary of State the previous month (December 12, 1960), was calling. "Yes, Mr. Rusk?" the newsmen heard the Senator answer in his imperturbable voice. While he talked with the Secretary-designate, Noyes turned to White and mused, "I wonder how he feels giving orders to an older man?" "Why don't you ask him?" suggested White. When the editor repeated his question, Kennedy looked astonished. "I don't see any problem!" he answered matter-of-factly.

Najeeb Halaby, a former Assistant Secretary of Defense under Republican Secretary Charles Wilson, had been waiting in the dining room with Walton. Halaby was anxious to work for Kennedy. As he had known the Senator only in a social way, Halaby had been invited for a "get-acquainted" interview with the possibility of being appointed administrator of the Federal Aviation Agency. They "sat down" together and, after a forty-five-minute exchange of ideas, he was offered the job. Kennedy decided to release the news immediately, but as his secretary was guarding the insistent telephone and was unable to type, Walton obligingly hammered out the text on his ancient typewriter. When the corrections were finished, the Senator escorted Halaby to the front steps, handed reporters the announcement and posed for joint photographs.

Shortly before one o'clock, Rowland Evans, another political columnist and an intimate Kennedy friend, slipped through the garden gate unannounced and was promptly apprehended by Secret Service agents. After properly identifying himself, Rollie was permitted to enter the house where the Senator immediately invited him to luncheon. This casual invitation was somewhat embarrassing to their mutual host. Walton, a popular bachelor and continually invited out, did not keep his larder stocked for any such glamorous emergency. Nevertheless, Katie Everett, his housekeeper for eighteen years, rose nobly to the occasion. She concocted a menu starring chipped beef and baked potatoes, which the future President of the United States ate with appetite.

The ambiance was magical, Rowland Evans recalled, at this last luncheon before John Fitzgerald Kennedy was to assume the heavy responsibilities of the Presidency. Through the tall, curtainless windows, they could see the drab gray skies and frozen lawn. But inside the cozy glow from a coal fire flickered across the butter-colored walls. Utterly relaxed, the Senator told three hilarious unprintable stories in quick succession. They were the type known to the Kennedy circle as "Dave Powers stories."

Then the conversation moved to more staid subjects. The President-elect, worried because he still had to give away several hundred-dollar tickets for the evening's theatrical Gala, summoned his secretary and told her precisely how he wanted them distributed. This minor matter resolved, he brought up two problems which particularly interested him. The first was how to make the best use of Negro diplomats. The second, which he discussed with great skill and perception, was how best to fill the numerous Assistant and Deputy Assistant Secretary positions available in both State and Defense Departments. He possessed all the essential facts about the men he named and, in his mind, juggled their potentialities against the jobs' demands. His extensive knowledge of the individuals and the implications of the work involved amazed even Evans, a sophisticated journalist who had known Jack Kennedy intimately for many years. "It was one of the most fascinating conversations I have ever heard," he stated emphatically.

When the meal ended, the Senator asked for a cigar. Walton, a nonsmoker, had none; he queried the Secret Service agents, but none of them indulged either. Finally, Walton stepped outside and conned the press. A half-frozen newsman delightedly sacrificed a magnificent stogie.

"A Nice, Decent Young Man"

One of the official inaugural functions that afternoon was the Governors' Reception, a 3 to 6 P.M. affair which was in full swing when the President-elect arrived. John Snyder, Secretary of the Treasury under Truman, was the chairman and the governors of almost every state, regardless of political affiliation, were present. Kennedy started down the receiving line greeting governors individually but was soon engulfed by a rapidly growing crowd of insistent well-wishers. They struggled to shake hands or at least to touch the person of tomorrow's President, behaving remarkably like a hive of drones fighting to nuzzle a queen bee. In the melee, Kennedy came face to face with former President Truman.

The future President, scarcely managing to maintain his balance among the shoving people, immediately invited the former President to come home with him for a visit. Truman accepted with alacrity. Before the crowd was aware of what was happening, Secret Service agents encircled the two men and spirited them to a waiting limousine. The falling snow had not as yet built up to disaster proportions and the car raced through Rock Creek Park to N Street.

In the pleasant library where, through French doors, they could see a single mammoth magnolia tree weighted with the first snow, they sat on either side of a crackling wood fire and talked. When Mr. Truman departed, thirty-five minutes later, the bareheaded Senator stood beside his guest on the doorstep while reporters asked the former President whether he had given the President-elect any advice. "Advice is the cheapest thing in the world," Truman snapped, "but I let him know that I would do anything officially that he wants me to do." Mr. Truman went on to describe John Fitzgerald Kennedy as "brilliant" and "a nice, decent young man," adding, "He knows the history of government as well as anyone I've met and that includes me."

Testament of Freedom

By dusk, the snow was falling so impenetrably that Bill Walton, who had been promised a ride with the Kennedys, wondered how he would get to the Inaugural Concert in Constitution Hall, much less the Inaugural Gala which was being staged simultaneously at the National Guard Armory on the opposite side of Washington.

*Mrs. Kennedy leaves her N Street house in the midst of a
blizzard to attend the Inaugural Concert.*

It was past seven when the telephone rang. "Billy Boy," said the familiar, bantering voice, "this is the Senator speaking! I can't stop by for you because only Constitution Avenue is being cleared, but if you can get to N Street in fifteen minutes, I'll take you!"

It was five long blocks across town and three down from 29th and P streets to 3307 N Street. Dodging snowdrifts, Walton ran all the way.

The Inaugural Concert had been completely sold out; but when, miraculously ahead of schedule, the Kennedys and Walton arrived at Constitution Hall, only a few hundred of the 3,800 ticket holders had managed to struggle through the storm. Nor had all the National Symphony Orchestra musicians made it. A chartered bus failed to pick up the Howard University Choir. Mischa Elman, the violin virtuoso, cradling his Stradivarius, was stranded in the Dupont Plaza lobby. His solo in a Vivaldi concerto had to be omitted from the program. Howard Mitchell, the conductor, tramped a mile and a half down 16th Street from the Roosevelt Hotel. He remembers that every street corner was blocked with stalled cars which he had to detour around through perilous drifts of snow.

The welcoming committee had not arrived, so minor concert hall staff members escorted the President-elect to the Secretary-General's room, a backstage enclave where important guests are received privately. Mitchell was startled to see them. "How did you manage to get here, Senator?" he exclaimed. "I had a little help!" replied Kennedy with a smile. While they waited for both musicians and audience to arrive, Mitchell was kept busy answering a barrage of Kennedy questions.

Though not a dedicated music lover, the President-elect was intrigued by the program of his own Inaugural Concert. The two main numbers had been chosen to complement his historic and literary interests. The opening selection, an overture titled "From Sea to Shining Sea," was based on the theme of "America the Beautiful." The opus had been commissioned for the occasion by Howard Mitchell and the National Symphony Orchestra and underwritten by a Ford Foundation grant. The composer, a young American named John La Montaine, had won the 1958 Pulitzer Prize with a Concerto for Piano and Orchestra. He had, since, studied musical composition on two successive Guggen-heim grants. He met the Kennedys at the concert, when they were presented with a hand-written score of his overture.

The second selection, "The Testament of Freedom — a Setting of Four Passages from the Writings of Thomas Jefferson," was composed by Randall Thompson in honor of the two hundredth anniversary of the birth of the third President. It was first per-formed in April 1943, at the University of Virginia. The four excerpted passages were: (1) A Summary of the Rights of British America in 1774; (2) The Declaration of Causes and Necessity of Taking Up Arms; (3) July 6, 1775; (4) Letter to John Adams, Monticello, September 12, 1821.

These ringing words of Jefferson, whom John Fitzgerald Ken-nedy so admired, were printed on a separate page in the concert program. The Senator, after glancing at them, slipped the pro-gram in his pocket.

While the Kennedys and Mitchell passed the time backstage in casual conversation, Constitution Hall was filling slowly. Mitchell later estimated, though perhaps optimistically, that be-tween twelve hundred and two thousand determined ticket holders finally were seated. The Georgetown University Glee Club made it to the Hall under police escort in a bus which had careened along sidewalks and the wrong way down one-way streets. Pianist Earl Wild, who was to play Gershwin's "Rhapsody in Blue" as a finale, arrived breathless after walking miles. Before the concert ended, all but six members of the orchestra were accounted for — most of them having come on foot after aban-doning their cars.

"Turn on the Lights So They Can See Jackie"

Once again the three — Senator and Mrs. Kennedy and Bill Wal-ton — were isolated in the warm limousine. Snow was still falling when they left the Concert Hall and rode along Constitution Avenue, past the floodlit Washington Monument, whose needle-tipped summit with its winking red light was obscured. They circled the Capitol and sped on to the distant National Guard Armory. Not a car moved on the broad avenue; but scattered work gangs, on duty to remove the continuing snowfall, warmed themselves at fires kindled in oil drums. Here and there a knot of hard-core enthusiasts, crusted white as icicles, had risked frostbite to glimpse the earlier cavalcade of theatrical stars en route to the Inaugural Gala and now remained on to cheer the Kennedys.

"Turn on the lights," the Senator suggested to Walton, "so they can see Jackie." Then he drew the program from his pocket and, in the dim light, read the stirring Jeffersonian phrases which he had just heard musically intoned. The President-elect may have been comparing the Jeffersonian prose to the Inaugural Message he himself was to deliver at noon the next day, for when he had finished, he shook his head and said ruefully, "Better than mine!"

The Inaugural Gala started an hour and forty minutes late (and ended at 1:40 A.M.). When the Kennedys' limousine drew up to the Armory entrance, a welcoming committee headed by Frank Sinatra and Peter Lawford, the President-elect's brother-in-law, were waiting to do the honors. Again the Kennedys were shown to an anteroom to wait until the show was ready to commence. As they waited, Leonard Bernstein raised his baton and the orchestra crashed into a "Fanfare for Inauguration," his own musical arrangement. John Philip Sousa's rousing march, "The Stars and Stripes Forever," followed, and then the music switched to "Walking Down to Washington." Most of the cast strutted down the aisles in groups of five, followed by a rear guard of college glee club members, all singing lustily and waving multicolored balloons. When the cast was lined up on stage, the presidential party stepped into their box, piped aboard (so to speak) by "Anchors Aweigh," the United States Navy's song.

Sinatra and Lawford had set up headquarters at the Statler Hilton long in advance and had been working frantically on the show. Their "Gala" was not one of the official events planned and underwritten by the Inaugural Committee: technically it was a "private affair" to which an "invitation," i.e., ticket, could be bought for one hundred dollars. The main purpose was to raise funds to help pay off the National Democratic Committee campaign deficit. A financial statement of the Inaugural Gala was never published by the Democratic National Committee. Though the Armory seats were sold out and the cast donated its services, the expenses — such as luxurious hotel accommodations and chauffeured limousines — were believed to have been astronomical.

With Sinatra and Lawford teamed as producers, the Gala had tremendous appeal for both Broadway and Hollywood, and so many stars had rushed to volunteer their services that it had been difficult to select a cast without giving offense. The fabulous final lineup ran the gamut from Mahalia Jackson, who sang "The Star-Spangled Banner," to Sir Laurence Olivier; from Jimmy Durante to Helen Traubel; from Harry Belafonte to Bette Davis. The harassed Sinatra took time out from his job as producer to sing a parody on his superhit "That Old Black Magic," turning it into "That Old Jack Magic," and Ethel Merman, hitherto a well-publicized Nixon fan, climbed on the Kennedy bandwagon by belting out "Everything's Coming Up Roses." Even Eleanor Roosevelt contributed to the program. She joined Helen Traubel and Frederic March in a reading entitled "A Moment with Lincoln," which was based on the Farewell Address Lincoln delivered when leaving Springfield for Washington.

The intermission was very gay. The orchestra dashed into "The Silver Bell Waltz," a favored tune which Lincoln had requested at his Inaugural Ball. Pretty usherettes with rhinestone crowns pinned atop their stylish hairdos, served the refreshments, while the President-elect box-hopped and friends dropped by to congratulate Mrs. Kennedy.

After the Gala, Mrs. Kennedy returned directly to Georgetown to spend her last night in the N Street house. The Senator continued on to a private supper party given at Paul Young's restaurant by his father and mother. The Gala cast, all available Kennedys, and all possible members of Jack's incoming official family were there — about three hundred in all. Jack enjoyed himself immensely, and it was 3:28 A.M. when the Secret Service agents clocked him in at home.

A Memorable Standout

On Friday, January 20, 1961, the cloudless sky was a piercing blue, the sun shone brilliantly on the pristine snow, and the daytime temperature hovered in the low twenties. At 8 A.M., John Fitzgerald Kennedy arose from his bed, where he had slept soundly for scarcely more than four hours. He was forty-three years old, six feet tall, and weighed about 170 pounds; on the rare occasions when he wore a hat, an unusually large size, seven and five-eighths, fitted him comfortably. Admiring friends noted when he stripped for swimming that he had the build of a light heavyweight fighter. Recently two physicians, Dr. Janet Travell and Dr. Eugene J. Cohen, had certified that he was in excellent health.

On this special day, he was to become the youngest of thirty-five Presidents to be inaugurated; the first President of the United States to have been born in the twentieth century; the first Roman Catholic to be elected; and the sixth Harvard graduate to attain the highest honor the American people could offer.

He showered, put on a business suit and went down to breakfast in the library. His tray was set on a luggage rack in front of the fireplace. The menu, as usual, was orange juice, lean strips of bacon, toast with marmalade, coffee with cream and sugar, and two poached eggs — a recent addition.

A few minutes later Jacqueline Bouvier Kennedy, wearing a dressing gown, joined him. She was thirty-one years old and five feet seven inches tall, a gracefully slender brunette with a notably erect carriage. One of her former schoolteachers, remembering her as a very young girl, described her aptly: "She was someone you'd never forget. She was very lively and full of mischief; had great, green eyes and wonderful hair." On this special day, she would become the third youngest of thirty previous First Ladies of the land.

Her tray, placed opposite his, contained her everyday breakfast: orange juice, toast and honey, and coffee with skimmed milk.

They looked through the morning newspapers. The news was almost exclusively stories and photographs of the Inauguration and the previous night's festivities and the awesome blizzard. In the Washington *Post* on the page opposite the editorials was printed a three-line item, perhaps the most significant of all. It was the President's daily schedule of appointments. On this special day, it read: "At 11:20 A.M., President-elect John Fitzgerald Kennedy will arrive at the North Portico to pick up President and Mrs. Eisenhower and to drive to the Inaugural ceremonies on Capitol Hill."

For eight years, Eisenhower's public life had been capsuled in this space, and now the spotlight would be turned on Kennedy.

At 8:55 A.M., the Senator left for Holy Trinity, a Jesuit church some four blocks away, where the Reverend Richard J. Casey would celebrate a special low mass. On his return from the service, Kennedy went to Miss Helen Montgomery's house across the street at 3302 N. Since the November election, Miss Montgomery, who lived with an eighty-six-year-old father and two lovebirds, had thrown open her home to the scores of reporters "covering" the Kennedys around the clock. She sheltered them from wintry weather, served them gallons of coffee, permitted the use of her telephone and made her front windows available as observation posts. She herself spent much of her time sitting at a window, energetically knitting bootees for the new Kennedy baby and keeping a sharp lookout across the way. Now, at the request of the newsmen who had benefited by Miss Montgomery's hospitality, the President-elect was to unveil a commemorative plaque.

The brass plaque was inscribed: "In the cold winter of 1960–61, this house had an important role in history. From it was flashed to the world news of preinaugural announcements by President John Fitzgerald Kennedy. Presented by the grateful newsmen who were given warm haven here by Miss Helen Montgomery and her father, Charles."

When the informal ceremony was over, Miss Montgomery was quite undone. "Oh, Senator, I am overcome," she stammered, "I mean President-elect, please forgive me, I am overcome — this is simply wonderful!" Then for the last time as Senator, John Fitzgerald Kennedy entered this N Street house.

The President-elect had worried about dressing appropriately for his Inauguration. Traditionally, throughout history, both incoming and outgoing Presidents had worn formal clothes and high silk hats. President Truman disliked top hats and cutaways, because he thought them personally unbecoming, but nevertheless he went along with custom. General Eisenhower, used to uniforms for every occasion, broke with tradition and substituted the less formal morning coat and black Homburg. Therefore, should he, the youngest man ever elected President of the United States, return to the conservative style or continue the informal Eisenhower approach?

Shortly after his election, the Senator had posed this question to Edward H. Foley, chairman of the Inaugural Committee. Foley chanced to have discussed this problem with eighty-four-year-old Senator Carl H. Hayden of Arizona, president pro tempore of the Senate, member of the Joint Congressional Inaugural Committee, and senior member of the Senate. Senator Hayden had replied to Foley, "Ed, tell that young fella he should wear a cutaway coat and silk hat. I want him to come down looking like a President."

Scarcely two hours before the Inauguration, a crisis arose which almost ruined the elegant effect which Senator Hayden so desired. Kennedy, relaxing after the strenuous campaign, had put on weight. Unmistakably, some of the avoirdupois was carried under his chin. Struggle as he might — holding his breath, stretching his neck — he was unable to fasten the wing collar which had been ordered especially to complement the cutaway. Evelyn Lincoln, his secretary, alerted the senior Mr. Kennedy. A car raced off and returned with an assortment of parental neckware, none of which fitted. After frantic burrowing through bureau drawers, miraculously a suitable collar was discovered.

John Fitzgerald Kennedy, finally dressed for his Inauguration, looked every inch a President. In his cutaway coat, light pearl waistcoat, and gray striped trousers, he was magnificent. He wandered into his wife's room, where Jacqueline Kennedy, with Provie in attendance, was also dressing for the Inauguration.

Some time before, Mrs. Kennedy had written to Oleg Cassini, who was to design so many of her clothes, that she wanted "a beige coat with just a simple dress underneath." Cassini sketched a coat with a slight flare at the hem, big cloth buttons and a tiny ring collar of sable to match a small sable muff she already possessed. The new First Lady "hated most hats" but had liked a white felt pillbox she had worn on the triumphant ticker-tape parade through Wall Street, seated beside her husband on the folded-back top of their car. She reordered this same pillbox, which afterwards became wildly popular, in beige. Mrs. Kennedy added long, beige gloves and plain, low-heeled pumps.

The simplicity of her costume would make her a memorable standout. In contrast, every elaborately hatted and expensively befurred woman on the President's Platform would appear less elegant. For she alone would not be wrapped in fur. "I just didn't want to wear fur," Mrs. Kennedy told a friend afterwards. "I don't know why, but perhaps because women huddling on the bleachers always looked like rows of fur-bearing animals." Whatever the reasoning, her appearance was also magnificent.

Shortly before 10:30 A.M., the President-elect's official escort arrived to take them to the inaugural ceremonies. They were Senator John Sparkman of Alabama, chairman of the Joint Congressional Inaugural Committee of 1961, and the Speaker of the House of Representatives, Sam Rayburn of Texas. They came a bit early, because the previous evening President Eisenhower had telephoned personally, inviting them all to drop in for coffee before proceeding to the Capitol. At 10:55, the Speaker's limousine left the N Street house, with the Kennedys seated side by side in back and the two genial Congressmen on the jump seats. They drew up under the North Portico of the White House at 11:03. President Eisenhower was standing just inside the door waiting to welcome them. He wore a cutaway and his face was unusually pink and smiling.

Dwight David Eisenhower was seventy. He was the oldest man to have served as President of the United States. At noon, for the

Jacqueline Kennedy enters the official stand at the Capitol before the Inaugural ceremony. She is greeted by her sisters-in-law Mrs. Peter Lawford and Mrs. Sargent Shriver. Her brothers-in-law Robert Kennedy and Sargent Shriver can be seen in the background. Mrs. Nixon, Mrs. Eisenhower and Mrs. Johnson are already on the stand. Former First Lady Mrs. Woodrow Wilson is standing behind Mrs. Johnson, and Mrs. John McCormack, wife of the Speaker of the House, can be glimpsed behind Mrs. Lawford.

first time in fifty years, he would be free of official responsibility. This special morning he had awakened at his regular hour, six-fifteen, and breakfasted, as usual, on orange juice, four ounces of rare steak, toast and coffee.

When the Kennedys arrived, Mrs. Eisenhower was in the Red Room with a score or more of guests. Among them were the Lyndon B. Johnsons, Richard Nixons, and members of the Joint Congressional Inaugural Committee, Senator Styles Bridges, Republican of New Hampshire, and Representative Charles Halleck, Republican of Indiana. The three Kennedy military aides, teamed together for the first time, and the outgoing Eisenhower military aides were also present.

Everyone remained standing for a few minutes after Mrs. Kennedy had shaken hands with Mrs. Eisenhower and murmured a few words. The atmosphere was painfully strained, and, though coffee and small cakes were served (Senator Sparkman remembers the "cookies were awfully good"), the refreshments did little to relieve the tension. Mrs. Kennedy tried to be as unobtrusive as possible. She glanced around quickly, looking for an inconspicuous place to sit. There was nowhere, except a sofa already occupied by Mrs. Nixon and a woman whom Jacqueline could not, in the stress of the moment, identify. She slipped onto the couch beside Mrs. Nixon who, most of the time, continued talking to her other neighbor.

When it was time to leave for the Capitol, President Eisenhower was helped into his overcoat and gingerly grasped his silk hat. He sat in the place of honor, on the right side of the limousine, for the last time. During the ride down Pennsylvania Avenue, the President, the President-to-be, the Speaker and the Alabama Senator enjoyed the crowds and talked of little that was significant, except for a brief moment when the two leaders discussed various military implications of D-Day.

Mrs. Eisenhower, Mrs. Kennedy and Senator Bridges followed in the second car. Mrs. Eisenhower was scarcely seated when she remarked brightly to the Senator, "Doesn't Ike look like Paddy the Irishman in his top hat?" The Senator, who was always most courteous, looked visibly distressed. Mrs. Kennedy made no comment.

During the remainder of the drive Mrs. Kennedy said very little. Mrs. Eisenhower chatted on effortlessly and the Senator responded politely.

"I Knew I Was Hearing Something Great"

The inaugural setting was splendid. The immense, sugar-white Capitol dome, topped by the robust bronze Goddess of Freedom, was silhouetted against the backdrop of a theatrically blue sky. Below stretched the pillared façade of the elaborately renovated East Front. An impressive dais, called the President's Platform, had been erected across the lower sweep of the great stairway. On the left were seated members of the Senate while the four hundred and more members of the House of Representatives stood at the right. The scarlet-jacketed United States Marine Band faced the platform. Behind them, seated on wooden bleachers or packed together on the icy ground, were some fifteen thousand dedicated and thoroughly chilled spectators.

On the President's Platform itself was seated a company of distinguished personages: the Chief Justice and Associate Justices of the United States Supreme Court; members of the President's Cabinet; Armed Services top brass, and the entire Foreign Diplomatic Corps. Some of the diplomats were dressed in gilt-bedizened diplomatic uniforms and carried plumed hats. Others, seemingly inadequately protected against the freezing weather, wore vividly hued native robes. Each of these groups had assembled in a room especially assigned to them within the Capitol and had been ceremoniously escorted to their seats.

Down at the front of the platform were the very special guests: three former First Ladies (Mrs. Eisenhower became the fourth after the swearing-in ceremony) ; former President Truman; Mrs. Earl Warren, wife of the Chief Justice; members of the Kennedy and Eisenhower families; and Mr. and Mrs. Joseph P.

Seated in the first row of the official stand for the Inaugural ceremony are Mrs. Johnson, Mrs. Kennedy, President Eisenhower, President-elect Kennedy, Vice-President-elect Johnson and Vice-President Nixon.

Kennedy, the first couple in history to watch their son become President of the United States. Eclipsing even this shining company were the brightest stars, the outgoing and incoming Presidents, the Vice-Presidents, and their quartet of wives. The President-to-be would be escorted down the stairs last.

Mrs. Kennedy sat quietly between President Eisenhower and Mrs. Johnson. Directly behind her was her new and affectionate admirer, Mrs. Woodrow Wilson. Some weeks before, Mrs. Kennedy had called on Mrs. Wilson. The twenty-fourth First Lady was captivated and found her young successor "poised and mature as well as beautiful." So enchanted was she that, despite her advanced age, Mrs. Wilson attended every possible inaugural function, braving the blizzard to get to the Concert and ignoring subfreezing temperatures to ride from the Capitol to the White House in the parade.

When former President Truman marched down the steps, he spied Mrs. Wilson, squeezed his way to her between the tightly wedged rows and kissed her. Back in his seat, he tapped his toe in time to the lively music and confided, in a penetrating voice, that his overcoat was twenty-five years old and he hoped no one would steal it.

Vice President-to-be Lyndon Johnson left the Rotunda with his overcoat unbuttoned and his top hat wedged firmly across his forehead. As he began to introduce his three ladies to various notables, the Marine Band accorded him a flattering fanfare. He had turned to chat amiably with his opposite number, Dick Nixon, when a spectator waving a ten-gallon hat shouted from the bleachers, "All the way with L.B.J.!" The Senator grinned but Mrs. Johnson shook her head admonishingly.

President Eisenhower sat with his silk hat in his lap and a muffler pulled up to his ears. "Oh! Ike's head looks so cold!" exclaimed a sympathetic feminine voice.

Richard Nixon was remarkably composed. Outwardly he acted almost as if it was his own Inauguration. He was to stand scarcely two feet from his victorious rival during the swearing-in ceremony. Afterwards, he would be the first to congratulate President Kennedy and, with admirable fortitude, summon a wide grin.

At last it was time for John Fitzgerald Kennedy to appear. Some minutes earlier he had started down the steps but, noting that guests were still assembling and fumbling for their chairs, he slipped back into the Rotunda. Now, in the dazzling sunlight, he came down the stairs and took his seat next to President Eisenhower and close to the lectern.

The previous day, the Senator had said that the blizzard had added "zip" to his Inauguration. Now, both fire and a too bright sun would add further excitement to the actual ceremony. Richard, Cardinal Cushing, had scarcely commenced the invocation when slender wisps of smoke started to drift up from the base of the lectern. Everyone, including the President and the President-elect, eyed this disturbing manifestation uneasily. Capitol police and Secret Service agents moved in swiftly. Crouching low they flattened themselves on the red carpet seeking the trouble. The Cardinal continued his lengthy prayer undisturbed, his harsh voice never skipping a syllable, while the men struggled almost comically near his knees. The smoke still floated upward and another workman was summoned. A motor which adjusted the podium to the speaker's height had short-circuited. The mechanism was locked inside and, before the key was found, His Eminence had finished and Marian Anderson was ready to sing "The Star-Spangled Banner."

Robert Frost, the octogenarian poet, had composed a special "Dedication for John F. Kennedy. His Inauguration." The poet spread his papers on the lectern and started to speak, hesitated after a few mumbled sentences and then stopped. Everyone in the front row of seats leaned forward anxiously to catch his words. "I can't see," Frost exclaimed, "the sun is in my eyes. I can't read!" The new Vice-President jumped up and held his top hat as a shield. It was no use. Frost announced in a shaky voice that, instead of his inaugural dedication, he would recite "The Gift Outright," a much praised poem, written in the thirties, which he knew by heart. He started: "The land was ours before we were the land's/ She was our land more than a hundred years/ Before we were her people/ She was ours in Massachusetts, Virginia/ But we were England's, still Colonials —" After the closing lines, Frost improvised a brief finale.

John Fitzgerald Kennedy became the thirty-fifth President of the United States fifty-two minutes late. When the time came, he stood up, removed his overcoat and placed his right hand lightly

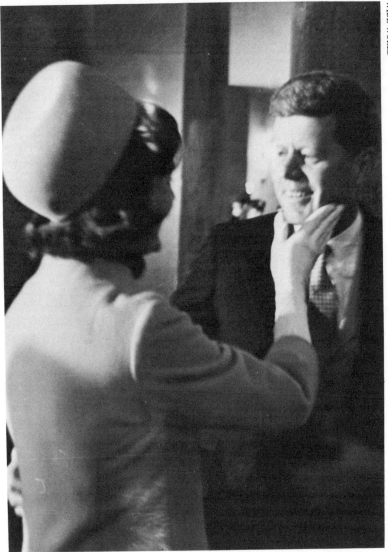

"Jack, you were so wonderful."

on a Douay version of the Bible which had belonged to his grandfather, "Honey Fitz" Fitzgerald. He repeated after Chief Justice Earl Warren the solemn words of the Presidential Oath. Then, bareheaded in the cold, he stood straight and proud to deliver his Inaugural Message. The shortest in history, the less than nineteen hundred words of the Inaugural Message were spoken in fourteen minutes.

His language was soaring, inspirational. His theme stressed individual sacrifice and a resolute dedication to peace. Many in the vast audience, watching the earnest, taut young man and swayed by the passion underlying his stern voice, cried — the tears half-freezing on their cheeks.

Until that chill hour on Capitol Hill, Jacqueline Kennedy had never heard the Inaugural Message in its entirety. "I had heard it in bits and pieces many times," she said, "while he was working on it in Florida. There were piles of yellow paper covered with his notes all over our bedroom floor. That day, when I heard it as a whole for the first time," she continued raptly, "it was so pure and beautiful and soaring that I knew I was hearing something great. And now I know that it will go down in history as one of the most moving speeches ever uttered — with Pericles' Funeral Oration and the Gettysburg Address."

When the ceremony was ended, the distinguished guests on the President's Platform were escorted into the Capitol. In the marble-paved corridor, near the great Rotunda, Jack and Jackie met for the first time as President and First Lady. It was a lovely, fleeting moment. "I was so proud of Jack! There was so much I wanted to say! But I could scarcely embrace him in front of all those people," she sighed, "so I remember I just put my hand on his cheek and said, 'Jack, you were so wonderful!' And he was smiling in the most touching and most vulnerable way. He looked so happy!"

Mr. Truman Gets an Autograph

A postinaugural luncheon honoring the new President and Mrs. Kennedy was given in the Old Supreme Court Chamber: a picturesque room inside the Capitol, still relatively unchanged though the Supreme Court had long since moved to its own magnificent building across the Capitol park.

The chairman of the Joint Congressional Inaugural Committee and Mrs. John Sparkman were hosts at the luncheon. Mrs. Sparkman and her daughter, Mrs. Tazewell Shepard, Jr., had painstakingly planned every detail. (At 3 A.M. on the day before the Inauguration, Mrs. Shepard's husband, a Navy captain on sea duty, was dramatically summoned from his ship to report immediately at the White House as naval aide to President Kennedy.) The invitation list was limited to about eighty. The twelve ranking guests were placed at a raised table facing the buffet so the others could see and talk to them, then serve themselves. The State Department protocol officer was responsible for the seating. "For once in my life I had *the* ideal seat," laughed Mrs. Sparkman, "with President Kennedy on my right and Vice-President Johnson on my left!" Mrs. Kennedy was placed on Senator Sparkman's right and the President on his left, while Chief Justice Warren sat on the new First Lady's right. As souvenir, beside each head table setting, was a silver ashtray engraved with the legend "Inaugural Luncheon 1961."

MENU

Cream of Tomato Soup with Crushed Popcorn
Deviled Crabmeat Imperial
New England Broiled Stuffed Lobster with Drawn Butter
Prime Texas Ribs of Beef
String Beans Amandine   *Broiled Tomatoes*

Grapefruit and Avocado Sections with Poppy Seed Dressing
Hot Garlic Bread   *Butterflake Rolls*
Patisserie Gâteau Blanche
Mints   *Coffee*

The buffet was magnificent but there had been one serious miscalculation in Mrs. Sparkman's meticulous arrangements: there was no time to enjoy the lovely food. The inaugural ceremony, previously so carefully clocked, had commenced twenty-two minutes late. The fire, overlong prayers, poet Frost's confusion caused further delays. And now, instead of eating, all the guests wanted to congratulate the Kennedys and Johnsons, shake hands and, perhaps, ask for autographs. Lean Leverett Saltonstall, the senior Massachusetts Senator, was a typical hardship case. He had piled his plate high but hadn't raised a forkful before he was ordered to leave for the Inaugural Parade.

But though many of his guests went hungry Senator Sparkman knew his luncheon had been a tremendous success and had only one regret. In his opinion, the most delightful incident of the Inauguration was not recorded. The scene occurred when former President Truman rose and bustled around the head table to solicit the new President's autograph. Kennedy, grinning and flushed with pleasure, signed Harry's menu with a flourish.

A Clock Struck Twelve

Shortly before noon on Inauguration Day, a White House truck drew up to the N Street house. Boxes, bags, bundles and Caroline's adored rocking horse were piled in. Last, placed gently, was John's white wicker bassinet, flounced with pink ribbon-run dotted Swiss. Thirty-one years before the cradle had been painted beige and elaborately beruffled in peach point d'esprit. In it, then, wide-eyed and grave with a fluff of faintly curling black

*Mr. Truman requests an autograph and in return signs the
Inaugural luncheon menu for the new President.*

hair, had lain a placid infant named Jacqueline Lee Bouvier. Soon, its occupant would be a long, lean, restless boy who had had a hard time getting born.

Behind the truck, in a White House car, rode Tish Baldridge, Mrs. Kennedy's maid Providencia Parades, and George Thomas, now the President's valet. With them, covered in protective plastic, was the First Lady's white silk and chiffon Inaugural Ball gown. This small cavalcade paused at the high iron gates. Far away, a clock struck twelve. As the final note shivered into silence, they passed through the gates and into the snow-covered White House grounds.

They were met in the Diplomatic Reception Room by Mr. J. Bernard West, the Chief Usher, and his staff. Provie refused to relinquish Mrs. Kennedy's Inaugural Ball gown and carried it upstairs still in its plastic cover. George handled his boss's white tie and tails with equal care. They spent the next few hours unpacking in the eerily quiet upper floors. Tish, meanwhile, tried to begin to cope with a tidal wave of flowers and inaugural gifts of all kinds. There were numerous volumes of pertinent history and a surprising variety of ornate guest books whose pages could scarcely contain the signatures of those invited to a single White House party. Patriotically inclined children had mailed literally hundreds of drawings of the White House to its new occupants. Over in the East Wing, where Mrs. Kennedy's offices were set up, there were stacks of welcome-to-the-White-House cards and several thousands of letters. Tish realized with dismay that, no matter how efficient the staff, it would be almost impossible to deal adequately with the fantastic amount of mail addressed to Mrs. Kennedy. But even in her wildest imagining she did not anticipate a total which would snowball to nine thousand letters a week.

As the hours drifted by, Tish and Provie became increasingly worried about Mrs. Kennedy. She was still so weak and they knew she had been exposed too long to the bitter cold.

*The President and First Lady ride in the Inaugural Parade.
Mrs. Kennedy glances up — perhaps at the Kennedy nieces
and nephews who were gathered in the windows of an office
building overlooking the parade route.*

"It Was Quite a Parade!"

Lieutenant General James Gavin, USA Ret., was the Grand Marshal of the Inaugural Parade and Bill Walton was his Deputy Marshal. They were to head the procession and had foregone witnessing the swearing-in ceremony in order to get the show on the road without delay. While the inaugural luncheon was in progress, Gavin and Walton, chilled and somewhat glum, had been immobilized in their open car. And though the President and his escort were scheduled to leave the Capitol at 1:30 P.M., it was 2:17 P.M. when Senator Sparkman finally wedged himself into the jump seat in front of the new President and his wife.

Late the previous night, over fifty cumbersome floats had been parked in streets and plazas around the Capitol. Since earliest morning forty bands, sixteen thousand marching men, plus the entire Cadet Corps of West Point and Annapolis, the Air Force Academy and the Coast Guard had been gathering at designated points nearby. Despite the awesome array of giant guns, tanks and missiles, there was a giddy, carnival atmosphere about the usually staid Capitol grounds. For here too was a motley assemblage of Indians, cowboys, beauty queens and Eskimos; horses, mules, dogs and a beguiling buffalo; middle-aged men bulging in fussy Old Guard Regiment uniforms and scores of pretty girls shivering in flimsy fancy costumes.

The most applauded float was a realistic replica of the Kennedy PT-109 boat. At the helm was Lieutenant Edward Thom, whose father had been killed when the ship was sunk. It was manned by nine surviving crewmen including fifty-four-year-old Patrick McMahon, whom the new President had rescued by towing him four hours through rough seas with the wounded sailor's life-jacket rope clenched agonizingly between his teeth.

"What this country needs," quipped an anonymous congressman, "is a winter capital!" Though soldiers had shoveled two hundred tons of rock salt (at sixteen dollars a ton) along Pennsylvania Avenue and melted stubborn drifts with flamethrowers, almost everyone participating in the Inaugural Parade would have agreed fervently with the congressman.

The temperature seldom rose above freezing and, with a stiff wind blowing directly into their faces, the bare legs of drum majorettes were blue, their baton-twirling fingers half-frozen. Miss Florida, who hailed from tropical Fort Lauderdale, confided that she wore flannel pajamas beneath her billowy gown and had borrowed a fur stole. Even the 3,600 hardy midshipmen from Annapolis were harassed by the weather. The middies prudently marched in galoshes which in a lapse of judgment were left unfastened. As they wheeled smartly around the corner past the Treasury Building and along the stretch fronting the presidential reviewing stand, first one galosh, then another, flipped off until, like raisins in a rice pudding, the snowy avenue was dotted with black overshoes.

The parade moved grandly down Pennsylvania Avenue. The crowd cheered, shouted, screamed, whistled, roared with a decibel intensity which muted the clashing cymbals and thumping drums of the United States Army Band and diminished to a whisper the slush-slush of the 3rd Infantry Regiment treading rhythmically over the hard-packed snow.

At last the long, black car came in sight and the crowd went wild. On the jump seat rode Senator Sparkman, his face one great grin. Behind, on the folded-back top, perched the new President, smiling and waving his shiny hat; and beside him the new First Lady, pointing excitedly with her muffed hand toward upper-story office windows where Kennedy nieces and nephews clustered; then to friends she had spotted in the grandstands.

To more thoughtful observers Jack and Jackie looked so young, so gay, so handsome, it seemed incredible that these two, the wife steadfast beside the husband, together now held the most powerful position in the world.

Behind this stellar attraction trailed bands, soldiers, state governors, monstrous floats: in fact every element essential to that gloriously martial, touchingly corny, deliciously cockeyed, all-American spectacular, the Inaugural Parade.

The President and Mrs. Kennedy were welcomed at the reviewing stand by the Grand Marshal and his deputy and members of the Inaugural Committee. Many distinguished guests were seated already, including Ambassador and Mrs. Joseph P. Kennedy, who had given a luncheon for family and close personal friends at the Mayflower. The President's father, who had remained discreetly in the background during the campaign, now for a brief moment came into his own. The former Ambassador was seated beside his son much of the time, his eyes shining with pleasure as passing units saluted their new Commander-in-Chief.

The President's three military aides, Brigadier General Chester Clifton (USA); Captain Tazewell Shepard, Jr. (USN); and Colonel (later Brigadier General) Godfrey McHugh (USAF) sat behind him. It was their first workout with the President as, of the three, only McHugh had known their boss more than twenty-four hours. (The Secret Service, representing presidential security continuity, offered the aides just two succinct suggestions for Kennedy's care. "Just stay close," advised Jim Rowley, the chief agent, "and give him soup, not coffee.") In rotation, the aides brought up members of the new Cabinet and official family. Some of them, like Army Secretary Elvis Stahr, had never met the President. Those who were presented sat beside Kennedy for a few minutes of pleasant conversation and then were replaced. As each person relinquished his or her seat, the President would say, "When the parade is over, won't you join us in the house?" From time to time, too, he would ask some close friend to escort a VIP into the White House.

The parade, which was touted in advance as the "most compact and precisely planned parade in modern history," had been scheduled to leave the Capitol at 1:30 P.M. Sunset that day was to be at 5:11 P.M., so the "tail element" had been clocked to pass the presidential reviewing stand at 4:46 P.M., when there would still be sufficient daylight to satisfy both marchers, spectators and TV cameras.

Gradually, guests in the presidential reviewing stand drifted away into the White House or home to dress for the gay evening ahead. As darkness fell, the cameramen informed an aide they could no longer take photographs and were pulling out. "I'm not leaving until the last man has passed!" exclaimed the President. Since he was the Commander-in-Chief, the Chiefs of Staff also had to remain. The tight little group of die-hards clustered together: the Vice-President and Mrs. Johnson, the Robert Kennedys, the Douglas Dillons, and a few long-time friends of the President. Dillon, a Republican and Eisenhower's Under Secretary of State, had switched to become Kennedy's Secretary of the Treasury. Dillon was enjoying the parade enormously and his engaging, diminutive wife, Phyllis, amused the President by recounting how terrified she had been of catching Dick Nixon's eye at the inaugural ceremony.

Together they watched the final units march past in the dusk. It was 6:12 P.M. when the last contingent swung by. The President left the stand and walked among them, shaking every outstretched hand. "It was quite a parade!" he kept saying over and over. "Thank you for coming!"

Strange Surroundings

At 3:27 P.M., Jacqueline Kennedy left the reviewing stand. She had had a glorious time in the parade, sitting beside her husband on the folded-back car top. But during the long, slow ride from the Capitol to the White House, she had been exposed to cutting gusts of wind and was thoroughly chilled. Now, after such deep emotional tension, she would have to prepare for the long, exhausting evening ahead: dress, have her hair coiffed, do all the endless small things which even a beautiful young woman must do to meet the challenge of the most glittering evening of her life. All this, too, in strange surroundings: a new bedroom, an unfamiliar house, a radically different way of life; and surrounded for the most part by strangers who instinctively were appraising her and, perhaps, subconsciously seeking flaws. She knew that she needed to rest; but she was closer to complete collapse than she realized.

Mrs. Kennedy was escorted from the reviewing stand to the White House by Colonel McHugh, the Air Force aide. They walked silently along the curving driveway, up the steps sheltered by the porte cochère. A doorman swung open the heavy half-door and Jacqueline Bouvier Kennedy stepped across the threshold for the first time as leading lady of the land. As Mr. West came forward to welcome her, she thanked Colonel Mc-Hugh for his attention. McHugh, deeply moved by the quiet drama, stood stiff and straight, until the slight figure crossed the gleaming marble foyer and turned the corner.

The Chief Usher escorted her upstairs. They discussed household affairs briefly in the empty hallway outside the Queen's Bedroom, which the First Lady would occupy until alterations to their special rooms were completed.

Then Mrs. Kennedy lay down to rest on the wide bed, hung with rose curtains, in which five modern-day queens had slept. Suddenly, all her reserve of energy seemed to melt away. As though trapped in some frightening nightmare, she was conscious but unable to move.

"When it was time to get ready for dinner — I couldn't get out of bed," she remembers with distress. "I just didn't have one bit of strength left and felt absolutely panicked. What could I do? Somehow I managed to get in touch with Dr. Travell. . . ."

Janet Travell was seated beside her husband in the presidential reviewing stand. She was summoned very quietly and hurried to Mrs. Kennedy's room. There she found her patient utterly exhausted and suffering from painful leg cramps. Dr. Travell ordered dinner in bed and prescribed a single, rust-colored pill. It was not until the following day that Mrs. Kennedy learned that she had taken her first, and what was to be her last, Dexedrine tablet.

A State of Giddy Euphoria

The first Kennedy entertainment in the White House was a high tea after the Inaugural Parade — an impromptu affair with an alcoholic assist for the nearly frozen. It was staged somewhat chaotically in the State Dining Room. Close friends and those present during the parade were bidden informally by the President, while members of both families had been invited in advance. Among them were Mrs. Kennedy's mother and stepfather, Mr. and Mrs. Hugh D. Auchincloss; her Bouvier aunts and a special first cousin, Michel Bouvier, only nine years her senior, but her godfather. He had substituted for his own father who died shortly before Jacqueline's christening. There were younger relations, too, who had flown in from jobs in Italy and Peru.

Early arrivals wandered haphazardly about the State Rooms on the first floor. Those who were not dazzled by the mere fact of being inside the White House found it drab and disappointing. The State Dining Room was so barren. Even soft candlelight could only mitigate, not banish, the chill of the "Williamsburg green" walls, a color which Mrs. Kennedy later described as "dentist office" green. The candelabra were dingy and needed replating. Several enormous and exceedingly ugly nineteenth-century porcelain urns stood out conspicuously. Flowers were almost nonexistent, though despondent potted palms drooped in many corners. Along the great corridor into which the five State Rooms opened stood a rigid row of pedestaled brass ashtrays. They harmonized splendidly with the palms and seemed to have been designed in the same era for the dual purpose of spittoon-cum-cigar-butt depository. And despite the historic cold outside, not a single fire burned in all the twenty-nine fireplaces of the Mansion.

Nevertheless, depressing though the décor might be, the occasion itself was so exciting that most of the guests were in a state of giddy euphoria.

Dinner Before the Inaugural Ball

The occasion which really launched the New Frontier socially was the dinner given before the Inaugural Ball by Mr. and Mrs. George Y. Wheeler (Mrs. Wheeler is now Mrs. Henry Suydam). Senator Kennedy had indicated his wish to be present. This would be his initial private social engagement as President, and his acceptance was supposed to be secret.

At first Jane Wheeler received a number of regrets, some from just-appointed Cabinet couples new to Washington. Then, when rumors of the President's impending presence grapevined around Washington, a second round of notes arrived from those who had declined. The new messages read, "Accepts with pleasure." "It was an educational experience for a hostess," Mrs. Wheeler commented dryly. Soon the disillusioned hostess found herself the target of a relentless campaign to wangle additional invitations. Jane had to turn down innumerable demands from known, as well as unknown, invitees of the "would-you-mind-asking-so-and-so" variety. "Some people actually sent me lists of people to invite!" she said. Jane did accede to a number of requests, mostly from the Kennedy clan and the First Lady-to-be who asked politely whether one or two old family friends could be fitted in.

This first gathering of the New Frontier had started quite casually. Smart, energetic Jane Wheeler, whose husband was a former vice-president of a radio and TV network, had been active in the "Citizens for Kennedy" program. In the final weeks of the campaign, she became an organizer of the "Kennedy Caravan," a scintillating group which included Ethel Kennedy, Arthur Schlesinger, Jr., the late Jeff Chandler, Angie Dickinson,

Joan Kennedy, Stan Musial, James Michener and Byron White, a Kennedy friend who was later appointed an Associate Justice of the United States Supreme Court. They made a wild and wonderful prop-stop tour in a small chartered plane through states like Kentucky, which Kennedy's political "pros" Kenneth O'Donnell and Lawrence O'Brien, had written off. Even though the old pros proved correct and none of the states the Caravan visited ended up on the Kennedy side, nevertheless their efforts were very much appreciated.

After the election, when Jane's energies had been channeled into inaugural plans, she mentioned to Ethel Kennedy that it might be fun to reassemble the Caravan members for dinner on inaugural night. Ethel agreed and startled Jane by going one step further. "Why don't we ask *him* to come?" A few days later, Bobby's wife relayed the word. "*He* accepts. *He* thinks it's a fine idea. *He* says, as a favor, would you mind asking the Cabinet?"

This request posed complications. The new top officialdom was scheduled to appear with President Kennedy at a string of Inaugural Balls. To invite them collectively to her house made Jane responsible for their promptness. She called Ed Foley, the inaugural chairman, to ask when her VIP guests should leave. "Nine o'clock!" replied Foley. "Then I might as well not have a dinner!" Jane groaned. "That's right!" Ed agreed cheerfully. "We've bought thousands and thousands of dollars of TV time. The people want to see their new President and his Cabinet. At Eisenhower's first Inauguration," he added, "some of the Cabinet, riding in separate limousines, got lost." Ike himself managed only the briefest TV appearance.

The inaugural chairman came up with a smart idea. He would hire a bus. Then the Cabinet could be kept together, and on time.

The bus was magnificent. It was red-carpeted, cozily heated and sprayed with delicious scent. It had a bar, a powder room, a small orchestra plus pretty Mrs. Sam Brightsman, wife of the Democratic National Committee's publicity director, to ride herd on the plush passengers.

It was in this deluxe vehicle that the Cabinet members and their wives became acquainted. They had been summoned from all over the country and before the Inaugural only a few could identify each other. They had met for the first time at a breakfast given by the Secretary of Labor-designate, and Mrs. Arthur Goldberg. The breakfast made a more than average impression because it was strictly Jewish and featured lox and bagels. ("The Goldbergs are very proud of that sort of stuff," explained a fellow Cabinet member.) Now, with the emotional inaugural ceremony behind, they could relax in this gay vehicle and enjoy each other. Orville Freeman, the Secretary of Agriculture-to-be, neatly described the ride as "a shakedown cruise for the Cabinet."

At the last tally, Jane Wheeler had dispatched over a hundred invitations to a "Dinner Before the Inaugural Ball." No mention was made of President Kennedy.

Ten circular tables were placed in the large recreation area of the Wheeler house on fashionably countrified Foxhall Road. They were covered with orange velvet cloths and centered with bowls of white camellias. The walls of the basement room were festooned with orange velvet garlands, and golden candelabra shed a becoming light.

The menu, complemented by superlative wines, was rightly described by an appreciative New Frontiersman as "out of this world." But again, as at the congressional luncheon, too few had time to do the gourmet dishes justice.

The President arrived, last and alone, after the guests had finished their cocktails. Everyone agreed that he had never looked better. He was gay, exuberant and totally confident. Near the fateful hour of nine, Ed Foley stood up. "Mr. President," he said, "I hate to interrupt this wonderful occasion, but we have to go." The President, relaxed and obviously enjoying himself, grumbled, "Ed, you've been pushing me around all day. Stop it! This is the first time I've had warm food in front of me since morning. I'm going to sit here another fifteen minutes!" "I'll give you five!" replied Foley. But it was nearer ten minutes when the President arose and the still hungry Cabinet members and their wives reluctantly followed suit.

"This Calls for a Celebration!"

It was well after nine when the President, accompanied by the Foleys, returned to the White House to pick up Jacqueline. The new Vice-President and Mrs. Johnson, who had preceded them, were waiting in the Red Room. Together, they would join forces for the round of Inaugural Balls.

Companionably, Kennedy and Foley lit cigars. They had drawn only a few puffs when the First Lady arrived, breathlessly, in a gentle flurry. She stood in the doorway poised as if for flight. Tall, slender and appealingly youthful, she was dressed in a sheath of white chiffon, the bodice sparkling with silver and brilliants, all veiled in a romantic gossamer cape which fell softly to the floor.

The President glanced up, drew a quick breath, and in reflex gesture, stubbed out his cigar. "Darling, I've never seen you look so lovely," he said in a low voice. "Your dress is beautiful!" He turned to the doorman who had guided his wife to the room. "Bring some wine!" The champagne appeared like magic. "This calls for a celebration!" exclaimed the thirty-fifth President of the United States as he raised his glass to the thirty-first First Lady.

On the arm of her husband, Mrs. Kennedy leaves the White House for the first time as First Lady for the round of Inaugural Balls planned for the evening.

Guests in President and Mrs. Kennedy's box at one of the Inaugural Balls include his parents, former Ambassador and Mrs. Joseph P. Kennedy; Vice-President and Mrs. Lyndon B. Johnson; his brother Edward and sister-in-law Joan Kennedy.

"You Looking at Us and We Looking at You!"

The President and Mrs. Kennedy made their first appearance at the Mayflower Hotel. Though planned in advance, this was a delicate courtesy to Mr. and Mrs. Truman, who were staying there. The former President was more or less a prisoner of his wife. The night before, during the blizzard, Mrs. Truman had put her foot down hard and refused to permit her husband to attend the Gala. She was equally adamant about his venturing from the snug Mayflower to the drafty Armory on inaugural night.

When the presidential party arrived, the excited guests stampeded into the main ballroom. Here they stood, elbow to elbow, staring as if hypnotized at the Kennedys. The orchestra struck up a swinging tune, but no one budged. Stanley Woodward, chairman of the Inaugural Balls, and his aides did their best to start the dancing. One of the aides stepped to the microphone. "Shall we dance?" he shouted. "No!" roared back the crowd cheerfully. Those at the back of the ballroom, in quite unladylike and ungentlemanly fashion, began to shove forward. They struggled to get closer to the presidential box where Jacqueline sat in her cool white chiffon beside Lady Bird Johnson, whose strapless gown was elegantly described as "Persian coral coupe de velour." The Cabinet was ranged behind them.

The crowds continued to stand motionless, staring in fascination at the guests of honor. Later the President, amused and flattered, quipped in an off-the-cuff speech, "I don't know a better way to spend an evening — you looking at us and we looking at you!"

At each of the four succeeding balls, the crowds reacted in a similar manner, mostly standing still and staring. President Kennedy neatly pinpointed this phenomenon in his final impromptu remarks: "The Johnsons and I have been to five balls tonight. We still have one unfulfilled ambition — and that is to see someone dance!"

Chairman Woodward, however, had a plausible explanation for the crowds' reaction. "Jackie was so lovely!" he mused over a final nightcap. "She stopped everybody dead in their tracks!" Woodward was aware, too, that John Fitzgerald Kennedy represented far more than political success: he had become the symbol of youth and a more shining future.

After leaving the first ball, the President detoured unexpectedly. He directed his car to the nearby Statler-Hilton where his party was not due officially for several hours. "I want to thank Sinatra personally — and all those Californians — who put on that great show last night!" he explained to Foley. "I'll only be a few minutes!"

The limousine stopped at the 16th Street entrance. The Kennedys and Foleys, escorted by Secret Service agents, walked up the stairs to the ballroom floor. The President hurried along the hall, his "shadow" inches behind. He was scarcely out of sight when Herbert Blunck, manager of the Statler-Hilton, arrived on the double. Spotting Foley he stammered, distraught, "Ed! You aren't supposed to be here now!" As he ushered them to a small, empty room reserved for VIP guests, Blunck hissed at Foley, "Why didn't you let me know you were coming early?"

Frank Sinatra was host at a dinner in honor of his co-performers. They were seated at the table when the President entered, unannounced. Sinatra, for once, lost his cool. For a moment he was stunned speechless.

Scarcely a quarter of an hour later, the President rejoined his wife and the Foleys. They set out again, as they had the previous night, through the snowy streets to the distant Armory, where the main Inaugural Ball was being held.

The enthusiastic crowd waiting for the Kennedys quickly got out of hand. Even the phalanx of tailcoated Secret Service agents could not clear a passageway through the aisles. So the President vaulted happily over the railings from one box to another with — as columnist Joseph Alsop phrased it later — "the agility of a mountain goat." En route to his seat by this strenuous method, he paused to thank each boxholder not only for their presence at the ball but also for their support in his presidential campaign.

At the Armory, the Cabinet members and their wives at last came into their own. Led by the inaugural chairman and Mrs. Foley, followed by the Inaugural Ball chairman and Mrs. Woodward, to thunderous applause, they crisscrossed single file over the immense floor. Veteran orchestra leader Meyer Davis, who had played both at the wedding of Mrs. Kennedy and that of her father and mother, was on the verge of tears, as he swung into a medley of sentimental tunes. Still no one danced. The guests stood transfixed, looking up at the handsome, smiling President, standing behind his young wife who, now and again, glanced up at him proudly.

As they were leaving the Armory for the third ball, Mrs. Kennedy faltered. One of the presidential aides assisted her into the car.

"I just crumpled," she explained ruefully. "All my strength was finally gone! So I went home and Jack went on with the others."

"Home" was now the White House; the limousine hurried them there. Again the Chief Usher was waiting to welcome her, and when the First Lady was safely inside, the others sped on to the Statler-Hilton, the Shoreham and the Sheraton-Park hotels. After the final ball, the President thanked the inaugural chairman: "I've never had such a good time in my life!" he exclaimed. "Come back tomorrow, Ed, and let's do it again!"

"Tell the President It's Time to Go Home"

It was a bit before 2 A.M. when the city desk of a Washington newspaper called a reporter who lived in Georgetown. "The Secret Service has just flashed that the President is rerouting his limousine and heading toward Dumbarton Avenue. Is he coming to your house?" "Heavens, no!" disclaimed the journalist. "Joe Alsop lives across the street from me. He's probably going there." The city desk buzzed again and again. "How about calling Alsop and asking who he's got with him?" the anonymous voice asked feverishly. "How about calling Joe and asking him what he's giving the President to eat?" insisted another voice. "Call him yourself!" was the ungracious retort.

The reporter was annoyed. She had invited out-of-town guests for an after-the-ball nightcap; but when President Kennedy's change of direction came over loud and clear on the police radio, the target block on Dumbarton Avenue was closed off and all vehicles except the presidential limousine were stopped at the corner. The journalist's guests, minus overshoes and wearing party footwear, had to flounder through knee-high snowdrifts. And still later, after 3 A.M. when they longed to call it a day, they were faced with the same soggy trek back to the corner.

A policeman was posted in front of the Alsop house. Jokingly, the journalist opened a window and called to him, "Officer, please tell the President it's time to go home! Tell him it's Mrs. Thayer that says so!" The policeman stopped flapping his arms and stamping his feet. "Lady, I sure wish I could," he bellowed back. "I'm freezing to death!"

It was 3:22 A.M. when the black limousine, with a mighty lurch, bucked through the snow and slowly crunched toward Pennsylvania Avenue and "home."

Earlier that evening, outside the National Guard Armory, Joseph Alsop had encountered a member of Mrs. Kennedy's personal staff. The staff member and her escort had managed to park nearby, so they drove Alsop home. The columnist, then a bachelor, was a personal friend and ardent Kennedy supporter. He had invited a few friends to drop by his house for a nightcap after the Inaugural Ball. His guests had arrived singly or in pairs and were sitting comfortably relaxed, drinks in hand, when the doorbell rang. Alsop opened the door and there, silhouetted against the snowy street, stood a figure familiar to everyone in the room. Yet there was something strikingly unfamiliar about the tall, smiling man. The essence of his physical being had changed. His bearing had a new aura of authority which seemed almost tangible. As if quickened by this hidden force, instinctively, everyone rose. They stood, a bit uncertainly, glasses grasped awkwardly, until the President made a small, almost imperceptible, downward motion with his hand.

The President, who had eaten so little during this eventful day, agreed without urging that he was hungry. But as Alsop had been host at a dinner party earlier that night, no supper had been prepared. Several of the female guests were delegated to the pantry where they began opening cartons of frozen terrapin. This epicurean selection was to set a splendid gastronomic tone for the New Frontier. The following morning, when the press finally pinned down the President's late evening host, Alsop replied coolly, "Yes! The President was hungry!" Then added grandly, "So I fed him terrapin!"

3

The First Days

"Please Tell Her I Didn't Burst In on Purpose"

During the first ten days President and Mrs. Kennedy were in the White House, the list of their social engagements gave only a slight indication of their activities. In Tish Baldridge's pristine notebook, the following events were listed:

Sunday, January 22nd, 1961.	Dinner guests: Mr. and Mrs. Franklin D. Roosevelt, Jr., Mrs. Ned Russell, Mr. William Walton, Mr. Joseph W. Alsop.
Monday, January 23rd.	Mr. and Mrs. Hugh D. Auchincloss for tea. Mr. and Mrs. Charles Bartlett for dinner.
Tuesday, January 24th.	Georges Balanchine for tea.
Wednesday, January 25th.	No engagements.
Thursday, January 26th.	No engagements.
Friday, January 27th.	Coffee at 4 P.M. with the recently released RBY-47 pilots and their wives.
Saturday, January 28th.	Dinner with Senator and Mrs. John Sherman Cooper at their Georgetown house.
Sunday, January 29th.	Reception for Cabinet and Sub-Cabinet members and their families.

At 9 A.M. the day after the Inauguration, when the thirty-fifth President of the United States entered his office in the West Wing, Dave Powers walked with him. "It was like being Alice in Wonderland," said this most Irish member of the Kennedy Irish Mafia, describing his big moment. "He looked ten feet tall to me, and he seemed to grow every day." The new President, wishing to orient himself, peered into all the surrounding offices before a

first meeting with his staff. He also made an important telephone call. In response, at 10 A.M., in nineteen-degree cold, Harry Truman came tramping jauntily up the snowy White House drive, his cane crooked over his arm. He had walked a mile from the Mayflower Hotel. It was the first time he had been invited to the White House in the eight years since General Eisenhower had succeeded him. White House reporters, taken completely by surprise, swarmed about him. Mr. Truman paused just long enough to make a sharp dig at Ike — and to put in a plug for the Kennedy Inaugural Message. "It will be one of the great ones," he snapped. "I've read 'em all. It was short, to the point, and in language anyone can understand. Even I could understand it, and therefore the people can."

President Kennedy, who had walked partway down the driveway to greet his distinguished guest, escorted him through the reception room and into the executive offices. As he stepped into the building, Mr. Truman grumbled, "They've changed this all around. We used to go straight in, and now you have to go in a circle. I'll have a time finding my way out!"

At the end of their visit, President Kennedy suggested paying a call on his wife. Mrs. Kennedy was occupying the Queen's Room until her own was readied. She was resting after the exhausting inauguration activities, propped up in the enormous canopied bed, warmed by a pretty bedjacket, and her hair was covered with a frivolous little cap. Dr. Janet Travell stood at the foot of the bed, talking with her patient of the previous evening, when suddenly there was a light tap, the door opened abruptly, and in stepped the President and Mr. Truman. Startled when they saw Dr. Travell, the two men retreated to the threshold. From this safe vantage point, Mr. Truman, obviously embarrassed, complimented the First Lady on her husband's Inaugural Message. Then he recalled that when his mother had visited the White House she had stayed in this same room. "The big bed scared her," he said; "she wouldn't sleep in it and insisted on using a bed in the little sitting room." Then he murmured a polite goodbye and fled.

The President followed him, very much amused by the incident; but Mr. Truman, who represented a more conservative generation, kept saying to his host over and over, "Please tell her I didn't burst in on purpose!"

Those first days, before the remodeling of their private living quarters was completed, Mrs. Kennedy found the Queen's Room the sole cheerful oasis in the otherwise depressing Mansion. Those who were privileged to see it agreed it was the warmest, most likable and only private room totally without what Mrs. Kennedy and Bill Walton had aptly described as "Early Statler" furniture. Since she had to rest much of the day, she made it her command post. Here she welcomed close friends, attended to her correspondence and summoned the first of many knowledgeable people who later were to be of greatest assistance in carrying out her still unformed plans for restoring the White House.

The private part of the White House was then at its nadir. Remodeling blocked off part of the living quarters. All the Eisenhowers' possessions had been removed but the familiar furnishings from the N Street house had not arrived. Two days after the Inauguration, Mrs. Henry Parish, the decorator, described the Oval Sitting Room (now the most beautiful of the private rooms) as "stark." The only furniture in the room was a center table, two chairs and two television sets. Everything was spotlessly clean, as if no one had entered the door." Mrs. Kennedy described her surroundings more dramatically. "It's like the Lubianka!" she said dolefully to John Walker, director of the National Gallery of Art. The discomforts of White House dining were equally discouraging to Mrs. Kennedy, who was accustomed to an attractive dining room, gay with flowers, delicate linens and china, as a setting for the delicious food she always served. "I saw what it was like eating off trays with four butlers hovering around —"

During that first week a few of their most intimate friends were invited to dine informally. Some were tremendously excited merely at being in the White House, but others, less impressionable, agreed it was not precisely cheerful.

By Sunday most of the out-of-town guests had dispersed, and that evening the Kennedys were hosts at their first small dinner. This night and on Monday were the only times they entertained in the downstairs Family Dining Room. These dinners had proved so unappetizing that, until the private kitchen was ready and René Verdon, the chef they recruited, was installed, their food was prepared by Pearl, their Georgetown cook, and they dined upstairs on trays.

The menu for this first dinner was almost the last of the unimaginative, old-fashioned meals served during Mrs. Kennedy's régime. The President, however, slipped the menu into his pocket, saying it was a souvenir worthy of being kept. Joe Alsop, one of the guests, saved his menu too, and, stepping completely out of character, made the somewhat corny gesture of asking the others for their autographs. The menu was very much like a conventional hotel table d'hôte, including side dishes and, to commence, the inevitable status symbol of the gastronomically uninitiated, Turtle Soup. It read:

MENU

Cream of Turtle Soup

Celery   *Olives*

Filet Mignon

Sauce Piquante

Parsley Potato Balls   *Beans with Mushrooms*

Profiteroles au Chocolat

Demi-tasse

There were only five guests: Mr. and Mrs. Franklin D. Roosevelt, Jr., Mrs. Ned Russell, Joseph Alsop and William Walton. They were very special friends. President Roosevelt's son Frank was not only very close to the new President but had campaigned hard for him in tight spots like the West Virginia primary, where the Roosevelt name still carried great prestige. Mary Russell, widow of a popular newsman, was one of a select group of ladies who had volunteered to help answer Mrs. Kennedy's staggering amount of campaign mail.

Before dinner the guests were ushered upstairs into the small Lincoln Sitting Room, adjoining the Lincoln Room which the President occupied during the remodeling. The sitting room was then nondescriptly furnished with obvious reproductions, but cocktails and caviar more than compensated for the dreary surroundings. Finally, it clearly became time to dine, but neither the host nor hostess seemed quite sure of what move to make. "Do I have to tell them," murmured Mrs. Kennedy, "or do they tell me?" After dinner was announced, they started toward the small elevator which would take them down to the Family Dining Room on the first floor. Automatically the President drew to one side so the ladies could precede him through the door. But Sue Roosevelt and Mary demurred. "Oh, no! *You* must go first, Mr. President!" they chorused. Reluctantly he obeyed, but once through the door he dropped behind them again.

The Family Dining Room, with its burgundy-red carpet, matching curtains and pale walls, was a gloomy spot. It was chilly and, in that high-ceilinged room, the voices of the seven people at the table echoed so loudly that, in a sympathetic reflex, they found themselves whispering. "Who knows?" ventured one of the guests, "what we say may be recorded!" And since no one in honesty could compliment their host or hostess on the quality of the cuisine, they all said nice things about the wines. The wines, they were told, had been brought from the N Street house.

After dinner the First Lady and her two feminine guests had coffee in the Green Room. Three straight-backed chairs had been set in a semicircle. There was no fire in the fireplace. It could scarcely have been less cozy. Meanwhile, the President and the other three men faced a small crisis. No one could find the masculine equivalent of a powder room. Since they knew each other well and felt somewhat silly about asking a butler, they went scouting around the foyer and in other less obvious locations. Not finding their objective, they turned indignantly on Frankie Roosevelt. His family had lived in the White House more than twelve years, why didn't he know? But he didn't, and for good reason. There is no powder room, either masculine or feminine, on the main floor of the White House!

When this impasse had been resolved, they all went downstairs to watch a color film of the Inauguration in the White House moving picture theater. The guests found it quite exciting to be sitting there in the darkened room, elbow to elbow with the principals in the flamboyant show that flashed across the screen.

Monday, Charles and Martha Bartlett dined alone with the Kennedys. The Bartletts were perhaps their most intimate friends. Charlie was a journalist, like so many close to the President, and they had met years before in Palm Beach where the senior Bartletts as well as the senior Kennedys owned villas. Charlie and Martha had been matchmakers: they had tried unsuccessfully for several years to introduce the busy Massachusetts Congressman to the equally busy Jacqueline Bouvier. And finally one summer evening in 1951, the Bartletts did manage to lure both Jack and Jackie to dine in their tiny backyard in Georgetown.

The Family Dining Room was warmer than it had been the night before. The atmosphere was so comfortably relaxed that the President took off his coat, and his friend did too. The Bartletts were enchanted at being in the White House and scarcely noticed what they ate, but afterwards the new First Lady commented, "The food was pretty awful!"

The President was in great form and told Bartlett what a kick he got out of sleeping in the great Lincoln Bed. "They call it Kennedy's bed, now," he said with a grin. Charlie, intrigued, asked whether he had slept well in it the first night and if he had had any interesting or unusual dreams. "No! I just jumped in and hung on!" the President replied gleefully. He was truly thrilled to be living in the White House. "All the money in the world couldn't pay for living like this," he said reflectively. "Just think, only six months ago I was begging people to shake my hand — and now they're lining up to get in and see me!" He mentioned again, with obvious delight, his enjoyment of the extra attention from so many servants. "They were all standing by while I showered and shaved!"

As the four friends were having coffee in the Green Room, their conversation took a serious turn which impressed the Bartletts. The main concern of both the President and his wife was how best they could use all the power and facilities granted them to help the people. The President was frustrated already by the possibility that he might only have four years in which to accomplish all the things he wished to do. Both Kennedys discussed plans for saving Lafayette Square. The Eisenhower administration had planned to renovate this lovely park across from the White House by demolishing the graceful old houses where historic figures like Stephen Decatur and Dolley Madison had lived. They planned to erect boxlike government buildings which would have dwarfed the nearby White House.

The Kennedys were equally distressed by the ugliness of the White House interior and especially the undistinguished modern reproductions which bore so little relation to their historic setting. Mrs. Kennedy was impatient to transform the White House into a place which everyone would want to visit, and where children could learn something of their country's history. This was only her fourth night in the White House, and already she was brimming over with tentative plans to persuade friends and wealthy collectors to contribute suitable paintings and fine furnishings.

After coffee the First Lady took Martha Bartlett on a tour of her new domain. The President and Bartlett went out together into the cold for a walk around the perimeter of the White House enclave. Secret Service agents trailed them discreetly. An elderly woman, startled to see the President, stammered, "God bless you, Mr. President!" The two men paced side by side companionably, and the President told what he considered a very funny story. That same morning there had been an air-raid drill and, en route to the bomb shelter, he had been escorted by an aide who had also served under President Eisenhower. As they walked from the presidential office, Mr. Kennedy, looking out toward the Washington Monument, noted the high ironwork fence enclosing the White House grounds. "How far is it down to that fence?" he asked. "It's a brassie and a seven iron, sir!" replied the Eisenhower-conditioned aide.

Though Bartlett laughed, he thought how extraordinary it was that he should be walking, this chill night, with the President of the United States. He remembered a telephone call to Palm Beach in early January. As their conversation ended his friend had asked whether he had received an invitation to the Inauguration. Charlie replied that he had and that it was a most impressive document. "Yes," said Jack Kennedy, "it almost makes you think it's going to happen!"

It had happened, and now, together, they crossed the narrow street, closed to traffic by guardhouses on either end, between the White House and the Executive Office Building. The President was trying to decide where to have his press conferences. They

climbed upstairs to the immense, outrageously gilded and bal-
conied Indian Treaty Room, where President Eisenhower had
met the press. President Kennedy finally decided on the larger,
more modern auditorium in the new State Department building.

There was no microphone, but President Kennedy mounted
the platform and, standing behind the rostrum, said a few words
while Bartlett listened critically from a back seat in the room.
Then they eased downstairs to the mail room and watched the
overstuffed bags of official mail being delivered. Skirting the
West Wing on their way back to the White House living
quarters, they spotted Walt Rostow, one of the new New Frontier advisers, returning to his office presumably for a late evening
of work. The President was pleased by this unscheduled demon-
stration of zeal and invited Rostow to report to him, personally,
every Thursday.

At midweek, on the spur of the moment, Bill Walton was
asked to dinner again. He had invited Martha Gellhorn to dine
with him and so was urged to bring her along. A dashing blonde,
the divorced wife of Ernest Hemingway was a successful author
in her own right and rated as a scintillating catch by eager local
hostesses.

They took a taxi to the White House. Martha was muffled in
mink. Walton, as usual, was overcoatless. He did not bother with
a wallet but stuffed keys and a few dollars in his trousers pocket.
White House dinner guests seldom arrive in taxis, so when the
nondescript vehicle pulled up to the spiked iron gateway, it was
stopped. The occupants were asked to identify themselves.
Walton, walletless, had not a scrap of evidence to prove who he
was. Miss Gellhorn's purse contained only the conventional cos-
metic aids. The guards were skeptical. Suddenly, Martha flung
open her coat. Inside, in swirling letters, her initials "M.G." were
monogrammed. The White House guards smiled in relief and
swung the heavy gates open.

"Our First Night Out!"

Saturday evening, the first time the President and Mrs. Kennedy dined out, set a precedent. It was the first time that a President of the United States had dined in the home of an opposition party senator. The Senator was John Sherman Cooper, a Republican, of Kentucky. His wife, Lorraine, was a Californian who had come to Washington some years before, after living in New York. Lorraine and Jackie had had a bond in common from the moment they met: each was interested in a senator, and later each married her senator. Besides, Lorraine Cooper possessed the qualities which the younger woman admired. She was an internationalist with great personal chic, exquisite taste in décor and a flair for delightful hospitality.

The previous June, Lorraine had asked Jackie casually, "Why not come to dinner before the Second Dancing Class?" (The Second Dancing Class was one in a series of three fashionable subscription dances held every year.) "I'd love to," Jackie replied. After the election, never expecting Jackie either to remember or to be able to come, Lorraine had made up the guest list for her dinner party. But one day shortly before the Inauguration, Jack Kennedy had telephoned. "Well, dear," he drawled, "I hear we're dining with you on the twenty-eighth."

So Lorraine Cooper added to her guest list until she had collected twenty-four remarkably interesting personalities (plus eight Secret Service men who were to dine belowstairs). And, as it tends to happen in official Washington, this so-called social gathering sparked a number of unexpected results.

Secret Service agents combed the handsome old Federal house from cellar to attic. The morning of the dinner they noted grimly that the front steps and sidewalk were perilously slippery and the snow-piled street scarcely less so. The Coopers' butler, hoping to melt the snow, had poured on boiling water and created a miniature skating rink. But magically, within hours, a street-cleaning squad appeared and removed even the lowliest snowflake.

The guests were seated at three tables for eight. The champagne was Dom Perignon, a Kennedy favorite, and the written menu for the dinner prepared by Mrs. Cooper's Spanish cook, Louise, was a play on the fact that before Senator Kennedy became President, both Kennedys and Coopers lived on N Street. There was Smoked Salmon; Chicken N Street; Gnocchi; Purée of Peas; Endive Salad; Brie Cheese; Gay Street Pudding; Fruit; and Coffee. The Chicken N Street was, as the hostess described it, "sort of stewed in its juice," while Gay Street was the old-time name for N Street, and the pudding itself was a "sort of trifle with vanilla sauce."

Senator and Mrs. Cooper and their twenty other guests were assembled some time before the President and Mrs. Kennedy arrived. When they stepped through the wide doorway together, into the high-ceilinged, candlelit and very romantic room, even those who had known Jack and Jackie many years caught their breath in quick delight. "Everyone thought they looked out of this world," recalled the hostess, "so beautiful, both of them, and enveloped in radiance which seemed almost tangible."

Together they walked among the guests, greeting those whom they knew and being introduced to the others by Mrs. Cooper. Among the guests were the British Ambassador, Sir Harold Caccia and Lady Caccia; the British Ambassador to the United Nations, Sir Patrick Dean and Lady Dean; David and Evangeline Bruce; Barry and Mary Bingham of the Louisville *Courier* family in Kentucky; Philip Graham, president of the Washington *Post* and his wife, Katharine; Edward Morgan, the broadcaster and his Wendy, an authentic beauty; the Averell Harrimans; and Joseph Alsop and Marietta Tree.

Here in these warm and friendly surroundings were many gifted and experienced people. The President was in a hurry to fill important posts. He had many to offer — in the wake of the Republican exodus — and little time to talk with potential appointees. Curiously, he had never really known either Averell or Marie Harriman before; but Harriman was to become indispens-

able as a troubleshooter and Roving Ambassador. Barry Bing-
ham, whose father had been Ambassador to Great Britain, was
quietly offered, though he did not accept, two major embassies.
David Bruce, who had distinguished himself as envoy in both
Paris and Bonn, already had been considered for Secretary of
State. But partly because of age, he had been passed over for
Dean Rusk and now he would go to London as Ambassador. And
Marietta Tree was soon appointed to the United Nations.

The Kennedys, of course, did not continue on to the dance.
The next morning a White House messenger brought Lorraine
Cooper a note from Mrs. Kennedy. It read: ". . . such an
incredibly lovely evening — and such a happy time for us — our
first night out! Much love to you and John — Jackie."

Senator Cooper had been Ambassador to India in the late
fifties, and not long after their dinner he and Mrs. Cooper
escorted the President to a preview of an Indian film, *The Road
to Apu.* The President was to be the guest of Indian Ambassador
C. M. Chagla at the preview; but as Mrs. Kennedy was ill and the
President engaged for dinner at the White House, it seemed
correct for the Coopers to accompany him on to the theater. But
when President Kennedy telephoned "you pick me up," Lorraine found herself in an amusing situation. Senator Cooper had
no chauffeured car: on nights out they hired a taxi. It would
scarcely be impressive for the President of the United States to
arrive at a gala opening in a taxi. Undoubtedly the sidewalk
would be red-carpeted, the Indian Ambassador and other notables standing at attention, while photographers poised to record
the moment of greeting. So quickly Lorraine called Tish Baldridge and suggested that a White House limousine be sent to
their house first, and then they would pick up the President. At
the White House entrance on Pennsylvania they found him
standing alone and bareheaded in the dark cold. The Coopers
could not see the Secret Service men who must have been nearby,
and he seemed strangely isolated.

After the preview he brought them back to show them the
White House. The main floor was in darkness when they arrived,
but as they walked, with the President in the lead, room after
shadowy room mysteriously flooded with light just before they
reached the threshold. They never saw who was responsible for

Mrs. John Newton Pearce, the first White House curator, surveys a storeroom and checks each item acquired during past presidential administrations for clues as to its origin and historic value.

the illumination, but it was, somehow, very beautiful, and the President seemed to enjoy the quiet show immensely. Then he insisted on taking them upstairs to see Jackie. He banged loudly on her door. "I've brought friends back!" he called. "Oh! No!" they heard her groan faintly through the door. "It's just the Coopers," he said reassuringly. The President opened the door, and there, sitting up in bed, was the First Lady. The Coopers remained for the briefest moment, and, as usual, they had fun together.

Spelunking

Traditionally, with each new administration, Congress appropriates a sum of money from which $50,000 is allotted the First Family for redecorating their private rooms and an additional $25,000 to underwrite repainting the dazzling President's House. But eight years had passed since the Truman Renovation of the White House; and what were described as "extraordinary repairs" were now indicated. To cover this contingency a total of $100,000 was made available to the Kennedys, part to be spent on the public rooms, the remainder in the private quarters.

Shortly after the election, Mrs. Kennedy had telephoned Mrs. Henry Parish, her New York decorator, for help in brightening the rooms which were to be her home during the next four years. The decorator had never been inside the White House and had little to go on except her knowledge of Kennedy taste. She did, however, discover a set of handkerchief-size White House blueprints in the New York Public Library. And until Mrs. Kennedy forwarded photographs from the Chief Usher's album, Mrs. Parish used these inadequate aids to re-create, as best she could, the intimate atmosphere of N Street in the wide reaches of the White House living quarters.

Through the intervening months swatches of materials were

mailed to Washington or Palm Beach for approval. On the frigid Monday after the Inaugural, requested to "just drop in," Mrs. Parish arrived unannounced at the White House, burdened with suitcases crammed with still more samples. The bags were unpacked and the carefully labeled contents laid out for Mrs. Kennedy's inspection. There were fabrics for draperies, under curtains, upholstery and strips of carpeting, correlated for each room, plus a sizable variety of other such decorative schemes to choose from.

In less than two hours Mrs. Kennedy, whose decisions were swift and incisive, had selected everything except the materials for her husband's bedroom. This she left to the President.

When it came luncheon time and there seemed to be no sign of a meal being served, Mrs. Kennedy turned to Mrs. Parish. "Do you think it is possible to have luncheon here or do we have to eat out?" Mrs. Parish, who knew nothing of the ways of White House living, was equally baffled until she spotted a bell. She pushed it hard several times and, like magic, Mr. West, the Chief Usher appeared. He assured the ladies that they could, indeed, be served luncheon right where they were.

Mrs. Kennedy chose the menu, just hamburgers and vegetables. The two trays were set on individual tables and a pair of solicitous butlers hovered over each one. Both Mrs. Kennedy and Mrs. Parish were nonplussed by this rather incongruous show of grandeur. In an aside, the First Lady murmured that she thought the four butlers could be better employed elsewhere!

They had scarcely lifted their forks when the President appeared. He greeted them with a cheerful "Hi!" Then glancing at the hamburgers he announced rather smugly that *he* had ordered a glass of Metrecal for luncheon. The President walked off briskly toward his bedroom, but in a remarkably short time sauntered back. Nonchalantly, he paused at each tray and literally devoured whatever food remained. His appetite appeased, the President approved everything his wife had selected, and, for his own room, decided on a deep blue toile-de-Jouy printed with a spate of cherubs. He felt compelled to explain, "I've always loved angels!"

Those first few days in the White House, David Finley, then chairman of the Fine Arts Commission, was the first of many knowledgeable and influential persons who were to help Mrs. Kennedy — not only with her still nebulous restoration plans, but also in making the White House more cheerful for everyday living. A Southerner, very much of the old school, Finley had been closely associated with Andrew Mellon, the Pittsburgh philanthropist who established the National Gallery of Art. He had been its director until a few years before. Mrs. Kennedy was still confined to her bed when Mr. Finley came to call, and he sat somewhat uneasily nearby, recounting the privileges to which she was entitled. Mrs. Kennedy could use any of the White House furniture stored in various warehouses; borrow paintings from the National Gallery and the Smithsonian Institution; count on government-owned greenhouses in the Washington area to supply plants and flowers.

But most important of all, they discussed the mechanics of forming a committee which would solicit and receive donations for reviving the White House interior. When Mr. Finley took his leave, he promised to send the First Lady a fine eighteenth-century American walnut highchest to start her project rolling. The Chippendale style chest-of-drawers arrived promptly the next day and was placed eventually in the President's bedroom. It was the first gift to the White House under the Kennedy régime and was, perhaps, the only piece of furniture to be accepted without official preliminary authentication.

Mornings in that post-Inauguration week, when Mrs. Kennedy could muster sufficient strength, provided her first opportunity to inspect all the White House rooms. She knew they totaled 132, including eighteen bedrooms. But there were also innumerable closets and cavernous storerooms which sheltered unused paraphernalia, the overflow of White House living: china, silverware, glass, sets with pieces missing; rugs and strips of carpeting, worn or faded or both; linens that had been ordered, then overlooked because they were not in immediate need.

Legally, since the Theodore Roosevelt administration, White House furnishings, of even the least intrinsic value, could not be sold, given away or otherwise disposed of. Any such discarded objects were stored in government warehouses, where they would, presumably, gather dust throughout eternity. Such residue as remained in the White House had either been in use since the 1948 Renovation or was kept at hand for some unpredictable occasion.

This curious accumulation, like all government possessions, had by law been inventoried annually. That is to say, a list of "goods on hand" had been made: so many forks, knives, spoons; so many dishes, wineglasses, chairs, tables, benches. But there had been no attempt to catalogue them, i.e., make a "complete enumeration of items arranged systematically with descriptive details." And certainly no attempt to determine their provenance, or origin, had been made.

So during the following weeks, Mrs. Kennedy went on what friends liked to call "spelunking" trips through storage space and out-of-the-way rooms. She made many discoveries — though of course they were not literally "discoveries." The majority of these finds were merely objects which, in the flux of changing administrations, had been temporarily forgotten because there was no comprehensive catalogue of White House furnishings.

When, for instance, a bundle of tarnished flatware was retrieved from some dark recess, the inventory detailed the precise number of pieces it contained. But until they were cleaned and "researched" by means of old photographs and original bills, no one could be sure that this silver was part of the table settings ordered from Paris in 1817 by President Monroe. Since the silver was inventoried, obviously it had not been lost. Just as obviously, because it was impossible to set a complete table with the few remaining pieces, the flatware had not been used for some time.

Two bundles of Aubusson rugs were brought to light from the cellar. Specially woven for the Red Room and the Green Room, they had been ordered by Theodore Roosevelt in 1902. But they faded badly and had been replaced with plainer carpeting. Now, for a brief span, until exquisite (but impractical) antique rugs were donated for the three State Rooms, Mrs. Kennedy had the Aubussons put back in their original places.

On one unforgettable occasion Mrs. Kennedy and an assistant penetrated a downstairs men's room. There, hidden from public view, stood a squad of ghostly white marble busts. Gentlemen all, they were draped in the ancient Greek manner, without restraint of collar or tie. This company, chiseled more than a century earlier, included Presidents Washington and Van Buren; ex-

Mrs. Kennedy rescued this collection of marble busts from a closet off a White House men's dressing room. The busts are of President Van Buren, Columbus, President George Washington, John Bright, and Amerigo Vespucci.

The First Lady discovered the remaining pieces of a china service which Abraham Lincoln had bought for the White House. Mrs. Kennedy used this china in the new President's Dining Room, in the private living quarters. The plates and serving pieces are banded in royal purple.

plorers Amerigo Vespucci and Columbus; and John Bright, a British statesman whose likeness had been commissioned as a gift for his ardent admirer Abraham Lincoln.

Inside or out, the White House was not designed as a place to exhibit statuary. Nevertheless these statues had accumulated over the years; and after Theodore Roosevelt, no one knew, much less cared, about placing them advantageously. Most probably, after the 1948 Renovation when there had been so much to do, the little band of marble men had been overlooked and, for want of a suitable display spot, were hurried into a walk-in closet off the men's room.

Mrs. Kennedy marched them right out, had their nicked noses and chipped ears mended, and provided them with smart marble-ized wooden pedestals which the White House carpentry shop improvised from a classic design. Cool and serene, these marble busts and others, more valuable historically, now gleam in various corners and galleries of the Executive Mansion.

In February, scarcely two weeks after the Kennedys had come to the White House, Mrs. Kennedy made the first of several "discoveries" which the press played up with some exaggeration. Later, after several other "discoveries" were accorded a similar splash treatment, Mrs. Kennedy's office suggested that reporters first check with Mr. West, who not only knew most but cared most about White House furnishings.

The initial "discovery" was in a ground-floor room used as a broadcasting studio. The find itself was a massive desk topped with green baize to protect it from photographic equipment. Under the baize the desk proved to be elaborately carved and an inscription indicated it was made from timbers taken from the H.M.S. *Resolute* and presented to President Rutherford B. Hayes by Queen Victoria in 1878. The *Resolute* had been abandoned on an arctic exploring expedition (the inscription spelled out) ; recovered by the captain of a United States whaler; then purchased, outfitted and sailed to England as a gift to Her Majesty by the "President and People of the United States, as a token of goodwill and friendship." When the ship was broken up, Victoria returned the compliment by having the desk made and presenting it to the President of the United States as a "memorial of the courtesy and loving-kindness which dictated the offer of the *Resolute.*" It is a charmingly sentimental story.

The President, as well as Mrs. Kennedy, was delighted with this "discovery." On February 6, 1961, the desk was taken to President Kennedy's office, where it fitted in comfortably with the new nautical décor which included paintings of naval battles and, in place of honor on the mantel, a model of the *Constitution.*

The actual facts were that the *Resolute* desk, except during the 1948 Renovation, had been almost constantly in use since the day Queen Victoria presented it to President Hayes. In later years Herbert Hoover had kept it in his study, now the Lincoln Room; and Franklin Delano Roosevelt had placed it in the Oval Room, which had been *his* study. Then the desk had been moved to the Broadcasting Room, where it served as convenient prop during the newscasts Dwight Eisenhower taped under the watchful eye of Robert Montgomery. After General Eisenhower left the White House, the desk had remained in the Broadcasting Room all of fifteen days before Mrs. Kennedy spied it. None of these moves and countermoves, however, had ever been recorded.

The second big "discovery" was valid and, though not reported accurately by the press at the time, it was of genuine historic importance. Soon after the 1960 election, when Mrs. Kennedy had determined on her restoration project, she had asked the Library of Congress to send her all their material on the White House. Among the many magazine articles, one was of special interest. In the January 1946 issue of the *Gazette des Beaux Arts,* a Dr. Hans Huth described the suite of furniture which President Monroe had ordered from Paris in 1817. A French cabinetmaker, Pierre Antoine Bellangé, had made fourteen chairs and a marble-topped pier table of gilded wood embossed with olive branches. These were to replace the original Blue Room furniture which had been destroyed three years previously during the British sacking of the White House. Under the stress of succeeding administrations and successive sales of White House furnishings, most of the chairs and the pier table seemed to have vanished. Mrs. Kennedy hoped to trace them, and what had attracted her attention to Dr. Huth's article was his claim that the table was still in the White House (as of 1946).

Mr. West, when consulted, believed he knew the whereabouts of the table. One of his staff fetched it from a government warehouse. The table was large and in obvious disrepair, so it was deposited in the White House carpentry shop. There, shortly afterwards, Mrs. Kennedy had the excitement of "finding" it. Newspeople, reporting the discovery, embellished the story with considerable fantasy, claiming that White House carpenters had been using the venerable table as a workbench.

Actually, the mystery of the disappearance of the Bellangé chef-d'oeuvre was easily solved. But only Mr. West had the answers. It had been removed from the Blue Room in 1902 when Theodore Roosevelt had sponsored a major architectural reconstruction and had brightened and simplified the White House interior décor. For some years afterwards it stood in the Diplomatic Reception Room, then was moved to the East Lobby. During the 1948 Renovation, the Bellangé table had been stored with all the rest of the furniture in a warehouse, and there it had languished for over a decade. The decorators in charge after the Truman Renovation knew little about the history of White House furniture. The shabby old table could never have fitted in with the glittering new reproductions they installed in the Blue Room.

Mrs. Kennedy had the pier table beautifully refinished. And when its photograph was reproduced in newspapers across the country, it evoked a gratifying response: soon three of the original Bellangé chairs were presented to Mrs. Kennedy. They had been bought at different White House auctions; now they were returned to their familiar places in the Blue Room.

Since there was no curator or other such person knowledgeable about White House possessions except Mr. West, it became increasingly apparent that a complete cataloguing of the warehouse contents as well as of the Mansion itself, was an absolute necessity. At this time, the White House housekeeper, Mrs. Mabel Walker, who had held her job since the Franklin Delano Roosevelt era, was close to retirement. She had been in command a long time but her ways were not the swift ways of Mrs. Kennedy. So Mrs. Walker was to finish off her long service in an important job which she accomplished with great efficiency. She was to compile the first comprehensive catalogue of all White House furnishings in various government-owned warehouses and also to supervise the photographing of each piece of furniture, silverware, china and even accessories. This catalogue, added to the scrapbooks Mrs. Kennedy initiated for flower arrangements and menus, would make White House management infinitely easier for future tenants.

Warming Hospitality

During the first week the Kennedys were in the White House there were two callers who would set the tone of the new administration. Both were men, one American, the other foreign; and each had reached the pinnacle of his individual art.

For President Kennedy's Inauguration, the rugged poet Robert Frost had composed a special poem. Now he came to say good-bye and wish the President well. To mark this occasion, the silver-haired poet and the young Pulitzer Prize winner were photographed together in the Green Room. It was the first time in many years that both President and caller had posed for pictures in the residential part of the White House.

Mrs. Kennedy's first caller was Georges Balanchine, the Russian-born director and moving spirit of the New York City Ballet. The ballet company was in Washington for a brief engagement. An ardent balletomane, the First Lady longed to attend but could not because of her health. As a young girl, Jacqueline had gone to ballet classes and had become so proficient that, at the spring recital to which parents were invited, she had tiptoed a solo number to Debussy's "Golliwogs' Cakewalk." Though quite aware she could never be a professional dancer, she had begun collecting a small library of books on the ballet and for a while hoped she might become part of this enchanting world by designing ballet and theatrical costumes.

As First Lady she was in a position to make a more important contribution. She invited Balanchine to tea and asked him,

"What can I do for the ballet?" Balanchine enjoyed the meeting immensely. Later, queried by a reporter, he described his hostess as a "beautiful representative of youth," then added, half in fun, "She looked like a pussy-cat." Balanchine meant this as a compliment, but the reporter, fearing it might offend Mrs. Kennedy and jeopardize her patronage of the ballet, struck the remark from her copy.

Later, when Mrs. Kennedy's social program was under way, ballet performances were staged in the East Room as after-dinner entertainment on a number of outstanding occasions. And when Mrs. Kennedy left the White House, she had been planning to invite Margot Fonteyn and Nureyev to dance a pas de deux as finale to some brilliant, never-to-happen evening.

On January 25, President Kennedy made a dramatic announcement. The two United States fliers whose RBY-47 plane had been downed over the Barents Sea the previous July had been released from the Lubianka Prison. They had been shot down and taken prisoners by the Soviets after their plane had strayed off course over northern waters. The United States had made protracted efforts to free the fliers; and now, unexpectedly, the Kremlin had released them. The President had telephoned their wives, Connie McKone and Gail Olmsted, in Topeka, and with their husbands they were invited to afternoon coffee in the White House. They came several days later; but Mrs. McKone and Mrs. Olmstead were so brimming with joy and relief at having their husbands home and safe that neither could summon the small talk needed at a White House reception.

Seven years later, Nikita Khrushchev, now toppled from power, recalled with relish his role in releasing the fliers. He stated that *he* had been responsible for the Kennedy victory. He disliked Nixon and determined to help Kennedy win. If he had freed the fliers earlier, Nixon could have taken the credit. So he determined to hold them until after the election. Nixon was defeated by a popular vote of less than 200,000. Khrushchev, not understanding the intricacies of the United States Electoral College, believed that more than this number of votes would have been swung to Nixon if he had given the fliers their freedom.

On Friday, January 27, the Kennedys' first house guest arrived. He stayed a week. He was Lemoyne Billings, the President's

Robert Frost was President Kennedy's first caller. Presidential visitors were usually greeted in the West Wing Executive Offices. But Frost was the first to be greeted and photographed in the residential part of the White House. This meeting of President and poet was recorded in the Green Room.

roommate at Choate. Since schooldays "Lem" had spent many weekends and much of his leisure time with either his friend or another member of the Kennedy family. He was close to each and every one. Though Lem was still a bachelor, Jack Kennedy's marriage had scarcely interrupted this routine nor was he fazed by the election of his friend to the Presidency. He stayed at the White House whenever he wished and for as long as he wanted. He frequently accompanied the Kennedys to their country retreat for a weekend of rest and relaxation. At first, until the White House staff became used to his comings and goings, he made them decidedly uneasy: for he would arrive unannounced, go upstairs alone and sometimes select his own third-floor guest room.

Lem felt that his presence in the White House was ideal. He was a built-in extra man whom the Kennedys didn't have to ask down, but who was always available. Sometimes he went along on an overseas state visit. On the Kennedys' visit to France and Austria in the spring of 1961, Billings followed in a commercial plane, carrying with him a model of the U.S.S. *Constitution* which the President would present to Khrushchev in Vienna. He took the greatest interest in Mrs. Kennedy's White House Restoration. Sometimes, though, he was teased outrageously.

One summer Billings returned from Europe full of excitement over an encounter with Greta Garbo. He intimated that when they both were visiting on the French Riviera, he had grown to know her quite well. Some days later a friend called Mrs. Kennedy and asked if she could bring Greta Garbo to dine. The small dinner was set in the new President's Dining Room upstairs. Lem was invited without being told the identity of the other guests. Miss Garbo was tipped off about his admiration and asked to pretend that she had never met him. Lem was rocked on his heels when she came through the door. He started forward eagerly, but a cool voice cut him short. "Have I ever met you before?" drawled the mysterious Swede. For the six dinner guests it was the start of a marvelous evening, and it made a story Lem Billings tells well.

Saturday, January 21, the day after the Inauguration, in an unusual procedure aimed at getting the administration off to a quick start, the Senate had convened specially to confirm the members of the Kennedy Cabinet. Except for thirty-five-year-old Robert Kennedy, the Attorney General-designate, whom a single senator believed unqualified, all ten Cabinet members, plus Adlai Stevenson, who was to be Ambassador to the United Nations, had been unanimously approved. In a three-minute ceremony, Chief Justice Earl Warren had administered their oaths of office under one of the giant crystal chandeliers in the East Room.

On Sunday, January 29, that same ceremony was repeated with the fifteen members of the subcabinet. This time, however, the Cabinet and all the wives and children attended. All together, there were over three hundred guests. It was the first occasion on which President and Mrs. Kennedy met their official family.

Feminine reporters who had been covering White House entertainments for many years could scarcely believe their eyes. One blasé veteran topped her story with the most corny headline — "Now the White House Is a Home." For the first time a bar had been set up in the State Dining Room. Ashtrays were strategically placed and, also for the first time, guests were allowed to smoke in the State Rooms. Logs glowed in all the fireplaces. The flowers attracted flattering attention too. They were so different from the expected massive arrangements of a single variety in each vase. There were full-blown tulips in silver bowls everywhere; while tulips and red carnations in the Red Room; white tulips and yellow carnations in the Blue Room.

There was no pomp and circumstance. The President and Mrs. Kennedy came down from their private quarters unannounced. As they moved through the rooms, a military aide accompanied them and presented individual guests. The Cabinet wives noticed with pleasure that Mrs. Kennedy's gown was simple but exquisite. It was an uncluttered black velvet sheath with a bateau neckline, the velvet embroidered and reembroidered in an all-over silky, spiderweb pattern.

The minor transformation of the White House which so agreeably impressed reporters was really little more than a pathetic but determined effort of Jacqueline Kennedy's understanding friend, Mrs. Paul Mellon, and of her decorator, Mrs. Parish, to "gay up" the old Mansion instantly. Every afternoon that week Mrs. Parish toured the State Rooms, making sure that fires were laid and ready to light; draperies drawn in the great arched windows; the new Lowestoft ashtrays conveniently placed and the sad, potted palms truly banished.

Mrs. Mellon, daughter-in-law of the late Andrew Mellon, was a trained horticulturist and a genius with flowers. She had brought her garden supervisor and a maid from her Virginia country place. Together, they created the floral effects which Mrs. Kennedy preferred — loose, informal arrangements, often called "Flemish," of many harmonizing varieties in each vase. This profusion of airy, delicate blossoms cheered the uncheerful rooms.

When warming beverages had been served in the State Rooms on that chilly inauguration afternoon, headlines had trumpeted this tradition-shattering event. The President had been annoyed. "You got me into trouble the first day!" he grumbled to Tish. The social secretary countered that all the guests had enjoyed themselves. Some time afterwards President Kennedy admitted he had "given her a hard time" over the cocktail question. "Now," he continued, "everyone says it's the best thing we've ever done." Later, when an abstemious senator detailed complaints from a number of constituents, Tish replied diplomatically: "— we would greatly appreciate your explaining to those interested enough to write to you on this subject, that wines, cordials and punches have been traditionally offered to distinguished foreigners visiting the White House as well as on many other social occasions. We are therefore only following a custom established by previous White House administrations as well as that long established by foreign governments for official entertaining."

Now, in the White House, the fires were often lit in the twenty-nine fireplaces, the rooms were sweet with the scent of flowers and the visitor was received with warming hospitality.

4

The President's Household

"Mr. West"

On July 16, 1790, Congress created the first authority responsible for the President's House. This act empowered President Washington to appoint three federal commissioners to administer the newly delineated District of Columbia and erect suitable government building therein. The commissioners in turn sponsored an architectural competition aimed at producing appropriate designs for an Executive Mansion. They gave the prize to James Hoban, an Irish-born architect from South Carolina, and with his plans subsequently supervised construction of what was to be called the White House.

The office of commissioner was abolished in 1802 and through succeeding administrations the White House was managed by varying federal agencies and specific individuals on their rosters. These agencies and individuals, at the direction of the President, exercised authority only over structural and landscaping changes. In parallel but more personal fashion, there was always one official upon whom the Chief Executive conferred direct administrative and fiscal responsibility. The title for such an important post varied with the times — from the old-fashioned "Steward" to the even more anachronistic and thoroughly misleading designation of "Chief Usher." The Chief Usher of today would have no time to "usher," for he is in command of one of the most complex public buildings of this era and is directly responsible to the President for the handling of an annual budget that averages three-quarters of a million dollars.

Two wings, the West and East, extend from either side of the familiar porticoed Mansion. These were added in 1902 and just before World War II; they house, respectively, two hundred workers in the President's Executive Offices and over one hundred employees attached to a variety of offices, including the Social Office; the military aides to the President; the White

House Personnel, Finance and Tours Offices; and chiefs of the White House Police and Secret Service detail. The government-operated General Services Administration maintains both wings. The Chief Usher's separate domain is the frost-white, picture-postcard central part of the President's House. Here is set the extravaganza which attracts round-the-clock world attention. Here is a museum through which, three hours daily, several million tourists shuffle each year; an apartment where the First Family attempts to live a private life; a hotel filled with constantly transiting guests; an auditorium for press conferences; a theater for films; and a portable stage sometimes set up for official after-dinner entertainments. In this Mansion, in a single day, there might be breakfast for congressional leaders; luncheons served simultaneously in three separate dining rooms; a formal dinner for nearly two hundred guests, and a reception for businessmen. The house is so security-conscious that it is guarded by two hundred special police and an unnumbered squad of Secret Service agents.

The Chief Usher must act as a catalyst between differing and difficult personalities. He must establish a special rapport with the First Family so that the White House is run according to their wishes. He must know all the answers to all the questions pertaining to his astonishing stewardship and, above all, really "care" for the house over which he rules. To accomplish this miracle he must combine the finesse of a diplomat with the shrewdness of a politician, a sense of humor with genuine kindness.*

---

* The Chief Usher would also have a role in the continuation of the White House Restoration project. So that the work which she had undertaken could not be nullified by the succeeding administrations, Mrs. Kennedy had, in the beginning, seen to it that legislation would be enacted to protect this project. An Executive Order setting up a Committee for the Preservation of the White House was signed later during the administration of President Johnson. The Order provided that the permanent membership of the Committee was to be made up of the director of the National Park Service, the curator of the White House, the secretary of the Smithsonian Institution, the chairman of the Commission of Fine Arts, the director of the National Gallery of Art and the Chief Usher of the White House, with an additional seven temporary members to be appointed by the President. Members were to serve without compensation, and their responsibilities included the preservation and interpretation of the museum character of the principal corridor on the ground floor and the principal public rooms on the first floor. The Committee was also charged with making recommendations as to the funiture and decorative objects used or displayed in these areas of the White

J. Bernard West managed all this. He was quick, smooth, stylish; laughed easily and was, predictably, very kind. He had spent twenty years of his now high-ranking government career in the White House, and to every conceivable query his answers were both immediate and helpful. With the aid of four assistants skilled in management, plus a staff of seventy, there seemed to be nothing he could not accomplish and very little that he did not know about the House.

Shortly after Mrs. Kennedy initiated the restoration project, Mrs. Charles Wrightsman, an early co-enthusiast, described Mr. West: ". . . the only one who cared was Mr. West. Once he saw that Jackie was really interested, he brought out all these old photographs and little notes he'd made of *what* had been *where* — and even old stereopticon slides."

Mrs. Kennedy, on her part, was most appreciative of Mr. West's abilities and of his understanding of the White House.

Early or late, almost every day when Mrs. Kennedy was resident in the White House, one or more memos from her would appear on Mr. West's desk. Mr. West, or "J.B.," as his friends call him, enjoyed each one immensely. Though inevitably most of her penciled notes entailed extra work, they gave a lift to his day. He delighted in anyone who was genuinely interested and was especially pleased that a First Lady should devote not only time and talent but affectionate care for the White House.

Some memos to Mr. West were long, others brief; but all showed her enthusiasm and unflagging attention to even the most minute details. Through them all threaded never-ending requests for rehanging pictures and moving chandeliers; solicitude for the comfort of guests; and an apologetic obbligato of concern for troubling him. "By this spring — next summer or next winter — we will be ALL finished and you can live in peace!" A selection from hundreds, possibly thousands, of these memos follow:

RUGS — The color of a rug selected for one of the rooms being "restored" did not please Mrs. Kennedy. She wanted it out, quickly.

House for both décor and arrangements best suited to "enhance the historic and artistic values of the White House."

Mr. West.
Can you call the State Dept. — see if they would like it for a grand office or reception room there — or in an embassy they may be doing abroad. Tell them there is a misunderstanding and it came to us in wrong color — make it seem like a terrific favor that we are offering it to them — then if they accept!

Mr. West.
There is a tear in rug in West Sitting Hall — by round wooden table where phone is — could it be fixed — set to NY I guess — maybe when we are gone a week at Easter.

Mr. West.
Would you tell decorator to keep looking for a rug for Blue Room — as I think I would like to find one a bit stronger — without so much pink — someday —

CHANDELIERS

Mr. West.
When we do Blue Room this summer — 1. put Blue Room chandelier in Green Room. 2. put Green Room chandelier in our 2nd floor dining room. 3. put one now in our dining room outside Treaty Room. 4. I need cords, silken ones, to hang pictures on in 2nd floor Oval Room. [for] chandeliers also in Red, Blue, Green and dining rooms (Family & Private), Halls etc. wherever they are necessary. Could a silken cover be made for chandelier — same idea as in Oval Room.

Mr. West.
1. When you take chandelier out of upstairs Oval Room, would you put it in the East Hall. 2. Can you ask if the Blue Room chairs we are having copied for front Hall should be mahogany or white and gold like others — then tell copier. 3. Can you send a picture of the long, downstairs gallery by movie room to Boudin [an uncompensated restoration consultant] tell him our plans for Smithsonian to hang WH data along walls — should frames be white or gold or just behind glass screwed along wall.

(Citizens wishing to tour the White House have to queue up along the ground-floor gallery before mounting to the State Rooms on the first floor. The gallery walls were bare and Mrs. Kennedy thought those waiting so patiently should have something attractive and of historic interest to distract them. Smithsonian Institution experts, carrying out her ideas, framed charming displays of White House memorabilia, which were hung along the walls. These displays, which were changed occasionally, became very popular.)

LIBRARY

Mr. West.

Putting a panel in bookcase facing you as you come in room was suggested — to hang 3 Indians on. I think this is a great idea — so will you have it made and painted — what I would like is to have it invisibly hinged — & be able to open it invisibly — like door to bathroom in Treaty Room — as then we could put books behind it.

By this spring we will be ALL finished & you can live in peace! Also if there is a money problem we will wait until we get a new batch of $ from guidebook.

(The "Indians" Mrs. Kennedy mentioned were three of five extremely rare portraits of Indian chiefs painted by Charles King Bird in 1821. The then Secretary of War had ordered a study made of the Plains Indians. A number of the paramount chiefs journeyed to Washington where they were received by President Monroe, who presented each with a large gold medal hung on a chain. The chiefs proudly wear their medals in the portraits.)

HEAT

Mr. West.

Can you tell Usher's office to adjust thermostat in my room, West Hall, Oval Room etc, our living quarters — so that heat is at 65. — It is either suffocating or great gusts of cold air blowing through airconditioners when I ask to have the heat turned down — Ask them not to cool blowing air conditioners on to accomplish this — as everyone gets a crick in the neck — greatest brains at Army Engineering Corps can figure how to have this heated like a normal, rattletrap house.

(Alas, Mrs. Kennedy could seldom keep the private living areas at the cool 65 degrees she desired. During the Truman Renovation the type of air-conditioning used in public buildings had been installed. It operated on zone control and, when the thermostat was changed, inevitably the apparatus emitted blasts of either frigid or torrid air.)

Almost weekly President Kennedy was host at breakfast for

congressional leaders in the smaller Family Dining Room, adjoining the State Dining Room. At these meetings the President often had notes to read and, as the chandelier was not electrified, light from the side brackets was insufficient. The room was being "restored" when Mrs. Kennedy wrote this memo, and the "divine picture" she mentions is a notable portrait of President Tyler.

Mr. West.
Tyler may have to go but as it is such a divine picture we can use it in Red or Green Room. Chandelier should be attached as JFK can't read there. — Rug with bright, blue border should be used — see if the secretary between windows (which isn't wanted there) can be given back to dealer in exchange for something we need.

Impatient at the delay in getting orders delivered, Mrs. Kennedy sent off a memo:

Mr. West.
If there are any little things which we discussed and didn't firm up, please give definite orders for them right away — or check with me. All I care about is getting everything *except a couple of 3rd floor bedrooms done by the New Year. (Please order Mr. du Pont's chintz & get curtains made for double North Guest Room.) Let's get all this decorating over with & we can all enjoy life. We will have one day at picture hanging in Blue and Green Rooms & we can all rest in peace after that. Thanks.*

Mrs. Kennedy disliked anything "corny" or saccharine; and calling the florists' workshop the "Bouquet Room" instead of simply the "Flower Room" fell into both categories:

Mr. West.
Can we call the Flower Room the Flower Room *& NOT the Bouquet Room — let's change before the latter sticks.*

One by one the third-floor guest rooms were "finished." Mrs. Kennedy supervised the smallest details.

Mr. West.
Red toile bedroom. 1. Please have telephone extension made long enough to go on bedroom table. 2. Tell Curator we need 1 more small Empire chair — similar to other in room — (or stool) to go in

front of dressing table. 3. Please get 2 scrapbaskets covered in red toile (like blue toile bedroom one), a straw one for small country bedroom (this should be straw color — not white) — white one in 3rd floor bathroom is fine — can have in all 3rd floor bathrooms. We still need white straw laundry hampers in those bathrooms — with tops that close —

Mr. West.
Could you call or write Mrs. Mellon — say I asked you to ask her permission — if I could write to the 2 young men who did the Xmas tree (get their address). Tell her it is about the pullman car brass and brown glass ash tray stands for East Room. Say I thought as they see so much — in the theatre, props, lights etc. they might know of something inexpensive & good taste — then you could write them — enclose pictures of stand & tell them how many we need & that ash trays must be lifted out. Thanks.

Suggested replacements for the ugly ashtray stands proved so expensive that finally Mrs. Kennedy herself designed the new ones. Adapted from an old plant stand, they were dark wood, with three plate-sized circular trays, the upper one scooped to hold a removable glass ashtray, alternating on either side. Real bargains, they were made in the White House carpentry shop.

EAST ROOM CURTAINS

Mr. West.
I noticed how awful East Room curtains looked at concert today when drawn — that is true of all curtains which are roped back in daytimes — they are full of wrinkles when drawn — I think we should have silk undercurtains — opaque — we could draw for evening — leaving yellow ones looped back in daytime — could you send Boudin East Room foto with curtains looped back in daytime — explaining problem — & ask him what he suggests for evening & let's get them by New Yr. when we will be having evening entertainments again.

They should have first priority — over Queen's Room — lovely silk undercurtains — as all the beauty of that room is lost when wrinkled curtains are drawn. Thanks.

Raw silk glass curtains were made for the East Room at "top priority." Quite naturally their pristine freshness made the old yellow draperies look dowdy by comparison; new ones simply had to be ordered. This was one of Mrs. Kennedy's last projects and they were not hung until after she had left the White House.

These shimmering gold curtains, approved by both Mrs. Kennedy and the Fine Arts Commission for the White House, took more than two years to complete. They were ordered through a New York firm but were woven in Paris because there were no looms in the United States sufficiently large to weave a pattern which did not repeat even once in its sixteen-foot length. They arrived in 1965, cost $25,000, which was paid for by the White House Historical Association. The gold silk damask matched the gilt cornices which had been installed over the East Room windows in 1902. (These cornices had been mostly obscured during the past eight years by the yellow draperies ordered at the time of the Truman Renovation.)

The pattern itself, woven in lighter gold threads, included a fantasy of butterflies, flowers, wheat, a rooster and numerous cupids busied in various activities. The heavy curtains were both lined and interlined, and an ornate eight-inch gold coiled fringe at the bottom gave extra weight.

During the ten days it took to install the curtains, the East Room was repainted in the same off white, the floor was resanded and the chandeliers and urns were cleaned. The East Room, rejuvenated, looked larger and more formal. Since by law the old draperies could not be sold or disposed of, they were stored, to wait perhaps for some government museum which might be inspired to re-create the famous East Room.

Mr. West.
Could little chest of drawers in Q. dressing room be painted black before Mon. I just want it to look more pulled together by time Maharani of Jaipur comes Oct. 23–27. Gold doesn't matter & mirror is OK — just blacken chest. P.S. Jaipurs will be bringing HIS valet — will you find place for him. Could spread in Lincoln sitting room be ready Oct. 23 — for day bed — otherwise put my fur rug on it & some green & yellow pillows.

When you send Healy Lincoln to be restored — have press release through Pam about Peale that will be there & when Lincoln comes back will find suitable place for Peale — who gave it etc. etc. etc. — great value etc.

Mr. West.
JFK approves Cabinet Room curtains — does not like muddy color of rug — I guess all molding things are fine too — I don't know what's new but I like all.

HIS OFFICE — *We don't want white chairs — he wants to see sample of rugs — He says curtains are OK but I think perhaps they should be a creamier color — as it makes everything else in room look so dirty — & we can't make sofas white.*

I just think design might be a bit feminine for Pres. office — I like something less draped — more like Cabinet or Red Room curtains — perhaps cream heavy taffeta with some braid — so could nother model be sent for Pres. office & go ahead making Cab. curtains —

Mr. West.
The sun is going to fade the walls & curtains in Green, Blue & Red Rooms — so the minute the tours are over could you have the blinds drawn & in summer I think they should be drawn for the tours (the white pull down blinds).

Also in the Blue Room make sure the braid on curtains is turned in as if the braid faces out it gets sun-burned.

Mr. West.
Mr. Kennedy, my father-in-law, is coming to stay with us this week. Please find out date and arrival time from Mrs. Lincoln — have her ask his secretaries these questions —
1. Does he need a hospital bed — If so put it in the Lincoln Room — on window side of present bed — tell her we will have victrola in his room — I'll put one of my portable ones there —
2. Does he need any other things? Medical lifts etc. in bathroom — if so have her give Dr. Burkley the list & where & how to install them.
3. I will meet him at the plane so let me know time & I will go in a convertible as he can only sit in front seat — Lincoln convertible I guess or whatever is around.
4. He will stay in Lincoln Room, Anne Gargan in Queen's — His nurses will stay on 3rd floor — I think there are 3 — in 3 north guest rooms I guess would be easiest.
5. — they will eat in mess to avoid troubling the household — You could leave a note in their rooms at mess hours & they can sign JFK — & we will pay for their meals — If it is all done on a cash basis there — Tell waiter to just add up their meals and bill JFK.
6. Anne Gargan & he will eat breakfast in room, lunch & dinner with

children — those are his meal hours & I will sit with them & he enjoys being with them.

7. I will tell nurses whenever they want to go out — they can walk out gate & get taxi — Maybe you could put a Washington Tour booklet in each of their rooms — then they won't use ushers' office as information bureau — Is there a TV in sitting room on 3rd floor South? Little middle room — if not — put one there and they can watch at nite —

8. Drink tray put it on Mr. K's side — but in dining room on a suitcase stand — I don't think she drinks & he just has make-believe cocktails. Tray should have Gin & Tonic — Coke — Ginger Ale, Rum, Scotch, Ice, cocktail shaker — Lemon juice — (I think this comes in a mix already in a bottle) — Sugar syrup in a jar.

9. If his Secret Service man comes — & I imagine he will as he is a companion — Jerry Behn can figure a place for him to stay — If he brings a male nurse he can sleep wherever you put men on 3rd floor. I don't know what his nurses setup is now —

10. Please see that Cornelia gets a few days off — she has none off up here & has been a saint. Also this winter could she never be off on Wednesdays — as then she can help me with the children.

MEMOS — SHORT SHORTS

PRIVATE LIVING

Mr. West.
Please put 4–5 vermeil boxes for cigs — on tables — the most ornate Victorian ones (1 is in Queen's Room now) If necessary take some from commode in our West Hall — All men love this room more than anywhere so we must have it usable.

Mr. West.
In the Queen's Room, Lincoln Room, 3rd floor hall and guest rooms we need cigarette boxes. All modern china ones look so tacky — could we find some flat ones which are not too vulgar — I wonder if Baccarat cylindrical cut glass ones would be all right for Queen's Room — and perhaps black lacquer for 3rd floor — but something to replace ones with flying fish & dollar bills on them — thanks.

Mr. West.
In future will the usher's office arrange to find out from the Pres.' office when he has meetings upstairs & have a butler there with coffee

ready or to ask them if they want drinks. — Each time he has a meeting I have to call to get someone up.

Mr. West.
This summer let's get rid of drinking fountain in 3rd floor hall. If staff need it it can go in linen room or their sitting room. Children won't miss it — it must go.

Mr. West.
When the man comes to do Q. Room's spotlight over mantel — would you also have him put one in Oval Room — to shine on our Greek head on the mantel. It would be nice to do this soon as the Pres. would like it.

Mr. West.
I think protocol should be — they announce
Pres. & Mrs. K.
Minister of Cultural Affairs
for France & Mme. Malraux
& we 4 go into receiving line — Make sure there is a 2nd aide so I hear names — Also check to see if Malraux will make a toast — if so we must have interpreter.
Pres. will make one so have interpreter.

Next is possibly the only memo whose instructions were not carried out. Mr. West resisted the change by a clever delaying action. The East Room's expanse of shimmering flooring is still very blond.

Mr. West.
— also could you please look into the possibility of really darkening the East Room floor — so it would stay — Aug.–Oct. would be good for this — on State Visits it would make it stop looking like a roller skating rink & we could keep it waxed like it is.

Mr. West.
I told Mrs. Wrightsman her bronze cleaner could clean bronzes on Blue Room fireplace — also Blue and Green Room mantel clocks & candelabra — as they will look dingy by comparison — & he is the Metropolitan Museum expert & says they should be cleaned — So will you let him have them when he calls you.

Mr. West.
Will you wheel down our pathetic group of lamps again — so we can choose some for the Q's Sitting Room and the Lincoln —

These lamps, mostly reproductions, had been bought at the time of the Truman Renovation. As an economy move, Mrs. Kennedy used some of them but had an expert come down from New York and fit them with especially delightful shades.

CHILDREN

Mr. West.
Mrs. Lincoln has a paper with autographs the astronauts gave for Caroline — Could you get it from her — have it framed in a little gold frame & put on my desk —

Mr. West.
Caroline's 2 favorite toys that she sleeps with were left at Hyannis Port over Thanksgiving — in either her bedroom or playroom. A stuffed gray poodle — a Raggedy Ann doll about 12 inches long. Could someone up there find them & have them sent to us at Palm Beach after Monday —

After an untold number of instructions to Mr. West, Mrs. Kennedy signed off.

Mr. West.
I want to do not one single thing & recuperate for 6 mos — so you will have that to look forward to. Thank you. JBK.

Bright with Flowers

"So much about the restoration of the White House was known," Jacqueline Kennedy said, "but what I thought was just as important to leave to the next President's family was a smoothly running house where everything was beautifully done, so that, if the future President's wife didn't care much about these things, still the White House would be nothing to be ashamed of."

Obviously, the White House Restoration became Mrs. Kennedy's long-range responsibility, but two less demanding projects were even closer to her heart. There was so little really personal about redecorating the historic Mansion. The undertaking was so vast, many experts had to be consulted, and the results approved by committees. But flowers and food were different. These were familiar subjects; and with them, in a noticeably short time, she could accomplish her own minor miracles.

Both President and Mrs. Kennedy loved flowers. Each had grown up in country places with delightful gardens, carefully tended trees and smooth green lawns. Their N Street house had been bright with flowers which Mrs. Kennedy arranged herself in a variety of unusual containers. The potted palms, ferns and the rigid floral juxtapositions which had been accepted by White House residents during so many administrations were almost physically as well as aesthetically depressing to Mrs. Kennedy. She had definite ideas on how she wanted flowers displayed in the White House — and on the understanding care which she knew the gardens and grounds needed. During the first weeks of her time there she reorganized the whole concept of flowers in the White House and left to her successors a year-round master plan of floral decoration.

Mrs. Kennedy learned that the head gardener, who had been with the White House for almost forty years, bore the double burden of supervising the grounds outside as well as the flowers inside. It seemed only sensible to divide these responsibilities. The National Park Service, it was decided, would handle all outdoor upkeep, and the floral arrangements inside were to be undertaken by three young men on the gardening staff who had previously assisted with the flowers. The senior of these, Elmer (Rusty) Young, was selected by Mrs. Kennedy to be chief of the Flower Room.

The Flower Room, a miniature florist's workshop on the ground floor of the White House, was efficiently reorganized, and a special closet built for the vases, bowls and urns, some of which Mrs. Kennedy had chanced upon during her voyage of discovery through the White House. To familiarize Rusty Young with her ideas on arranging flowers, the First Lady lent him several books from her collection on still-life art and a marvelous ancient tome on Flemish flower arrangements borrowed from Mrs. Mellon. Rusty Young found Mrs. Kennedy's ideas easy to follow. "He has a feeling for color and mass and can do bowls of flowers, which look like Dutch still lifes, with whatever materials are on hand," the First Lady complimented Young. "He only needs a suggestion, a few words or a few flowers held in front of a container, to know how to finish an arrangement."

Jacqueline Kennedy's concept for White House flowers was fresh and new. She thought they should give the impression of being just picked from a garden and therefore preferred seasonal blooms to exotic hothouse varieties.

"With Mrs. Kennedy our orders changed a great deal," explained Rusty Young in a triumph of understatement. "There were more apple and pear blossoms, forsythia, pussy willows — and every kind of marguerite daisy —" The rainbow of blossoms and flowers which now appeared in the White House was tremendously exciting: the tree and shrub blossoms included deutzia, mock orange, weigela, plum, pear, cherry, apple, forsythia, flowering crab apple and crab apple with berries. In spring, too, there were lilacs, hyacinths, freesia, ranunculus, anemones, sweet peas. In summer, gallardia, coreopsis, stock, heliotrope, zinnias, gypsophila, summer lilac, sweet William, geraniums, dahlias, Canterbury bells, foxglove, heliopsis, calendula. While in fall and winter there were tuberoses, bouvardia, blue lace flowers, dahlias, anemones, oriental oranges, stevia, gerbera daisies! *

Beside this galaxy, blue cornflowers and geraniums were almost always kept on hand. The President liked a knot of cornflowers in his buttonhole when he wore a formal business suit. He treasured a small silver vase given him by the President of Ireland. He kept it on a lamp table in his office and enjoyed having it filled with blooms from the geraniums which bordered his Rose Garden.

The new arrangements which Rusty Young created for the First Lady were enchanting. A jardinière in the main hall might contain White Majestic daisies, sprays of lavender, cymbidium orchids, white stock, fuschia-colored stock, Bermuda lilies, purple

---

* There were two varieties of flowers, snapdragons and gladioli, for which Mrs. Kennedy had such an aversion that neither was permitted in a White House arrangement. The First Lady held what she called "florists' roses" in almost equally low esteem.

anemones, and pussy willow. While on a sofa table in the Red Room, a vermeil urn might be filled with white stock, single white chrysanthemums, white carnations, white freesia, white candytuft, white tulips, open red roses and pussy willow. One of Mrs. Kennedy's favorite arrangements was a handled Lowestoft mug, placed on a very small table in the Diplomatic Reception Room and containing blue cornflowers, yellow and orange epidendrum orchids and gypsophila (baby's breath) .

Sometimes more than four dozen flower arrangements were made in a single day; and occasionally more than a hundred, including duplicates for use in case of summer rain, when tables were set up both on the lawn and inside. Flowers were cosseted to keep as long as possible. But Mrs. Kennedy felt that the thousands of tourists who filed through the State Rooms every day should see the White House flower-filled and at its prettiest. Therefore, when practicable, the flower arrangements were first put on display in the morning of an official function. They were placed in a large refrigerator immediately after the entertainment and several days later were rearranged in a new design.

The master work plan was started a few weeks after the new arrangements were considered a success. *First,* a list was compiled of the various containers which were to be used in each room. Each was always placed in the same room and in precisely the same spot. For instance, the valuable vermeil urns which hitherto had been locked in glass-fronted showcases, were now to be used in the Red Room and in the Hall outside the Treaty Room; Lowestoft bowls were for the Green Room and the Monroe *bronze-doré* pieces were to shine only in the State Dining Room.

Second, photographs in color were made of every flower arrangement used at an official function. The pictures were dated, described and filed in three scrapbooks: one for Mrs. Kennedy, a second for the housekeeper, and a third for the Flower Room.

After a year, when this plan had rounded out, the same arrangements could be copied each succeeding month without guesswork or calls to florists to find out what was in season.

It had always been the pleasant custom for the President and First Lady to send White House flowers to friends or those they wished to compliment: on arrivals or departures; on happy or sad occasions. Mrs. Kennedy's quick eye soon noticed that the lovely flowers were sent out in the unglamorous type of papier-mâché vase which florists provide "for free." Because so many such gifts were made, it was a minor but not financially unimportant problem to solve. (The Kennedys were to send out a weekly average of six such offerings.) Finally, Mrs. Mellon found the answer in a series of handled wicker baskets which were smart, yet inexpensive. She picked them up on her travels in the Caribbean and brought them back to be copied. The small baskets became a White House trademark and a status symbol to the recipient. Eventually, the favored models were standardized.

When the flower arrangements were settled, so to speak, Mrs. Kennedy turned her attention to standard plants which could be trained over wire frames or trimmed in ornamental shapes. The huge, marble-paved lobby which spread from the North Portico entrance (off Pennsylvania Avenue) had always been bare and drafty. It needed greenery: but elegant greenery, in contrast to the old, shaggy palms, for through this doorway came chiefs of state and other highly placed notables. At the First Lady's suggestion, the National Park Service began to grow standard plants, among them Ficus (a Brazilian fig) and Fastidiu. The Ficus plants, which were four to five feet tall, were planted in wooden tubs and cut in ball-headed shape. Others were coaxed to grow on wire frames shaped like pyramids. They looked very grand indeed.

All the plants, shrubs and trees used on White House property were supplied by the National Park Service. In Mr. Kennedy's second year in office, Mrs. Kennedy thought there should be some one definite place where White House plants could be grown and maintained. She inspected various government-owned plots of land, and in 1962 greenhouses were built in an outlying section of Washington. The greenhouses were not exclusively for White House convenience but also to stock other park reservations. An open area surrounded the new greenhouses, and Mrs. Kennedy was sufficiently perceptive to see that it was put to good use. Here plants and stock flowers like small chrysanthemums were grown and sent in generous quantity to the White House.

The Kennedys, like so many average American families, had lawn trouble. Both were accustomed to lush, green grass: the

President in Hyannis Port, the First Lady at her mother and stepfather's summer place in Newport. But the grass which flourishes in a cool New England climate does not grow well in Washington. That which they had had planted was, unknown to them, susceptible to a blight, evident only in the sunny parts of the lawn and showing up in small purply-brown spots. At first the gardeners were able to disguise this with a spray of green coloring, but by late July the offending splotches had spread too widely to be covered up.

As she was leaving for Hyannis Port, Mrs. Kennedy penciled a staccato memo to the imperturbable Chief Usher:

Mr. West.

The White House lawns are a disgrace. I am sure that you are working on them — but something truly drastic must be done by Fall —

1. It is a sea of brown as one looks across the South Lawn.

2. Clover, weeds and crab grass are mixed in.

3. On the hillsides there is a completely different type of stringy, long green grass. — It is driving the President crazy — and I agree with him. In Glen Ora where we have one man who cuts the lawn every two weeks, it looks like green velvet — and this place does not look as well as cowfields in Virginia.

Months ago the complaint of crab grass came up — the lawns are now worse than ever — and patches of soggy, dying, expensive turf are not solving the question. This summer please solve this.

1. Probably the lawns must be re-seeded — the proper seed must be found. Surely some expert in the Agricultural Department — Park Service can provide advice —

2. A method to water the lawn must be found — and not by having miles of snakelike green hose everywhere — with sprays shooting up so no one can walk near them — also it is ugly and undignified for the President's house.

3. Is sinking water spouts too expensive? It is done in Palm Beach but I don't know if that is practical this far north —

If helicopters leave a mark perhaps a piece of canvas could be laid to protect the grass.

I have never bothered much about lawns — but every place I have lived — with a part time gardener — the lawn has been beautiful — so surely with twelve gardeners that is possible at the White House —

By the East Wing — the hill and gardens are truly atrocious — we

are on our way restoring the inside of the White House now — so
please make a major effort this summer on the lawns —

AND — the big problem now is LAWNS — am sure you will solve
it —

Thanks   JBK

Eventually, professors from all over studied the problem and decided that the only solution was steam sterilization. This involved digging up the top foot of soil, then steaming, sterilizing and replacing it, and re-seeding it from scratch. In spite of all these efforts, the lawn still gives trouble today.

In her memo to Mr. West on the painful subject of lawns, when Mrs. Kennedy had pointed out in no uncertain terms that the East (Wing) Garden was "atrocious," she little thought that this same garden would be redone and one day known as the Jacqueline Bouvier Kennedy Garden.

That first spring they were in the White House, the President had asked Mrs. Mellon to renovate the Rose Garden, which was just outside his office windows. The garden had fallen on lean days, for many of the rose plants had been personal presents to President Eisenhower, and he had taken them with him to Gettysburg. The garden was extensively replanned, reconstructed and replanted to provide President Kennedy with a lovely setting enclosing an area sizable enough for him to greet large groups. The garden was very much the President's own enthusiasm; as Mrs. Kennedy wrote to Mrs. Mellon from Florida: "— the beauty of it seems to affect even hardbitten reporters who just come there to watch what is going on. Jack took Princess Beatrix of the Netherlands to it (I hope she wasn't wearing spike heels) and, of course, he is still planning to drag the Grand Duchess of Luxembourg down there at midnight on April 30th."

The Rose Garden was finished and now Mrs. Mellon was to design a garden for the First Lady. The East Garden was outside the long, ground-floor gallery through which tourists enter the White House. Irvin Williams, the White House horticulturist, who had worked with Mrs. Mellon on the President's project, described it as "a really dreary place." To cheer up the tourists Mrs. Kennedy had bulbs planted in the fall for spring blossoming, and through both summer and winter the plants were to be

the Jacqueline Bouvier Kennedy Garden, which was transformed by Mrs. Paul Mellon from the undistinguished East Garden and finally completed after Mrs. Kennedy had left the White House.

changed. But now she wanted a corner where she could have a bit of privacy after the tourists had left, where she could relax, and where Caroline could play unnoticed.

Mrs. Mellon decided to make the garden an enchantment, a fey place that was something out of Alice in Wonderland. It was to be a woman's garden, with a pergola. There was to be an herb garden to please René, the chef, and a small plot which Caroline was to have as her own. There would be some topiary, geraniums, tiny bulbs planted under the trees, perhaps a wicker chaise longue, and for the children a string hammock dyed tomato red. There would be a small cutting garden and a croquet lawn. Amusing Victorian benches were resuscitated from the cellar. One had belonged to President Harrison, another to President Lincoln.

It was to be a simple garden, without too much upkeep involved. No sooner was it half-done than birds flocked there and took over. There were mockingbirds and mourning doves and cardinals.

Mrs. Mellon had partially described her plans to Jacqueline Kennedy, who wrote back from Florida: "— I have complete confidence in your East Garden. All I would do is to look at your plans and just agree with them, so go ahead — you have so much sense of which is fitting for the White House — dignified but not elaborate with scriggly French beds everywhere — so I know that what you will do there will be divine."

But the East Garden had still not been finished when Mrs. Kennedy left the White House. Afterwards, when Mrs. Mellon returned to the White House for the first time, she asked the new First Lady (Mrs. Johnson) to name it for Mrs. Kennedy. The garden had been Mrs. Kennedy's idea and so it became the Jacqueline Bouvier Kennedy garden.

Culinary Tours de Force

Mrs. Kennedy's greatest initial concern was to find a sophisticated chef. She had heard ominous reports of White House food — which she soon found to be all too accurate. She was aware that the culinary situation at the White House had been uncertain for some time. The Eisenhowers' head chef had resigned in 1957. His eventual replacement had been a Filipino who had served twenty-eight years in the United States Navy. His service record had been so excellent that he was hired by the White House, initially as a meat chef. He soon became a special favorite of Mrs. Eisenhower, less for his gastronomic ability than for his flair for decorating elaborate cakes which she delighted in presenting to charity bazaars, personal friends and members of her family. In July 1957 Mrs. Eisenhower had sent the Navy chef a thank-you note which he still treasures. "The President and I wish to thank you for the wonderful cake which you decorated for our 41st wedding anniversary. The big basket with pink rosebuds in the center and the two little doves on the handle of the basket are truly lovely. As for the lacy hearts in each corner and the innumerable flowers, it seemed impossible that these were made of icing and not real —"

Mrs. Kennedy, however, felt that a chef with broader experience would better suit their needs and, though the former Navy cook was to remain on the White House domestic staff, she was pleased when René Verdon accepted the job as head chef.

The late Henri Soulé, proprietor of the famed Le Pavillon restaurant in New York, had recommended him. A cheerful bachelor who was to "live in" at the White House (most of the staff "lived out"), he was French-born but an American citizen. During the twenty-eight years he had practiced his profession, Verdon had completed the usual gastronomic cycle of five-star

Providencia (Provie) Parades poses with René Verdon, the White House head chef, and Ferdinand Louvat, the pastry chef.

Mrs. Kennedy is photographed with Mr. J. B. West, the Chief Usher, on December 6, 1963, her final day in the White House.

restaurants in Paris, Deauville, London and aboard a French luxury liner. He had then been assistant chef at the Carlyle, a Manhattan hotel where the Kennedys always stayed. For higher pay he had moved on to the less fashionable Essex House. After he accepted the White House offer it took several months to establish René on the government payroll, and during this period his salary was paid personally by President Kennedy.

René soon became so understanding of everyday Kennedy food preferences that, when Pearl left the White House, he was named family chef as well as head chef, the latter a lofty position hitherto solely dedicated to preparing state entertainments. On occasion René traveled with the President, and once was flown to Costa Rica to conjure luncheon for a gathering of Latin American heads-of-state.

In sympathetic collaboration with Mrs. Kennedy, he was to help make White House dinners memorable and undertake such culinary tours de force as supervising, from a tent pitched on the lawn, the historic dinner given at Mount Vernon by President and Mrs. Kennedy honoring President Ayub Khan of Pakistan.

Later other specialty chefs were added to the White House staff with varying degrees of success. One, an Italian, possessed an irrepressible passion for cooking fettucine and carving fish, swans and other beasts, from ice. This is an art form which literally left Mrs. Kennedy cold; his tenure was brief. By contrast, Ferdinand Louvat, a pastry chef, proved a permanent marvel. Previously, all pastries, small cakes and cookies were bought, not made in the White House. But now Ferdinand turned out a thousand miniature éclairs, hundreds of bite-size tarts, seemingly by sleight of hand. One unforgettable afternoon, when the Black Watch Pipes and Drums and the Band of the Royal Highland Regiment marched and countermarched on the South Lawn, some seventeen hundred six- to thirteen-year-old children were invited to see the exciting performance. But perhaps Ferdinand was really the star performer. He dumbfounded Mrs. Kennedy by nonchalantly producing twelve thousand cookies!

The Finest in White House Living

White House housekeeping methods were as complicated as they were antiquated. A tactful overhaul was needed to adjust from the requirements of middle-aged presidential couples whose children were grown, to a husband and wife with mere babies, and to adapt to a President and First Lady who declined to accept for their distinguished guests less than the finest in White House living.

The First Lady was accustomed to a small, well-trained staff; she found the constant rotation of White House butlers and maids inefficient. Many household amenities, such as attractive everyday china, glassware and linens, were sadly lacking. Curiously, except for the massive brass cigar stands on the main floor, there even seemed to be no ashtrays. (A few days after the Kennedys were in residence, a wealthy woman, who was to become one of the most generous White House donors, pressed five one-hundred-dollar bills into Mrs. Parish's hand with the suggestion she buy some really handsome ashtrays.) However, all these details were minor problems which Mrs. Kennedy could easily resolve; to her, having good food agreeably served was the immediate issue.

"The kitchen was on the ground floor of the White House," Mrs. Kennedy explained. The 7- by 20-foot pantry, one flight up from the kitchen and linked by a tiny staircase, was incredibly inadequate. "This narrow butler's pantry was on the same floor as the State Dining Room," she continued, "—and on the night of State Dinners or any large dinner, the whole Family Dining Room, which was in between, was turned into a pantry —

"The first meals we had in the State Dining Room were so full of delays that I decided to cut the number of courses. For that reason we never had soup because it could not be served hot — I usually had a first course, meat course, salad and cheese (or pâté) and dessert. And among the wines served at every meal, one was American. — I really think this might have been too simple for the President's House but any other way we would have been at the table all night."

Selecting wine was difficult, too. The White House had no wine cellar. Because of a complex accounting system and an inadequate budget, it was impossible to buy in quantity and therefore no provision for storage had ever been made. The wines had always been purchased separately for each entertainment. Mrs. Kennedy immediately consulted Douglas Dillon, Secretary of the Treasury and proprietor of the celebrated Haut Brion vineyards in France, about what to purchase. The Secretary referred her to Frederick Wildman, a friend and connoisseur who owned a New York wine and gourmet food shop. Mr. Wildman spent a day in the White House with Mrs. Kennedy, adapting his selections to the budget presented by Mr. West. He suggested wines, imported and domestic, for every occasion.

"Mr. Wildman really made an incredible contribution!" said Mrs. Kennedy enthusiastically. Some time afterwards she read with pleasure that Isaac Stern, the violinist who had performed so brilliantly at the White House dinner honoring the French Minister of Culture, remembered the names of the wines served and had commented on their excellence.

In previous administrations, either a single horseshoe or an E-shaped table had been used for state and official dinners. These tables seated only ninety-six, but Mrs. Kennedy devised a new arrangement which made it possible to invite almost double the number of guests. She was sure the intimacy of smaller groups would spark more gaiety, so she had the White House carpenters make a number of round tabletops which, set on bases, could each seat ten. She banished the ungainly banquet board and substituted a long table at which twenty-two could be accommodated and at which the President presided. As it was impossible to set up all the small tables in the State Dining Room, she played hostess to the overflow in the Blue Room and had the two rooms linked by a public-address system which made it possible to interchange toasts.

The small tables were enchanting. They were covered with

buttercup-yellow linen veiled with white organdy overcloths, embroidered with wands of tiny formalized leaves. Flower-filled vermeil centerpieces complemented the old vermeil flatware. Some of the centerpieces were from the Margaret Thompson Biddle Collection (which had been bequeathed to the White House during the Eisenhower administration); other gilded bowls, embossed with a bamboo design, were given by the Paul Mellons. There were two dozen of the latter, and they were among the first White House gifts presented during the Kennedy régime. Before too long, Mme Porthault, the designer of ravishing Parisian table linens, donated an exquisite state tablecloth, of white, gossamer-light fabric with an overall gold-thread embroidery of delicate flowers.

During the first weeks in the White House Mrs. Parish had ordered the needed replacements of everyday china. The glassware, too, was much depleted and entirely inadequate for the newly increased number of place settings for official entertaining. Ever since Mrs. Kennedy had campaigned in West Virginia, where she had been distressed by the poverty in the coal-mining areas, she had wanted to make some contribution to the state. The Morgantown Glassware Guild, Inc., was an important West Virginia industry, so here she ordered the White House crystal with the suggestion that, in addition to their own designs, they copy a tulip-shaped champagne glass which she preferred. A White House release, dated May 20, 1961, stated:

> The glassware, which has been much needed for White House use, includes 6 dozen of each of water goblets, wine and champagne glasses. Mrs. Kennedy, who ordered the glassware out of gratitude and affection for West Virginia, knew of the Guild's work because of her visit to the State during last Spring's campaign.
>
> The Morgantown Glassware Guild originally made crystal called "Old Julian Street," which was patterned after designs suggested by Julian Street, a well-known authority on wine and author of several books on the subject. The glasses were simple in design, tulip-shaped and lacking in embellishment so that one could enjoy the color and taste of the wine without being distracted by the design of the glass.
>
> The glasses which the White House has ordered are similar

in design to the "Old Julian Street" crystal but will hereafter be called by the firm "The President's House" crystal.

Mrs. Kennedy plans to use the new glasses for the first time at the Senate Ladies' Luncheon on Tuesday, May 23rd, 1961.

Some time later Mrs. Kennedy said with satisfaction, "— this glassware was advertised and sold everywhere as the 'White House' wine glass — it only cost something like six dollars a dozen. But I didn't mind that at all, as I thought it was nice to help West Virginia and nice that people should see that those simple glasses were pretty enough for the White House."

The following year a widely known manufacturer of costly glassware offered to donate a complete set of very expensive crystal to the White House. But Mrs. Kennedy demurred. She wrote Mrs. Parish: "— the whole problem is still West Virginia — it still is NO — and will be until they aren't poor any more. It is funny — but in all the places we campaigned — & sometimes I was so tired I practically didn't know what State we were in — those are the people who touched me most — The poverty hit me more than it did in India — maybe because I just didn't realize that it existed in the US — little parched children on rotting porches with pregnant mothers — young mothers — but all their teeth gone from bad diet — I would practically break all the glasses & order new ones each week — it's the only way I have to help them —"

President Kennedy made a habit of checking accounts which seemed out of line. He was more than ordinarily interested in bills as so many were paid out of his own pocket. He was the only President of the United States except Herbert Hoover who did not keep his salary: from the day he had entered government service as a young Representative from Massachusetts, he had turned every paycheck over to charity. Now Kennedy found that an astronomical amount of money had been spent on food during his first months in the White House. He agreed with his wife that menu planning and the ordering of foodstuffs belonged under the direction of the housekeeper, who could more easily control costs, rather than in the domain of the social secretary, who had her own time-absorbing job quite apart from arranging meals.

Mabel Walker, who had been housekeeper since the Roosevelt era, was near retirement. She could not keep step with Mrs.

Kennedy's new ideas and so, during the final months of her career Mrs. Walker was delegated to cataloguing and supervising the photographing of such White House furnishings as languished in government warehouses. When Mrs. Walker was established in her new job, Mrs. Kennedy persuaded Anne Lincoln to take over as housekeeper.

It was an unusual choice for an unusual job. The daughter of a Park Avenue physician, a Vassar graduate, Anne was managing the New York office of moving-picture star Robert Montgomery when Tish Baldrige telephoned to offer a position on her staff. A year later Anne took over the responsibilities of the housekeeper. She had no professional experience but was backed by the Kennedys' belief, which so often proved right, that anyone who was naturally bright and on the Kennedy "wavelength" could handle almost any job "like a breeze."

As the housekeeper was directly responsible to Mr. West, Mrs. Kennedy outlined Anne's new duties in a memorandum.

Mr. West.

I want to get it all clear in the beginning so that Anne will know her domain, and the two offices (Housekeeper and East Wing or Social Secretary's office) can become independent and work more effectively that way. It seems to me, for the future, that MENUS is the most important of all to put under Housekeeper.

Tell Anne she doesn't have to bother about children's or our menus. — René does ours by ear and if it's a special evening with special guests — Anne should have him set up a proposed menu — otherwise he knows by now what the Pres. likes.

MY SUGGESTIONS FOR ANNE

If she doesn't have enough shelves in her office, please build her maximum amount.

1. She must keep up the Flower scrapbooks — 3 sets

2. She must have shelves for menus — past ones we have used in White House, official and private. I will turn over to her a box of recipes I have saved or used (which I want back eventually) and she must have a file of ideas. She should keep menu scrapbooks (like my black ones) the same as the Flower scrapbooks — 3 sets:

> *One for myself*
> *One for her and for the East Wing, I guess*

I suggest that Anne put her office in order and learn to know about house — see all silver, china and glass stored throughout the house — those butler's pantries on mezzanines — learn names of staff and shifts [of work], care of furniture etc. etc. — then she can take over menus when she is ready.

Before she definitely assumes command of menus — she could send me a set of proposed ones — for example:

    Press breakfasts
    Stag lunches 4 or 6
    State Dinners Fall Winter Spring
    Our small dinners for 6 or 8 — Fall Winter Spring
    Buffets — for receptions

and send a set of ones East Wing has used on similar occasions — so I can be sure Anne does it the way I want before she definitely starts.

She might need some secretarial help with all those scrapbooks etc. I believe that the Housekeeper is directly responsible to you — so you decide and arrange all that, her salary and whatever title you hit on.

Tell Anne as soon as the President leaves for the office, she is free to poke all around 2nd and 3rd floors — and can go anywhere — our private apartments etc. — and I wish she would, as that is the only way she will learn how the house runs — She can ask Provie any questions she wants —

Next week is a very busy one so I won't have much time — but week after that I will discuss anything with her or you —

The new housekeeper soon found that the basic difficulty of White House housekeeping was lack of money. The overall budget, a congressional appropriation, had been pegged at almost the same amount for many years. Presidents, wishing to avoid any implication of "high living," had been averse to asking for any increases. The budget, somewhat under $700,000, covered operating expenses but not entertainment costs: the State Department underwrote all White House hospitality for visiting chiefs of state and, on occasion, for foreign guests of slightly lesser rank. This covered the cost of state dinners or, sometimes, state luncheons. But official entertaining, which honored all other categories of guests, was charged to the President's $50,000 a year entertainment allowance, a sum which was really the untaxed half of the $100,000 Presidential salary, and usually had to be supplemented from his $40,000 annual travel stipend.

Obviously, as these two types of entertainment were paid for through separate accounts, known respectively as the "Extra Special" and the "Special Account," the food and wines had to be ordered and sales slips filed individually. Since White House living consisted of more than just partying, the housekeeper faced juggling a total of five different accounts. The third was the Family Account, under which all food and refreshments consumed by the President's family and private guests were charged directly to him. The fourth, or Staff Account, covered provisions ordered on a strict budget which went into at least one daily meal for each of the thirty-two members of the White House domestic staff. The fifth and final account kept the housekeeper in such necessary but unglamorous supplies as dust cloths, brooms, soap flakes and detergents.

Sometimes the housekeeper ordered for all five accounts in a single day, each purchase being billed separately. Because of this division there were few opportunities to save by buying in bulk. There was an equally minimal chance of profiting by sales, because all White House foodstuffs had to be bought from some seventeen wholesalers who had been cleared by the FBI. (Even these tried and true purveyors were not permitted to deliver to the Executive Mansion. White House trucks picked up all orders.)

The "Extra Special" and the "Special" accounts were the first to test the new housekeeper's ingenuity. Though she had no control over budgets or food prices, Anne could control what was spent on each individual entertainment. Checking costs became an important facet of her job. Though the State Department "picked up the tab," she tried to limit spending on state dinners. But an occasional splurge was called for when the President entertained a foreign leader, and she made up menus on which filet mignon, baby lobsters, pâté de foie gras and other de luxe items were repeaters. Somewhat to her surprise she was soon ordering nonchalantly such luxuries as 150 baby lobsters, 45 pounds of crabmeat, 15 pounds of beef tenderloin and, in a single breath, 90 pints of strawberries, 22 quarts of whipping cream, 10 gallons of vanilla ice cream, which added up deliciously to a gargantuan quantity of Strawberries Romanoff.

The marketing order placed for a state dinner which took place on a Friday (and therefore featured Lobster Thermidor rather than meat) seemed incredible. A Roquefort Mousse as well as Strawberries Romanoff were included in the menu for 180 guests, and the total added up to $2,267 minus the cost of extra butlers.

MARKETING ORDER

Lobsters	100
Cooked jumbo shrimp	4 lbs.
Fowl (base for soup)	1 case
Eggs	1 case
Leeks	5 bushels
Idaho potatoes	2 cases
Spinach	80 lbs.
Shallots	1 basket
White mushrooms	3 baskets
Chives	10 packages
Watercress	30 bunches
Escarole	20 bunches
Chicory	20 bunches
Parsley	2 bunches
Strawberries	90 pints
Parizot French mustard	10 jars
Sour pickles	6 jars
Roquefort cheese	20 lbs.
French bread	15 boxes
Saltines	6 boxes
Instant Sanka	6 jars
Coffee cream	2 qts.
Whipping cream	22 qts.
Vanilla ice cream	10 gals.
Mixed nuts	5 lbs.
Assorted chocolates	6 lbs.

Ordered for the Artists Who Performed After Dinner

200 regular sandwiches
5 gals. coffee

WINES

Inglenook Pinot Chardonnay	9 cases
Dom Pérignon	9 cases
White Chablis	2 gals.
Red Burgundy	2 gals.
Corona cigars	3 boxes
Asst. cigarettes	2 cartons
Cutty Sark	2 cases
Old Grand-Dad	2 cases
Beefeater gin	1 case

Though it was neither gastronomically nor visually apparent, the new housekeeper really cut corners on the "Special Account" which covered the official entertaining for which the President paid. (This entertaining might honor such top-rank personalities as the Vice-President, the Speaker, Supreme Court Justices or Diplomatic Corps members.) Anne managed these economies by simply avoiding high-priced cuts of meat, substituting chicken or perhaps less expensive cuts and never ordering vegetables or fruit out of season. The new chefs contributed substantially to overall economy, since now almost everything served was made on the premises. Scarcely any "baked goods" were bought outside, and Ferdinand Louvat, the amiable pastry chef, with two women helpers, turned out literally thousands of rolls, cakes and tarts in a day.

As a result of shrewd ordering, the new housekeeper reduced the cost of official — though not state — dinners to a remarkable low of eleven to fifteen dollars per person, which included liquor but not the wages of extra butlers, who received fifteen dollars an evening.

Sometimes the honor guests at a state dinner (for example, an Indian leader and his wife or a ruler from a religiously ascetic

Moslem state) observed dietary regulations which required specially prepared dishes. The State Department informed the housekeeper of any culinary quirks well in advance through an informative memorandum, slangily called a "Cheat Sheet." It not only detailed dietary rules but also included a thumbnail personal profile of the guest of honor which enabled Anne to brief the household staff on any unaccustomed manners of the visitors.

"I'm an old hand at planning vegetarian platters for Indian guests," she soon would say, "and at seeing that fruit juices substituted for wines are well sweetened."

The housekeeper's main worry about the elegant dinners, however, was neither cost nor exotic recipes. It was simply timing. State dinners were usually quite punctual. They moved along smartly because protocol officers rigidly regulated the timetable of a chief of state. Official dinners, on the other hand, could be a real hazard to culinary perfection. Without the help of split-second protocol timing, it seemed impossible for 150 or more guests to arrive, exchange greetings and sip one or two cocktails with any degree of punctuality. So official dinners were often an hour late in starting. A delay in serving meat, Anne discovered, might be parlayed successfully: but vegetables, and some desserts, just wilted. She experimented with the staying powers of vegetables and found that any variety steeped in a cream sauce remained hot and beautiful in a double boiler. Purées were other "lasters" and a Baked Alaska became more luscious if it relaxed for around forty-five minutes after leaving the refrigerator.

One of the first things that surprised Anne Lincoln when she took over her new job of housekeeper, was the rigid White House economy. "I was poking around closets, getting to know my new domain and trying to figure the mechanics of running it," she recalled, "when I found towels with pulled places; sheets mended to a fare-you-well." She realized that in the White House anything which was usable had to be saved and could not be thrown away. Even empty soft drink bottles were redeemed!

On one of her inspection forays Anne made a surprising discovery. Far back on a linen closet shelf she came upon about fourteen dozen hemstitched Irish linen sheets. They were brand new and had not even been unwrapped. After some tactful sleuthing, the new housekeeper believed the sheets had been ordered during the Hoover administration and, obviously, forgotten. Later, Anne surmised this impressive quantity had been acquired to help maintain an unusual White House tradition. As housekeeper she had to keep on hand, in the third-floor linen room, enough sheets and pillowcases to stock a small hotel. This generous supply was needed because the President and First Lady's bedlinen was changed completely, not only every morning but also after either had lain down for even a moment of rest. Sometimes, each of the beds was stripped several times daily. No one seemed to know when or through whom this habit had originated. It was an "old White House custom"; the maids took pride in it and would have been loath to discontinue it.

The linens in everyday use, which Anne had found in such a woeful state, looked as though they had been commandeered from some naval vessel. They were totally unsuited to the White House. "They were hopeless!" Mrs. Kennedy commented succinctly.

Gradually Mrs. Kennedy began to select a few lovely replacements, and before she left the White House some of her purchases had arrived. For the Queen's Room she chose pale pink silk sheets, appliquéd at the hem with satin sprays of lilies of the valley, one of her favorite flowers. For the less feminine bedrooms, in which close friends and relatives might stay, there were the finest linen sheets appliquéd with a shower of smart polka dots.

What pleased the housekeeper, as well as Mrs. Kennedy, was that these luxurious linens did not cost the White House a penny extra. The new acquisitions were paid for with money released from the budget when other items already budgeted were bought with funds derived from the sale of the White House guidebooks!

Sometimes the housekeeper was confronted by colossal as well as comic shopping problems which had little relation to the satisfaction of ordering wines, filet mignon or pâté de foie gras. One day, for example, Charles Fickler, the head butler, walked into her office and asked, "Could you buy me a few dish towels?" "Certainly, Charles," the housekeeper replied, "how many?" "Oh! About two hundred!" he replied nonchalantly. So Anne became a dedicated "ad watcher," searching both local and New

York newspapers for bargains and taking full advantage of white sales. If her shopping list was sizable, she found it cheaper to go to New York. There, as well as in Washington, her identity was seldom known even after her purchases were made, because packages were never sent to the magic address, 1600 Pennsylvania Avenue. Instead, parcels were delivered to a special room in the nearby Executive Office Building, where they were subjected to X ray and other security precautions before reaching the White House.

One afternoon an assistant chef burst into her office almost in tears. "I need a hundred tomatoes!" he cried. Tomatoes, stuffed with crabmeat, were on the dinner menu and several cases had gone astray. Quickly the housekeeper picked up the telephone receiver. A White House truck hustled to the grocer's and the errant edibles were retrieved.

The daily mechanical "musts" and the quick-step from party to party made White House housekeeping the dizziest merry-go-round of its kind. It was part of the housekeeper's job each day to help plan and smooth the way for two, four, perhaps even five, totally different entertainments, some of them given simultaneously upstairs and down, with guest lists ranging from a dozen to, maybe, a thousand people of differing ages and tastes.

The mechanical "musts" included checking to see that 18 bedrooms and 20 baths were tidied; 147 windows kept clean; 29 fireplaces laid ready for lighting; 412 doorknobs wiped clean, around 3,000 square feet of floor waxed, rewaxed and often waxed again; half an acre of marble mopped and remopped; yards and yards of red carpeting vacuumed literally morning, noon and evening; 37 rooms dusted and redusted, some of them at least five times in 24 hours.

Besides, in the hectic half hour between the instant when the last of 15,000, 20,000, sometimes even 25,000 tourists left the White House, and the first VIP luncheon guest arrived, the housekeeper was obliged to check the cleaning, waxing, dusting and polishing; to make sure flowers were perked up and rubber matting taken up and red carpeting laid down.

The cleaning squad, armed with mops, buckets and waxing machines, would line up like runners waiting for the starting pistol. As the last tourist disappeared, down came the stanchions and connecting chains which kept the crowds in check. The desk where the guidebooks were sold was rolled away. The rubber matting, along where tourists walked, was rolled up. Underneath, the imprint of thousands of feet had removed every grain of wax from the floors. In corners, everywhere, there was a weird flotsam: chunks of chewing gum, tinfoil wrappers, bobby pins, hairpins, nubbins of tar brought in from the street. The marble stairway and the foyer were surfaced with a dark tan film. Curiously, from so many people shuffling along slowly, a sort of effluvium seemed to emanate. Tables, mantels, everything in the State Rooms was covered with a whitish dust. All this was removed before the glowing red carpet was rolled down and vacuumed, and some of the flowers, wilted by the heat of so many bodies, were changed. As the men waxed, mopped, dusted furiously, the housekeeper was right behind, straightening, adjusting, centering, picking up the tiniest fallen petal, patting even the plumpest pillow.

Half an hour later it seemed impossible that thousands of people had moved, breathed and moved again through these serene rooms.

In the afternoons, again in the evenings before dinners which utilized the State Rooms, the housekeeper inspected all three for a final time, tugging the edges of the drawn draperies into a straight line, seeing that the fires were lit. Every day or so, the housekeeper and James Ketchum, the young White House registrar who later became the curator, inspected the seven guest rooms. Ketchum kept a sharp eye on the antiques, the housekeeper concentrated on small creature comforts. Expected guests were pampered with the latest magazines, different brands of cigarettes, assorted chocolates, and at bedtime a thermos filled with ice water. Anne also coaxed the White House florist to create special flower arrangements which harmonized with the color scheme of each room.

The White House staff, which the housekeeper directed, fluctuated in number but usually consisted of five doormen, six butlers, one pantry girl, three cooks, two stewards, one kitchen helper, six maids, two laundresses, five housemen, and an assistant housekeeper — a total of thirty-two. Like the housekeeper herself, they were all enrolled in the Unclassified Civil Service. Unlike the Civil Service, they did not have to take an entrance examination, but they were entitled to all pension and similar benefits. Again, unlike members of the regular Civil Service, Unclassified Civil Service people might be fired with relative ease. They all worked an eight-hour day in a forty-hour week, with overtime at time-and-a-half and double pay on holidays. They were entitled to two weeks of vacation, usually scheduled in summer.

On paper a household staff of thirty-two sounds more than adequate, but the housekeeper found she had to do considerable juggling to get the essential work done. Owing to the eight-hour limitation, unless overtime was paid, the housekeeper had to divide the staff into two shifts, one on duty from early morning until after luncheon, the second staying as late as needed at night. As each member of the staff had two days' leave each week, there were seldom more than fourteen or sixteen persons available. So when the President or his family made last-minute arrangements or invited unexpected guests, the housekeeper had to telephone frantically, either to ask regular staff members to remain overtime or to round up part-time workers who had been cleared previously by Security.

5

Official Living

Strictly Matters of Protocol

During the first two years of the New Frontier, President Kennedy met with seventy-four foreign leaders. This was twelve more than Franklin D. Roosevelt had totaled during his dozen years in office; more than Harry Truman in almost eight years; and slightly more than half the sum of those whom Eisenhower received in eight years. All these leaders, divergent as they were in nationality, race, color and culture, were entertained at the White House.

They were not only eager to meet the new President; soon it became almost equally important to meet Mrs. Kennedy. Her presence at the festivities became the status symbol of a successful visit; and when a specially impressive state function was desired, it was considered essential that the First Lady make an appearance. Sometimes this was difficult, since, besides her solo trip to India and Pakistan, during almost eight months of the less than three years Mrs. Kennedy was to spend in the White House, Dr. Walsh had forbidden her to undertake official duties. (One president of a South American country refused to bring his young and beautiful wife when he learned that Mrs. Kennedy would be abroad during his state visit.)

As the waiting list of foreign leaders desiring official invitations increased, the most pressing problem was that of time. Any changes in the established routines for visits were subject to strict protocol, yet obviously new approaches had to be explored. The President took a keen interest in all aspects of form. He worked closely with the new Chief of Protocol, Angier Biddle Duke, and eventually evolved a number of shortcuts to reorganize state visits on a more humanly bearable basis.

Duke, a hard-working man of wealth, had been apprenticed in the nuances of protocol by serving with a political appointee Ambassador in Argentina and Spain. Subsequently, he had served as Ambassador to El Salvador, a Central American country. Duke was the youngest in United States diplomatic annals to be nominated to this lofty rank. So he knew only too well what state visits were like.

The genesis of these visits was comparatively simple. The Washington ambassador of an individual country would inform the State Department that his emperor, king, president, or prime minister would welcome an invitation. The State Department then filed these names in a "futures" book, and once or twice a year the President was given an "outlook" of proposed visitors. Then, annually, two state guests were chosen from each of the five geographic areas of the world: i.e. North and South America, Europe, Asia and Africa.

The visits were three-day affairs involving a staggering number of ceremonial engagements and three lengthy dinners: the first at the White House; a second at the local embassy of the honored guest; and a third usually at the State Department. The obvious solution was to shorten the span to two days. "We are trying not to be victimized by precedent," Duke explained to fellow diplomats, "but, of course, the wishes of the guest come first, and the nature of the visit is always determined in consultation with the invited leader."

Previous White House occupants had left many details of these visits to staff members. The Kennedys took endless pains, planning individually for each guest and each visit, gleaning their most minute likes and dislikes months in advance and then adapting this information to menus, toasts, after-dinner entertainment and state gifts. The Kennedy touch appeared effortless. But in reality the behind-the-scenes work was unremitting.

The smaller the nation, it was soon discovered, the less the invited leader wanted his spotlit moment to be shortened. As a trial balloon, a number of countries were asked to submit a list of events they considered essential should state visits be pared down. Surprisingly, the smallest state of all returned a schedule which, in complexity and elaborateness, was equaled only by the state sojourn of Queen Elizabeth. But finally a compromise was made. A two-day visit was arranged for a "presidential guest" who was either a repeater at the White House or on such serious business that skipping the icing did not matter. For all others the three-day "glitter" treatment remained in force.

Sometimes, but not often, the President questioned a State Department suggestion for a state visit. He balked a bit in honoring the Grand Duchess of Luxembourg. The duchy over which she reigned was very small, and it seemed scarcely worth so much time and attention. However, an invitation was genuinely politic, and Her Royal Highness's visit proved a delight. For the Grand Duchess Charlotte had warm ties with the United States. A personal friend of the Franklin D. Roosevelts, she had been their White House guest on several occasions. During World War II, she had shown great courage when her land was invaded by the Nazis; she escaped to Lisbon, where she was spirited to safety aboard a United States destroyer dispatched by President Roosevelt. Quite apart from these sentimental reasons, as a matter of practical politics, it had been preferable to invite the Grand Duchess rather than, say, a German visitor, because the demands of international prestige automatically entailed a Gallic follow-up to any Teutonic invitation.

When Mrs. Kennedy learned that the Grand Duchess was a devotee of Shakespeare, she personally arranged a very special entertainment following the state dinner. The program was to be "Poetry and Music of Elizabethan Times." Mrs. Kennedy immediately wrote to Basil Rathbone, a British actor who had also achieved réclame in Hollywood, concerning Shakespearean selections he might read to the distinguished White House audience. One of their first selections was a presidential favorite, the famed St. Crispin's Day speech which Henry V of England delivered on the eve of the Battle of Agincourt and which Winston Churchill had quoted so dramatically more than five centuries later, during the Battle of Britain. (The President knew part of the oration by heart, a fact which Rathbone admitted later "scared the daylights out of me!")

> *If we are mark'd to die, we are enow*
> *To do our country loss; and if to live,*
> *The fewer men, the greater share of honour.*
> *God's will! I pray thee, wish not one man more.*
> *By Jove, I am not covetous for gold,*

Nor care I who doth feed upon my cost;
It yearns me not if men my garments wear;
Such outward things dwell not in my desires;
But if it be a sin to covet honour,
I am the most offending soul alive.
No, 'faith, my coz, wish not a man from England:
God's peace! I would not lose so great an honour
As one man more, methinks, would share from me,
For the best hope I have. O! do not wish one more:
Rather proclaim it, Westmoreland, through my host.
That he which hath no stomach to this fight,
Let him depart; his passport shall be made,
And crowns for convoy put into his purse:
We would not die in that man's company
That fears his fellowship to die with us.
This day is call'd the feast of Crispian:
He that outlives this day and comes safe home
Will stand a tip-toe when this day is nam'd,
And rouse him at the name of Crispian.
He that shall live this day, and see old age,
Will yearly on the vigil feast his neighbours,
And say, "To-morrow is Saint Crispian."
Then will he strip his sleeve and show his scars,
And say, "These wounds I had on Crispin's day."
Old men forget; yet all shall be forgot,
But he'll remember with advantages
What feats he did that day. Then shall our names,
Familiar in his mouth as household words,
Harry the King, Bedford, and Exeter,
Warwick and Talbot, Salisbury and Gloucester,
Be in their flowing cups freshly remember'd.
This story shall the good man teach his son;
And Crispin Crispian shall ne'er go by,
From this day to the ending of the world,
But we in it shall be remembered;
We few, we happy few, we band of brothers.
For he to-day that sheds his blood with me
Shall be my brother; be he ne'er so vile,

This day shall gentle his condition;
And gentlemen in England now a-bed
Shall think themselves accurs'd they were not here
And hold their manhoods cheap whiles any speaks
That fought with us upon Saint Crispin's day.

SHAKESPEARE, *Henry V*, IV. iii. 18–67.

Rathbone also read Ben Jonson's "Have You Seen but a White Lily Grow?" which was then sung by Robert White to the plucking of a lute. There were also duets by White and Helen Boatwright accompanied by the Consort Players, a group of six instrumentalists who performed on such quaintly named instruments as the cittern, virginal, pandora, and antique lute as well as on treble and bass viols. ("Consort" is an Elizabethan term for a group of musicians entertaining on a set of instruments of the same family.) The program included five poetic excerpts and sonnets which the First Lady selected: Marlowe's "Come Live with Me and Be My Love"; Shakespeare's "Shall I Compare Thee to a Summer's Day?" and "When Daisies Pied and Violets Blue"; John Donne's "Go and Catch a Falling Star" and "Death Be Not Proud"; and finally, Robert Herrick's "To Virgins, to Make Much of Time."

In her effort to perfect the program, Mrs. Kennedy listened to innumerable taped performances supplied by the Music Division of the Library of Congress. From these she chose individual numbers for the Consort group and for Rathbone, whose vocal resonance she had particularly liked contrasted to the tones of the medieval instruments.

This meticulous attention to detail was rewarded by a serene evening of great elegance. It began with the traditional exchange of gifts in the Oval Room. ("This was a nice ice-breaker," the Chief of Protocol commented, "because Mrs. Kennedy was so interested in everything. Often the children were allowed in to see the gifts — especially if they included objects like a jeweled sword —") The Kennedys gave their guest a beautiful paperweight made of azurite and malachite, strewn with turquoise flowers, standing free in golden grass. The Grand Duchess and her son, the Hereditary Grand Duke of Luxembourg, presented their hosts with two magnificent porcelain plates decorated with views of the feudal castle of Viaden and of Luxembourg City, which was then celebrating the millennium of its founding.

Quite apart from the unusual after-dinner entertainment, this had been a special evening personally for Mrs. Kennedy. It was April 30, 1963, and it was her first public appearance since the announcement of the expected birth of her child.* That morning, because of inclement spring weather, the First Lady had been forbidden by her physician to be present at the Grand Duchess's helicopter arrival on the South Lawn. The President's sister, Mrs. Sargent Shriver, acted as stand-in, and Mrs. Kennedy watched the colorful ceremony from Caroline's schoolroom window.

That evening the Grand Duchess trailed white chiffon, diamonds and frosty mink, and Mrs. Kennedy looked appealingly young in a lavender organza sheath with a standup belted effect at the waist. Appropriately, Dr. Spock was among the guests, and Caroline, wearing pink pajamas and robe, looked down on the party from high on the stairs.

The Grand Duchess enjoyed herself immensely. The *Almanach de Gotha* listed her age as sixty-seven, yet she liked to water-ski. She told her hostess, who was adept in this aquatic sport, "But not on one ski." Then Her Royal Highness added with a smile, "I had to laugh when one of your papers said, 'it's chic to be pregnant'!"

One minor shortcut in the new protocol concerned the President directly and not only became extremely popular with state guests but also provided an unforgettable spectacle for those assembled to greet them. Hitherto most modern Presidents had dutifully journeyed to the airport to meet the VIPs, then motored with them back to the President's Guest House (Blair House) through Washington's dismal outskirts. This trip often consumed the better part of two hours; it wasted the President's precious time and gave incoming guests an unfortunate first impression not only of Washington but possibly the United States as well. So it was arranged at the first touchdown airport to

---

* Patrick Bouvier Kennedy. Born August 7, 1963, at Otis Air Force Base, Hyannis Port, Massachusetts. He weighed 4 pounds 10½ ounces and was 5½ weeks premature. He developed an idiopathic respiratory syndrome and died two days later of hyaline membrane disease, at the Children's Hospital in Boston.

transfer state guests into a presidential helicopter. With the President's House as charming backdrop, when the whirlybird had settled gracefully on the South Lawn, the new arrivals were then accorded full military honors.

Since this type of plane-to-door delivery deprived the state guest of being photographed riding with the President of the United States and, if accompanied, deprived his wife of similar desirable exposure with the First Lady, a "mini-parade" was arranged. The presidential cars left the White House by a side entrance and drove along a single, but extra-long, flag-bedecked block on Pennsylvania Avenue to Blair House, the official residence for state guests. Once there, the President and his wife saw their guests up the front steps to the door.

A special protocol was built around Mrs. Kennedy, and the first decision made was on what occasions she was to appear. Some two-day and even some three-day visits were stag affairs. If the wives were included, it was obvious, especially for the grander occasions, that the First Lady should be present. She adhered to this basic principle except when her presence was banned for reasons of health.

Sometimes, to the distress of the protocol team, Mrs. Kennedy, prompted by curiosity, showed up where she was not expected. Ben Bella, the Algerian Prime Minister and representative of a Moslem country, was the first to arrive on the White House lawn by helicopter. Mrs. Kennedy did not want to miss the initial run of a Kennedy shortcut in protocol. But as ladies were automatically barred from the welcoming ceremony, she hid in the surrounding shrubbery, holding young John so that he, too, could peek at the exciting display.

The First Lady was anxious to meet the King of Morocco. King Hassan was young and had ruled his romantic North African country only briefly. Like Arab kings of great wealth and highest position, he was accompanied by an unusually large entourage, and therefore was scheduled to arrive from New York by train. The problem in protocol was that Moslem custom forbade him to bring his wife. (The King's wife was a young girl, daughter of a mountain chieftain, whom he had married when she was fifteen.) But, possibly to insure the presence of Mrs. Kennedy at the welcoming ceremonies, the well-informed King took the precaution of including a sister in his party. She was Lalla Aisha, who had been a pioneer in the emancipation of Moroccan women. Though, according to Islamic ruling, the Westernized Princess was accorded no personal rank, protocol placed her third, after the Moroccan Prime Minister, in her royal brother's entourage. United States protocol, on the other hand, could not permit Mrs. Kennedy to assume this lesser position.

So after many serious consultations between the Moroccan Ambassador to Washington and the Chief of Protocol, this grave matter was equally solved. Two identical platforms were built in the railroad station. On one, waiting to welcome the King, stood President Kennedy and Secretary of State Dean Rusk. On the other, in splendid isolation, stood the First Lady. When the foreign guests arrived, the King and his Prime Minister joined their Western opposite numbers on one platform while the Princess stepped up beside Mrs. Kennedy!

The guest list of those invited to the state dinner for the King of Morocco evolved after tremendous travail between the State Department and the White House. The basic elements in all state dinners, in addition to the visitors and their party, consisted of the Secretary of State, the Assistant Secretary of State in charge of this special area, various officials in charge of A.I.D. and Information programs of the country involved. In all there were anywhere from four to eight persons (and their wives) from the State Department at most dinners. The much lower ranking Desk Officer, a younger Foreign Service member, had direct business and cultural contacts with the country being honored. He supplied the names of interested businessmen, of colleges where students from Morocco were enrolled, of Moroccans who had been successful as American citizens. The Chief of Protocol, the Desk Officer and Mrs. Kennedy's social secretary would juggle names patiently, and Mrs. Kennedy's press secretary suggested members of the Fourth Estate. In the final analysis the President and Mrs. Kennedy completed the list. He would select members of Congress or national political figures. She would add shining lights from the cultural world. A personal friend or two would invariably be invited and often some personage from Washington residential society.

Even the smallest facet of a state dinner was planned painstakingly. The toasts offered by President Kennedy were considered of great importance. Often they were based on drafts made by the State Department with an eye to the objective of the visit from both the standpoint of the President and that of his guest. The drafts were studied carefully by the President, who then added the final leavening of humor, historical allusion and current reality, which made them serious, yet witty in a combination which was truly his own.

John Fitzgerald Kennedy had an unusually enjoyable time polishing his toast to the King of Morocco. It so happened that, back in the 1770s, Morocco had been the first country to recognize the young United States of America. George Washington immediately sent a message to the then Emperor of Morocco. The thirty-fifth President quoted the first: "It gives me great pleasure to have this opportunity of assuring Your Majesty that while I remain head of this nation I shall not cease to promote every measure that may contribute to the friendship and harmony which so happily subsists between your empire and this republic."

The state dinner honoring the King of Morocco was a memorable evening. The Princess and her ladies-in-waiting were resplendent in gold caftans with jeweled belts, His Majesty in a dress uniform jacketed in dazzling white. The after-dinner entertainment was a telescoped edition of *Brigadoon,* a musical in which bagpipers skirled on stage. The score for this 1947 Broadway show, now revived at City Center, had been composed by Alan Jay Lerner. And after the performance President Kennedy said that both he and Lerner had been fellow students at Choate School. Then he added, "— neither of us thought the other would amount to anything!"

The careful considerations of protocol, which had made the welcoming ceremony of the King of Morocco so intriguing, carried over into problems of those in the Kennedy official as well as personal family. President Kennedy wished the Vice-President and Mrs. Johnson to be paid the most meticulous attention. "I might forget," he told Duke, "so I want you to be sure the Vice-President and Mrs. Johnson are lined up right for photographers — and that they are on the guest list for all the private parties we're invited to."

Mrs. Kennedy, in a memo to Mr. West, asked him, "Will you tell whoever it is, after this — at *every* occasion when they play 'Hail to the Chief' and just announce the President — to please also say the Vice President of the United States and Mrs. Johnson — it is embarrassing to have them not announced —"

Mrs. Joseph P. Kennedy, the President's mother, presented a unique problem. Though, as the wife of a former United States Ambassador there was real precedent for rank, her protocol rating remained an enigma for some time. For never before had the mother of a President been as physically young and active. Most presidential mammas had been old and somewhat infirm and as a matter of course never attended parties. The senior Mrs. Kennedy, however, delighted in the social whirl and on a few occasions played hostess for her son at official White House functions. Not even the commanding Mrs. James Roosevelt had ventured this decorative role. Finally, Mrs. Kennedy's position, or lack of it, became acutely embarrassing to the protocol office. A carefully weighed decision was made, and the President's mother was ranked almost top of the list, after the Vice-President, the Chief Justice and their wives.

President Kennedy's three sisters, Eunice Shriver, Patricia Lawford and Jean Smith, did not fare as well. They had to assume their husbands' ranks which often left them far behind in the crowd.

Both the President and Angier Duke had an amusing brace of protocol worries about the First Lady. Respectively, their problems were hats and animals. The First Lady's husband always feared that she might turn up hatless on some important occasion. Though Mrs. Kennedy was less than lukewarm about hats, usually she wore some fetching bit of millinery. But once in a great while she emerged with her glossy head uncovered. When his wife appeared in this fashion the President delighted, as he did with his incorrigibly hatless sisters, in making a small, poignant moan: "What would Alec Rose* do to us in an election!"

The Chief of Protocol's problem with animals was that all too soon chiefs of state and other notables discovered Mrs. Kennedy's passion for birds and beasts of every description. An animal —

* The president of the Hatmakers' Union.

any kind of animal — became THE present. Horses, dogs, deer, ducks, tiger cubs, ponies, cats, goldfish, hamsters, rabbits were offered. The Kings of Saudi Arabia and Morocco, the Crown Prince of Libya and Eamon de Valera of Ireland, each wanted to give the First Lady a splendid horse. Desperately Duke pleaded with Mrs. Kennedy to make a rule — and stick to it — no live animal as gift. Mrs. Kennedy at first acquiesced, but she loved to make an exception. At the extraordinary National Horse and Cattle Show in Lahore, during her visit to India and Pakistan in 1962, she accepted from President Ayub Khan a vintage but beautifully trained gelding named Sardar. This infraction of their "understanding" gave Duke a bright idea. He suggested to Eamon de Valera that he *first* ask Mrs. Kennedy to visit Ireland and *there* give her a hunter. Duke's reasoning was simple. Since Mrs. Kennedy could accept few invitations for foreign visits, the incidence of cumbersome gifts would remain minimal. Subsequently, a similar suggestion was made to other nabobs wishing to give the First Lady horses. The Chief of Protocol's idea seemed to click.

Ceremonial Largesse

Since ancient times, when emperors and sultans and kings and caliphs first undertook visits of state, they vied with each other in the magnificence of the gifts they exchanged. This opulent custom continued unabated to democratic times and today, even the leader of the most liberal state arrives laden with handsome offerings for the President and his wife. Until recently, our new republican country was too self-conscious to return this ceremonial largesse in kind and the usual present to a state guest was either a Steuben glass bowl, or perhaps an autographed, handsomely framed photograph of the current President. After World War II, as United States overseas commitments increased and foreign chiefs of state began to beat a path to Washington, the official attitude toward gift-giving became more relaxed. The State Department, which pays the bill, increased the amount allotted for such tokens (and President Kennedy pressed them to raise it even higher!) and gifts were selected with more discrimination. The ultimate success of the gift, of course, depended greatly on the taste and concern of both the President and his First Lady.

Though the gifts which the President and Mrs. Kennedy gave their various distinguished guests were notably imaginative as well as beautiful and suitable, the First Lady had been searching for the, to her, perfect American state gift. Even the smallest country, she found, touchingly tried to give something magnificent — huge elephant tusks, tribal robes, boxes made of precious metals. The American state gift had to look splendid and also should be sufficiently sophisticated to give to heads of highly civilized countries. "Anything that was Early American," Mrs. Kennedy explained, "would look too rustic. Our modern things would look out of place in old surroundings."

President Kennedy was equally determined that the state gift should have a particular meaning for the recipient instead of being of a noncommittal ceremonial nature. He had brought a model of the *Constitution* to Khrushchev in Vienna and had ordered a dozen faithful replicas of George Washington's sword for leaders who were history buffs. But perhaps his happiest gift had been to President de Valera of Ireland. Jack Kennedy was very sentimental about his visit to Ireland and wanted an extraordinary gift. He was delighted when a Brooklyn monsignor offered a Civil War flag which the famous 69th Fighting Irish Regiment had carried into battle. To the President, just two generations removed from Ireland, it seemed, symbolically, the perfect gift.

For a while the Kennedys had thought of giving historic letters. Mrs. Kennedy made a superb find in a letter from Washington to the Vicomte de Noailles, brother-in-law of Lafayette, which her husband presented to President de Gaulle. (Out of patriotism, the owner of the letter had donated it to President Kennedy.) On his last official trip overseas, President Kennedy stopped in West Germany. Here he gave Chancellor Adenauer a historic letter from General von Steuben, a German who had fought in the American Revolution. Aware that a future guest, President Radhakrishnan of India, was both philosopher and scholar, the President devoted a great deal of time to the selection of a superbly preserved first edition of *Aesthetic Papers* which contained the essays of Thoreau and Ralph Waldo Emerson.

Such historic documents made wonderful gifts, but sources for them were precarious; an appropriate letter for the appropriate head of state could not always be come by. Then, one day, Mrs. Kennedy went to the Smithsonian Institution to discuss details of her White House Restoration plans with Dr. Leonard Carmichael, the secretary and director.

Dr. Carmichael wanted to show Mrs. Kennedy the First Ladies' Hall, where costumes of her predecessors are on display. On the way they had to walk through the Hall of Minerals. When she entered this fabulous dark cavern, Mrs. Kennedy halted abruptly, astonished at the sheer beauty of the spotlit displays. "I was overcome," she recalled. "It was like Ali Baba's cave!"

There were no lights in the great Hall except within the dazzling showcases. Here, ingeniously displayed, were some of the great gems of history: the insistently blue Hope Diamond, spilling on its diamond-studded chain from the half-ajar door of a miniature safe; the brilliant canary-colored Shepherd Diamond; a Bragança family jewel, the 427-carat Portuguese Diamond, glowing almost imperceptibly blue; a 138- and a 330-carat star ruby and star sapphire, both the world's largest; the weightiest of all black diamonds, still rough-cut; a 31-carat heart-shaped diamond which Empress Eugénie had set in a ring; a gigantic pink oriental pearl still fixed in a stickpin which had once adorned a Pakistani prime minister's cravat; a six-pound, thirteen-inch-diameter crystal ball, cut from a single rock; and, in odd contrast, the nubby little gold nugget, scarcely fingernail size, which had triggered the California gold rush.

In other cases there were even more vivid gems: stalactites of palest pinks and chartreuse green; tall-fingered chunks of azure blue and deep sapphire, of lilac shading to purple, orange, red, chalky white, chocolate brown and jet black. And, in the two entrance showcases, crystals ranging green through blue re-

David Webb designed this state gift, a paperweight of brilliant blue stone, decorated with gold and turquoises, which was presented to the Grand Duchess Charlotte of Luxembourg during her visit to the United States.

volved on circular platforms, so that every facet of their craggy makeup scintillated in the piercing fingers of light.

Mrs. Kennedy thought them more beautiful than the precious stones. Yet none were really of great value. They were merely minerals which could be found in the ground in different parts of the United States from Maine to California. She spent hours there with Dr. Carmichael and wrote down the names of the most lovely stones — azurite, a lapis lazuli color from Arizona; turquoise from New Mexico; hematite, a glistening black crystal; apatite from Maine, a fickle mineral which crops out in white, green, brown and sometimes purple.

Immediately, Mrs. Kennedy had imagined paperweights made from these stones, delicately feminine or more heavily masculine, each artfully embellished by a skilled, inspired jeweler. She telephoned David Webb, one of the most original young designers, explained her idea, and asked him to go to the Smithsonian and look at the stones she liked especially.

Each paperweight that David Webb designed had a plaque on the smooth underside which commemorated the occasion. They were bound with ropes of twisted gold and some were sown with fragile, stand-up flowers. They were more than splendid, and they were completely American.

Later, Dr. Carmichael was to recall that afternoon: "It was one of the great days of my life — to watch Mrs. Kennedy discover the potentialities of these gems."

"Gaiety, Informality and Culture"

During many previous administrations White House entertainments had been planned more or less to rubber-stamp each other. Now, each of the Kennedy state dinners, as well as each domestically oriented official function, was unique. The sole criticism: each set a precedent which was difficult to top. Those invited to an affair which might be rated as even a whisper less fascinating than a previous one inevitably felt hurt. A British journalist, a dinner guest at the White House, wrote back to London: "Mrs. Kennedy has substituted gaiety, informality and culture for the traditional stuffed shirt. The key to this new mood," he continued, "may be capsuled in the words on a book of matches at each place, 'The President's House.' It suggests the White House is now the lived in home of the President as well as an institution."

The new mood not only transformed state dinners starring foreign leaders, but also rejuvenated annual official events honoring important government functionaries during what was known as the White House Social Season. This busy period commenced immediately after Thanksgiving and ended before Ash Wednesday, with a brief respite during the Christmas holidays.

The main events had always been rather static: they included a series of four dinners and five receptions. The dinners honored in turn the Vice-President of the United States; the Chief Justice of the United States; the Speaker of the House of Representa-

President Kennedy and a windblown First Lady ride back to the White House after leaving their first state visitors, President and Mrs. Bourguiba of Tunisia, at Blair House following a motorcade through the city.

tives; and the Chiefs of Diplomatic Missions in Washington. They were white-tie affairs with monotonously predictable guest lists. Mrs. Earl Warren, wife of the Chief Justice, for instance, was the dinner partner of Vice-President Nixon for forty-two evenings during the Eisenhower administration. The receptions were scheduled at a conservative nine in the evening, and, though the elegance of white ties, tails and decorations was *de rigueur*, only punch, sandwiches and cakes were served. The receptions honored congressional, judicial and governmental agency members; high-ranking military; and lesser officials in the Diplomatic Corps.

The galaxy of imaginative Kennedy entertainments started off with a state dinner in honor of President Bourguiba of Tunisia which featured a Military Tattoo; continued on through a bright, modern ballet for Emperor Haile Selassie of Ethiopia, who was known to be an ardent devotee of the dance; another night when Pablo Casals played his cello after dinner; and a "cultural soirée" for André Malraux, the French Minister of Culture (May 1962), who later accomplished the impossible by sending France's greatest art treasure, the Mona Lisa, to Washington. The special guests for this dinner included such luminaries as the Charles Lindberghs; Nobel Prize poet Alexis Léger; the American painter Andrew Wyeth; poet Robert Lowell; playwrights Arthur Miller, S. N. Behrman and Tennessee Williams; art connoisseur August Heckscher; president James Rorimer, of the Metropolitan Museum; theatrical impresario Elia Kazan; French author Henri Bernstein; actress Geraldine Page; big business cultural aficionados John Loeb and David Rockefeller; and diverse supporters of culture like Charles Bohlen, the United States Ambassador to France; Representative Adam Clayton Powell, Assistant Secretary of State for Cultural Affairs Lucius Battle; and Georges Balanchine, the famous ballet dancer and choreographer.

After dinner the guests listened to an extraordinary musical performance: Schubert's Trio in B Flat Major, Opus 99, played by Eugene Istomin, pianist, Isaac Stern, the violin virtuoso, and Leonard Rose, cellist.

The dizziest evening was a dinner to which all the American-born Nobel Prize winners and their spouses were invited (April

29, 1962). The inspiration for the dinner had been Mrs. Kennedy's, but it was the distinguished guests who sparked the unexpected fun. Soon after they arrived at the White House, the Nobel Prize winners, in festive mood, succumbed to the gay rhythm of the United States Marine Orchestra. The musicians, stationed at the Cross Hall outside the State Rooms, were playing dance tunes "nonstop." As the first couple arrived, instead of proceeding sedately toward the East Room where the President and First Lady were to greet them, spontaneously, they sought each other's arms and began to dance. Soon the great hall was filled with the other Nobel Prize winners, all twirling recklessly on the slippery marble floor.

Even the least conventional White House guest had never defied protocol by dancing before dinner. But President Kennedy was to describe his uninhibited guests in glowing terms when he rose to give a toast: "— I think this is the most extraordinary collection of talent that has ever been gathered in the White House — with the possible exception of when Thomas Jefferson dined alone."

Some time afterwards playwright Arthur Miller explained the contrast between the relaxed Nobel Prize winners and the more shy literary and artist guests at the Malraux dinner. "All these people are used to earning their living by pushing a pencil or a fiddle, they are not used to talking. They were absolutely overwhelmed by being invited." Tennessee Williams had quipped, "If our mothers could see us now!" The President, in a toast to the talented guests at the Malraux dinner, had scouted the American impression that an artist's life was "soft." "Actually, creativity is the hardest life there is —" Then he made his audience laugh: "This is becoming a sort of eating place for artists. But they never ask *us* out!"

Carat for carat, the most glittering of all the Kennedy state dinners was the one in honor of the Shah of Iran and his beautiful young empress. One hundred dress-uniformed soldiers lined the White House driveway. Fifteen dancers from Broadway shows and the New York City Center Ballet had practiced in the White House for a week to perfect their performance of Jerome Robbins's *Ballets USA*. The Empress Farah Diba wore a golden creation almost entirely covered with ruby beading. She sparkled with what was surely several million dollars' worth of jewels which, the Shah disclosed discreetly, were part of the state treasure which underwrote the stability of Iranian currency. Mrs. Kennedy chose a simple, exquisite dress and pinned an antique diamond sunburst in her hair. The President and his wife stood side by side at the North Portico to greet their decorative guests. As the President caught sight of the glowing Empress, he chortled with irreverent glee, "She's outdone you! She's *really* outdone you!" In the same mood the President commenced his toast to the Shah: "The Shah and I have one thing in common. We both went to Paris with our wives and ended up wondering why we had bothered. We thought we might as well have stayed home —"*

The Kennedy transformation of the traditional official entertaining was gay as well as logistically sensible. The four dinners and five receptions that previously constituted the White House Social Season were replanned. Dinners honoring the Vice-President, the Chief Justice and the Speaker, were combined in a single gala evening. Both the Diplomatic Dinner and the reception for embassy staff members were canceled. The emergence of so many small nations had made the Diplomatic Corps unwieldy. It had become impossible to include all the chiefs of mission and their wives at a White House dinner and equally impossible to invite to a reception all the lower ranking diplomats in the 116 continually proliferating local embassies.

As an annual White House invitation was considered the just due of every foreign ambassador, Mrs. Kennedy made amends for having vetoed their special dinner by dividing the roster of envoys and asking each half to a separate afternoon reception.

The congressional, judicial and governmental receptions remained fixed on the conventional Social Season calendar, but the military party, which boasted the longest guest list, was rescheduled in warm weather to provide elbow room on the South Lawn for the crowds of high-ranking officers, almost entirely generals and admirals, from the mighty Defense Establishment.

---

* Mrs. Kennedy seldom met the wives of state visitors except at official functions. Empress Farah, still in her thirties and the mother of small children, was the exception. The Empress called informally at the White House, met Caroline and John, and spent several hours with the First Lady. They had much in common.

Under earlier administrations, a White House reception had been an ordeal which only the physically fit could truly enjoy. The President and his wife had "received" in the Blue Room. Hundreds of guests, in white tie and tails, long kid gloves and décolleté gowns, lined up two by two and often four abreast in the long, narrow East Room. They inched along under the crystal chandeliers, past the stiff portraits of the Washingtons, through the Green Room, finally to grasp the presidential hands. No liquid refreshments were offered and smoking was forbidden. After a perfunctory handshake, the guests were herded on their way, a bit faster, through the Red Room and into the gloomy State Dining Room. There they clustered in an impenetrable mass around the long table set with punch bowls and plates of little sandwiches and cakes, which vanished instantly.

The Kennedy receptions were marvels of elegant informality. There was no receiving line. As guests wandered admiringly around the White House State Rooms, they could sustain themselves at buffets set up in both the East Room and the State Dining Room. Butlers passed glasses of respectably sturdy punch (it would have been too difficult to serve hundreds of guests mixed drinks) and ashtrays were conveniently placed.

Instead of making an "entrance," as they did at formal dinners by stepping down crimson-carpeted stairs flanked by flag-bearers and followed by military aides, all to the stirring fanfare of "Ruffles and Flourishes" (which President Kennedy enjoyed hugely), the President and his wife used the small elevator and arrived from their private quarters unannounced. They made an unobtrusive "progress" through the rooms, mingling with their guests and escorted by one or more of the three military aides who made the proper presentations.

The only "set" aids to protocol were contrived at large receptions like the judicial, to which a sizable number of important judges had been invited. To prevent any oversights in introductions with resulting hard feelings in those who might be overlooked, the outstanding personages were gathered together by aides and protocol officers in the East Room to which the presidential couple first made their way.

The twin Diplomatic Receptions were unusually felicitous affairs. The wives of the ambassadors were at ease in pretty cocktail dresses, while the ambassadors were even more relaxed minus formal dress and diplomatic uniforms. The atmosphere was so genial that two innovations in standard protocol practices were introduced.

The first was a tactful minor nicety. There are two sets of foreign ambassadors in Washington: the first accredited to the White House; the second to the Organization of American States. The first takes precedence over the second with the inevitable result that the OAS-accredited ambassadors feel twinges of inferiority. To boost Latin American prestige and self-esteem, President Kennedy, after greeting envoys accredited to the White House in the East Room, received the OAS ambassadors in a special Red Room ceremony.

This gesture was appreciated especially since an unusually large number of envoys accredited to the White House happened to be absent from Washington. The chargés d'affaires of their embassies replaced them. Since a chargé d'affaires always ranks lower than an ambassador, the OAS envoys would resent being forced by the exigencies of protocol to be received by President Kennedy after the chargé d'affaires of their own national embassy.

The second innovation set a precedent: for the first time in diplomatic history, the President of the United States accepted the credentials of two foreign envoys at a party. Usually incoming ambassadors presented their letters of credence at a private White House ceremony. The long-established procedure was automatic, boring and time-consuming. The new arrival was introduced to the President, proffered a letter from his chief of state, then delivered a brief speech. The President accepted the document and replied even more briefly. They shook hands and exchanged a few words.

At the Kennedy Diplomatic Reception the two ambassadors, Zender of Switzerland and Karim Bandoura of Guinea, were placed last in the receiving line. In turn, the envoys offered their letters of credence, then made perhaps the shortest speeches in diplomatic history. As President Kennedy received each document, an aide handed him the script of his carefully prepared replies. The two ceremonies were completed in record and most agreeable time.

The President and Mrs. Kennedy

request the pleasure of the company of

Mrs. Thayer

at dinner

on Tuesday, April 30, 1963

at eight o'clock

Please send response to
The Social Secretary
The White House
at your earliest convenience

White Tie

FG

Mrs. Sigourney Thayer

will please present this card at
THE SOUTHWEST GATE
The White House
April 30, 1963
at 8 o'clock
NOT TRANSFERABLE

A White House invitation to the dinner for Grand Duchess Charlotte.

On January 21, 1963, the most headlined official function given by the President and Mrs. Kennedy honored the three branches of the government: the Executive, the Judicial, and the Legislative. Though the honorees were Vice-President Johnson, Chief Justice Earl Warren, Speaker of the House John McCormack, and their wives, the real star of the evening was the newly decorated Blue Room, which was unveiled to mark this impressive occasion. (The restoration of the Red and Green Rooms had been finished the previous year.) The 157 guests included Cabinet members, Senate and House leaders, directors of the most important government agencies, and the Associate Justices of the Supreme Court; they were seated both in the State Dining Room, where the President presided, and the Blue Room where the First Lady was hostess. Later, there was dancing in the East Room, but this was the sole grand-scale dinner Jacqueline Kennedy was to plan without a program of after-dinner entertainment. The guests, however, were admirably diverted by fine food, witty oratory and the privilege of being the first to view the new Blue Room.

The menu began with Filets of Sole Véronique; proceeded to Sirloin of Beef St. Florentin, accompanied by green beans and braised tomatoes; then to Salade Mimosa sustained by Brie cheese, and climaxed with a dessert fancifully named "Surprise Dolley Madison," which a nongourmet guest had fun describing as "just a bunch of egg whites blown up and a plop of strawberries on top."

The President set a gay tone with his toast, directing his remarks to the Vice-President, the Chief Justice and himself. All three had much in common, he commenced, since they were included in Richard Nixon's book *Six Crises;* all had aspired to the Vice-Presidency and only one had made it; all had aspired to the Presidency and "fortunately," he continued with a grin, "only one of us made it"; and all had desired a long tenure in office, but only one of them had made *that.**

Vice-President Johnson, seated beside Mrs. Kennedy, continued tongue-in-cheek: "It is with some apprehension that I came here tonight, Mr. President, since the last time I sat down

* The Chief Justice of the United States is appointed for life.

to dine with you it cost me a thousand dollars!* Tonight we can split it three ways." Mr. Johnson ended on a serious note: "May we who are honored here continue to draw unity from our division of powers and strength from unity of purpose."

The Speaker, gallant as always, tuned his tribute to Mrs. Kennedy. "She is a great diplomat and a great Ambassador — who has given an image of America which has made the world smile again." The Chief Justice, devoted father of six young Warrens, honored the rest of the presidential family by offering toasts to Caroline and John and to Mrs. Joseph Kennedy, who was present at the festive evening.

Of the trio of colorful State Rooms — Red, Blue and Green — the Blue Room had been the most difficult to restore. It is oval in shape, centered between the Red and Green Rooms, and its physical proportions are especially unmanageable. The ceilings are eighteen feet high and the walls are pierced by three immense windows and no less than five doors, two of which open into the Red Room, another pair into the Green Room, while a larger double door gives onto the Cross Hall and the North Lobby.

Though in recent times this impressive chamber has been known as the Blue Room, it was named as such only in the mid-nineteenth century administration of President Van Buren. In 1817, three years after the White House had been burned by the British, President Monroe ordered from Paris furniture, candelabra and many decorative accessories as replacements for the original furnishings. Among these items was a set of fourteen gilt chairs, part of a suite made by Pierre Antoine Bellangé, which were placed in what was then known as the Oval Room. Through contemporary paintings and scraps of material remaining on the old frames, it has been discovered that the chairs Monroe ordered were upholstered in crimson silk; but the color of the walls has never been determined. Yet it is believed with some assurance of certainty, that during the administration of James Madison the "Oval Room" walls were cream or buff and the woodwork accented with gold. Monroe was Madison's successor, and quite possibly he may have duplicated this color scheme when he restored the White House.

* Mr. Johnson referred to a recent Democratic fund-raising dinner.

During the Truman Renovation the Blue Room walls had been covered with a strident blue silk woven with a repeat design of the United States Seal in gold. This effort was not successful, and Mrs. Kennedy believed that a more subtle effect should be achieved to set off the brilliant hues of the Red and Green Rooms on either side. As the adjoining Red Room had been known for its vivid shade during so many years, the Fine Arts Committee decided that it was inadvisable to retain Monroe's crimson upholstery in the Blue Room. Instead they hoped to restore the room as nearly as possible to what it had been in the original White House during President Madison's administration. The walls were to be kept pale in tone, and, so that the room could still be known as the Blue Room, the traditional blue was to be retained in the curtains, upholstery and Savonnerie carpet.

The "treatment" of the room was taken from an Empire "document"* provided by Stéphane Boudin, head of Jansen, the famed Paris decorating firm, who acted as unpaid adviser to Mrs. Kennedy's White House Restoration project. After many experiments on a miniature scale model, the Blue Room walls were hung in cream satin vertically striped with the "mat," or reverse side of the material. A blue draped valance, with a tasseled Empire border in purple, encircled the room below the cornice line, and the curtains and valances in the high windows were similar in design. The Monroe Bellangé chairs were upholstered in a blue silk, specially woven with a gold eagle motif which had been found on a similar chair in the background of John Vanderlyn's portrait of President Monroe.

A superb set of bronzes — a chandelier, wall sconces and two large candelabra — were acquired to complement the Monroe mantel clock and candlesticks. Finally, the golden oak floor was stained a darker hue.

All these decisions in decoration might seem easy with taste and money at command. But actually, the curious proportion of the Blue Room made the task so difficult that Mrs. Charles Wrightsman, a member of the White House Fine Arts Commit-

---

* A "document" is a swatch or length of material documented historically as to its origin, color and design. Sometimes various materials used in an especially noteworthy room are included in a single document.

tee and a generous and imaginative perfectionist, commissioned a small-scale model, a sort of miniature stage set on which samples of wall coverings could be tried and curtains and valances arranged in various ways; and even tiny copies of the Bellangé chairs were made so they could be shoved around to achieve ideal placement.

Here, in the gleaming setting of the finished Blue Room, portraits of the first seven Presidents were hung for the first time. They included five likenesses painted from life and ranked as the most important acquisitions in the White House.

Toast to an Almost-Five-Hundred-Year-Old Lady

The most acclaimed of all Kennedy era state guests was not honored at a White House dinner. Yet she was more eagerly awaited and more enthusiastically received than any other visitor. She was the Mona Lisa.

Leonardo da Vinci's fifteenth-century portrait *La Gioconda,* was certainly the most famous painting in the Western world. No estimate could be placed on its worth. It seemed unbelievable that the French government would risk removing this priceless national treasure from the Louvre, much less ship the fragile wooden panel on which it was painted across the Atlantic. The government of France, however, did accept the awesome risk; and this unusual move was consummated in a far from usual way. Instead of being "loaned" to the National Gallery of Art or to New York City's Metropolitan Museum of Art, the lady of the enigmatic smile became the "guest" of President Kennedy. The Mona Lisa was designated as a personal loan, and her security became the responsibility of the President of the United States.

Somewhat incongruously, the Mona Lisa's journey across the ocean had been the dream, and finally the personal obsession, of a Washington *Post* political reporter named Edward Folliard for over a quarter of a century. Now, in 1963, because of the charm and prestige of Jacqueline Kennedy, though she had taken no direct action in this extraordinary matter, the dream was to become a reality.

The dream had been born in 1935 when Eddie, then a promising young reporter, was sent to Pittsburgh to interview Andrew Mellon, the financier and philanthropist who had served as Secretary of the Treasury under three Republican Presidents. Mr. Mellon also had amassed a fifty-million-dollar collection of paintings for which he wished to build a grandiose gallery in Washington and then present both to the nation.

On Washington's Birthday, 1935, when everyone was on holiday, Folliard met the former Secretary of the Treasury at his old-fashioned office in the Mellon National Bank. As Mr. Mellon smoked small black cigarettes, he described to the enthralled newsman how he had developed a compelling interest in Renaissance and pre-Renaissance art and had commenced purchasing paintings on his first European tour. Andrew Mellon told Eddie he had begun planning a National Gallery of Art in the 1920s and added that looking down the Mall from his United States Treasury office, he had selected a tentative building site. (The unassuming Mr. Mellon had never considered the use of his name in connection with the National Gallery of Art.)

It was two years before Congress accepted the Mellon art and the gallery itself would not be completed until 1941. Nevertheless Folliard, Irish and romantic and completely without personal means, immediately began to devise ways he could help enrich the still-to-be-built National Gallery of Art. His first, and enduring idea was to borrow beautiful paintings from every possible source; and of all the paintings he could think of, he considered the Mona Lisa the most uniquely desirable. He fell in love with the mysterious Florentine and luring her to the United States became an admitted obsession. At last in 1950 Folliard took direct action: he wrote a letter to popular Henri Bonnet, then Ambassador of France in Washington. He asked whether the Mona Lisa could be loaned to the United States. Bonnet replied sympathetically that this was an interesting project but difficult to realize. Quite possibly, for fear of being quoted, the Ambassador diplomatically skirted any direct mention of the Mona Lisa in his letter.

The next time Eddie Folliard asked that question of a member of the French government, he voiced it loud and clear in front of an important audience. It was May 1962, and André Malraux, Minister of Culture for France, was a visitor in Washington. The Minister and Mme Malraux had been honored by President and Mrs. Kennedy at a state dinner, a highly flattering accolade usually reserved for chiefs of state or prime ministers. Some days later Malraux was the honored guest at a luncheon sponsored by the Overseas Writers. Before posing his familiar request, Folliard had apprised Hervé Alphand, then French Ambassador, of his intention. Alphand nodded a go-ahead. So eager was Eddie that he was first on his feet for the usual postprandial question-and-answer session staged at such press affairs. He waited impatiently for Malraux's reply to be translated. The reply was worth waiting for. "Perhaps a loan could be arranged," the translator repeated, "since great works of art belong to mankind and not exclusively to France or any other individual country." This statement was definitely encouraging. Folliard would only have another six months to wait.

The previous spring, 1961, when President and Mrs. Kennedy had made their state visit to France, the Minister of Culture had charmed the First Lady; and he in turn had found her delightful. Malraux courageously had put aside deep personal grief (two sons had been killed in a motor accident) to escort Mrs. Kennedy on various sorties to National Museums. A highlight was an exhibition of Impressionist paintings at the Jeu de Paume Museum. Afterwards Mrs. Kennedy had captured newspaper headlines, the imagination of the art-loving Parisian public and the Minister's approval by daring to select as her favorite painting Manet's sophisticated *Olympia,* an explicit nude whose pale skintones were counterpointed by background figures of a Negress and a black cat.

This pleasant Parisian interlude had sparked the Malraux visit to Washington in 1962 and the imaginative state dinner which emphasized "cultural" rather than the usual diplomatic and political guests. The Malraux trip was an unqualified success; and perhaps now some courteous gesture of thanks might be in order.

Immediately after the dinner at which Folliard had asked his

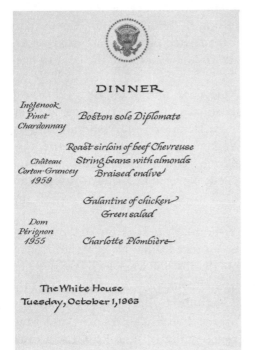

DINNER

Inglenook
Pinot
Chardonnay

Boston sole Diplomate

Roast sirloin of beef Chevreuse
Château   String beans with almonds
Corton-Grancey   Braised endive
1959

Galantine of chicken
Green salad

Dom
Pérignon
1955   Charlotte Plombière

The White House
Tuesday, October 1, 1963

A menu from the state dinner given in honor of His Imperial Majesty Haile Selassie, Emperor of Ethiopia, on October 1, 1963.

all-important question about the Mona Lisa, the director of the National Gallery of Art, John Walker, wrote to Malraux seeking clarification of his statement. The summer slipped by without a reply. One day when Walker was about to leave Washington airport for New York, he was summoned from his plane by a White House call. It was Mrs. Kennedy, breathless with the news that Malraux intended to lend the Mona Lisa, not to the National Gallery, but personally to the President. (President Kennedy later delegated his authority to Walker.)

The Washington *Post* flew Folliard to Paris to accompany *La Gioconda* on her great adventure. She was packed meticulously in a case containing a chemical which absorbed moisture and kept in her private air-conditioned cabin aboard the luxury liner *France*. On her departure, like any popular feminine traveler, she was sent a variety of floral tributes, each addressed personally to Mona Lisa. Folliard, in "seventh heaven," wired an ecstatic, almost maudlin, story daily; and on the eve of the ship's New York arrival a dinner was given in honor of the famous passenger. The pastry chef had made her portrait in tinted sugar, and everyone solemnly drank to the health of the almost-five-hundred-year-old lady.

John Walker met her in New York, and in an air-conditioned van, escorted by succeeding squads of state troopers as they transited New York, New Jersey, Delaware, Maryland and finally the District of Columbia, Walker and Folliard rushed the 250-mile trip with sirens screaming, through red lights and toll booths without slackening speed. Never had a queen or even an empress been as royally greeted, commented Eddie Folliard delightedly.

Though the Mona Lisa arrived in New York on December 19, 1962, in Washington she was tucked into an air-conditioned vault, because President Kennedy did not want to introduce her until after the New Year when Congress convened. The gala opening was scheduled at the National Gallery of Art on January 8, 1963, and beforehand, a dinner honoring President and Mrs. Kennedy was given at the French embassy. The First Lady wore a delectable pink chiffon strapless sheath embroidered with pearls. (A Secret Service agent held her matching stole — which he tried to hide behind his back, by folding and refolding it into a small square!) Almost without exception all top United States officialdom was present; and they dined sumptuously on Pâté de foi gras, Filet de Charcolais sous le Cendre with Sauce Renaissance, Coeur de laitue Mimosa, and Poires Mona Lisa for dessert.

After dinner President Kennedy made a graceful speech saying that the United States was "grateful to the leading artistic country in the world," and concluding, "the United States will continue to press ahead to develop an independent, artistic force of its own." André Malraux, the Minister of Culture, touched a more emotional note: "They [risks to the Mona Lisa] are real but exaggerated — but the risks taken by the boys who landed on D-day at Arromanches — to say nothing of those who had preceded them twenty-five years before — were much more certain. To the humblest of these, who may be listening to me now, I want to say, without raising my voice, that the masterpiece to

*The President and Mrs. Kennedy
receive their distinguished guests before
a dinner honoring the American-born
Nobel Prize winners in April 1962.*

*The Mona Lisa was shown at a special
exhibit at the National Gallery of Art
in Washington under the aegis of the
French government.
French minister of cultural affairs
André Malraux and his wife were
present with the President and
First Lady at the unveiling.*

*Pablo Casals performs at a White
House concert following a state dinner
for the Governor of Puerto Rico and
Mrs. Muñoz Marín.*

which you are paying historic homage this evening, Mr. President, is a painting which he had saved."

As he left the dining room, President Kennedy spotted Eddie and Helen Folliard, seated at a table near his mother, Mrs. Joseph P. Kennedy. With a gay wave of his hand, he called out, "Thanks for a nice dinner, Ed!"

The Mona Lisa evening which had commenced so gloriously ended in near disaster. Twelve hundred invitations had been issued to the National Gallery of Art. The Mona Lisa was hung in solitary splendor against a burgundy velvet background, on a wall erected in the Great Sculpture Hall, two-thirds of the way from the entrance. The twelve hundred guests, and certainly scores of gate-crashers, crowded uncontrolled. Those who penetrated the Hall could not get out; most of the guests were unable to get in; and everyone had difficulty in seeing the portrait because of its protective glass. The audio system failed abruptly and only President Kennedy's most rousing campaign voice could top the noise made by the shoving crowds. "I know the last time the Mona Lisa was exhibited outside Paris," he shouted at Malraux, "— in Florence, a crowd of thirty thousand people packed the gallery in a single day, while large crowds smashed windows. I can assure you that, if our reception is more orderly, though perhaps as noisy, it contains no less enthusiasm or gratitude."

John Walker was crushed by the fiasco of what had been planned as a scintillating yet dignified evening. He wrote President Kennedy a sad letter of apology. The First Lady answered for him:

Dear John,
What a sweet note. The President feels you have given him too much credit, and that it was a wonderful occasion. Please do not feel badly. That is the only thing that would really upset me.

You have been so wonderful and made so many undreamed of things possible, I could never tell you how much we appreciate all that. You musn't brood and make it worse in your mind. It was a fantastic evening. It is as Malraux said, part of the magic of the Mona Lisa, almost an evil spell. She made it worthwhile and continues to do so every day —

So please don't ever have a backward thought again, and just think how beautifully you have hung the picture, and how happy it makes everyone to have it there with you watching over it.

The day after the reception, despite cold and rain, some 35,872 people came to see the Mona Lisa; and during the twenty-seven days she remained on view, 674,000, or more than half the annual gallery attendance, came to admire her.

After Washington, a million people, it was estimated, filed by the Mona Lisa during her stay at the Metropolitan Museum in New York City. Then John Walker, as representative of the National Gallery of Art, accompanied the distinguished guest back to France. The Mona Lisa occupied a cabin between those assigned to Walker and a representative of the French government. Every night, Walker recalled, "some whimsical guy placed a pair of women's shoes outside the Mona Lisa's cabin door." Once in Paris, the director accompanied his charge to the Louvre. There, like an expectant father, he waited outside a laboratory, pacing up and down for an hour and a half, while the painting was macro*-photographed to ascertain if there had been any damage. Fortunately, the great adventure had not hurt the beautiful woman. The Mona Lisa went back to her accustomed place on the great gallery wall, luminous as always, and smiling just as enigmatically.

"Please, Mr. President, Put Your Hand Over Your Heart"

The most dramatic and assuredly the most famous state dinner in White House history was given by President and Mrs. Kennedy on a clear July night in 1961 at Mount Vernon, in honor of President Mohammad Ayub Khan of Pakistan.

* "Macro" means extensively developed, large. — It is a photographic process which "blows up" or greatly enlarges all details.

During her visit to his country, Pakistani President Ayub Khan presented Mrs. Kennedy with this bay gelding. When Ayub Khan paid his second visit to the United States, the First Lady accompanied him to Glen Ora to inspect Sardar and take a short canter around the Middleburg, Virginia, retreat.

This evening set a precedent; for though the Roosevelts had entertained their staff at Hyde Park and the Trumans had been hosts at the Mayflower when the Executive Mansion was under renovation, this was the first time that a state dinner had been given outside the White House.

The idea for the entertainment had been initiated in a roundabout way. Charles Wagner, a government architect, who had read about Mrs. Kennedy's flair for imaginative entertaining, suggested to the resident director of Mount Vernon, Charles Cecil Wall, that the First Lady might enjoy arranging a reception or, perhaps, a supper after hours when the Mansion was closed to tourists. George Washington's beautiful plantation, then deep in conservation problems, needed a dash of distinguished public notice. So Director Wall passed along the suggestion to Tish Baldridge, who mentioned it to Mrs. Kennedy in a breezy note.

A gentleman telephoned to say that Mount Vernon would be at your disposal any evening this spring or summer from 5:30 on for a private party. He said that it is fabulous in the early evening with the setting sun and the beauty of the river. The public is kept out after 5 and they are set up to cater and serve a supper. The rooms of the house are thrown open as though it were being lived in. You might want to keep this in mind for a little special entertaining of special pals.

Mrs. Kennedy returned a sedate reply: "Remind me if we have a State Visit or some VIPs this spring — Japanese are coming in June."

Almost immediately, however, the First Lady realized the dramatic possibilities of giving a state dinner at that most revered national "shrine." Within a few days she launched an operation whose seemingly impossible logistics would have daunted anyone endowed with less organizational genius.

The state visit of President Ayub Khan of Pakistan was not scheduled until July. This later date would allow sufficient time for the elaborate preparations required. Around 150 guests could be invited, and to ferry them up and down the Potomac from Washington to Mount Vernon would necessitate recruiting several government vessels. A simple menu must be chosen since the cooking as well as the dining equipment would have to be transported from the White House and set up on the Mount Vernon lawn. The National Symphony Orchestra could provide after-dinner entertainment though the difficulties of moving the orchestra and its instruments, building a stand and making sure of proper acoustics would be formidable. President Kennedy always enjoyed a military drill. At Mount Vernon, the home of General Washington, it would be eminently suitable, especially if the drill could be in Continental army style.

There would be innumerable small details, which could also make or break the evening. Like silver cups for mint juleps and Colonial liveries for the butlers who were to serve this Southern libation; perfumed spray to discourage summer insects; and essential, if less elegant, items such as portable lavatories, so necessary when many workers are employed; finally, especially elaborate invitations which would add up to an extra flutter of enclosures in each envelope.

Sanford Fox, the administrative officer of the Social Entertainments Office, who is also the most accomplished of the White House calligraphers, was responsible for the makeup of all White House invitations, including those to this remarkable festivity. An envelope containing the invitation to a conventional state dinner contained five enclosures. Those invited to the Mount Vernon Dinner received an extra three plus a superbly engraved program of the concert to be played.

The standard state dinner invitation included:

1. The invitation itself, a heavy, square card topped by the gold Presidential Seal, with the guest's name handwritten in banknote script to match the engraving;

2. A separate square of thin paper on which was handwritten in script, "On the occasion of the visit of ——" followed by the name or names of the guest or guests of honor.

3. A nontransferable admission card bearing the guest's name, the date and hour of the function;

4. A thick, plain card engraved simply WHITE TIE or BLACK TIE;

5. Another plain, thick card with the engraved message:

Anne Lincoln, White House house-keeper; Tish Baldridge, social secretary; and Pamela Turnure, press secretary for the First Lady return from Mount Vernon by boat during one of the planning sessions preceding the state dinner for President Ayub Khan in July 1961.

Mrs. Kennedy and Begum Aurang-b, the daughter of President Ayub Khan, make their entrance at the inner party held at Mount Vernon in honor of the Pakistani leader. President Kennedy and President Ayub Khan are behind them.

"Please send response to the Social Secretary, The White House, at your earliest convenience."

The Mount Vernon dinner required in addition a map showing guests how to reach the docks where the ships waited to carry them up the Potomac; a second set of instructions indicating how to reach the White House in case of inclement weather; a separate single sheet program for the orchestra, listing an alternative concert program to be performed in the White House instead of outside at Mount Vernon.

"The program for the Mount Vernon dinner was a marvel," Sandy Fox enthused. "It gave the feeling of living in George Washington's time." The program, as he described it, was "a combination of engraving and printing on a rough cover stock with a deckled edge which showed the Fife and Drum Corps on the West Front of Mount Vernon. Inside the program," he added, "was an oriental rice-paper fly leaf with the Presidential Seal."

All these details had to be checked and rechecked, each moment of the long evening timed and retimed. Again and again.

Soon Mrs. Kennedy began dashing off memos to Mr. West:

TABLES I think we should have yellow cloths if we have enough — otherwise white — and gold ballroom chairs — Small vermeil cachepots (Pres. adores such) with mixed freesia or whatever is in season — *not daisies* in middle — Can we use gold knives, forks, plates from the White House —

TENT I think we shall plan to have a tent over the tables — then if there is a light shower — we can stand on the piazza & go quickly under tent — a striped one — a gray & white would be nice — otherwise whatever you can get but not army drab —

Even the President took a hand at memo writing. He wanted the Mansion interior at Mount Vernon to look its very best. "See that they have all the Lowestoft bowls in house filled with flowers — very low — ask Mr. West to ask Mr. Pecora for suggestions." (Mr. Pecora was Mrs. Paul Mellon's horticultural expert.)

Some days before the dinner, Mrs. Kennedy and Mr. West had been checking the facilities at Mount Vernon. On the return trip down the Potomac the First Lady called out to Mr. West, who was seated well forward, "I suppose you're going to jump off the

White House roof tomorrow?" "No!" Mr. West shouted back, "not until the day after the dinner!" (Perhaps this exchange inspired the First Lady's Christmas present to Mr. West. It was a sofa cushion embroidered with the legend "You don't have to be crazy to live here. But it helps.")

There were to be 140-plus guests. Twenty of them were high-ranking Pakistani including the handsome President, his daughter and son-in-law. Among the American contingent, besides the President and Mrs. Kennedy, were the Vice-President, the Speaker, Secretaries of State, Treasury, Defense; the Attorney General; seven of the most powerful senators; ten representatives; the Secretary of the Navy; and such useful people as the Chairman of the Joint Chiefs of Staff; the directors of both the Budget and the CIA; a number of wealthy men of artistic significance, Henry Francis Du Pont, chairman of the Fine Arts Commission for the White House and Robert Dowling, director of United Artists Corporation. There were the ladies of these important men, a smattering of State Department officials, press, military aides and at least one society beauty.

Four United States Navy ships were tied up to the Washington dock. The two Presidents rode in the *Honey Fitz* (named after President Kennedy's maternal grandfather); Mrs. Kennedy, Begum Aurangzeb and her husband the Shahzada Aurangzeb (the Pakistan President's daughter and son-in-law) were on the Navy yacht *Sequoia;* while the Vice-President ranked in the *Patrick J* (named after President Kennedy's paternal grandfather) ; and Secretary of State Dean Rusk was host to Pakistani notables in a PT boat. Aboard each ship were a protocol officer and a presidential aide to introduce the guests and make sure they were served with appropriate refreshments.

Once docked at Mount Vernon the guests rode uphill to George Washington's Mansion in limousines which sped so close they almost crushed the toes of a double rank of United States Marines who, in faultless precision, snapped their famous "Rippling Salute."

Beyond the Mansion, the great tent, strung with garlands of greenery, its sides looped up, showed the tables for ten, covered in primrose yellow, centered with vermeil bowls filled with white and gold flowers. In back, what did not show was Chef René

Verdon, also in a tent, putting the final touches on the delicious three-course dinner which had been transported in army trucks from the White House. The mint juleps, in their silver-frosted cups, were being served on the piazza and on the broad lawn overlooking the river Washington had so much loved.

With a shrill of fifes and a brisk rattle of drums, the show began. The Colonial Color Guard and the Fife and Drum Corps of the First Battle Group, 3rd Infantry, marched toward the President and his guests. They wore replicas of Colonial uniforms and carried handmade copies of eighteenth-century drums and drum slings used in General Washington's army. They executed an intricate drill and, to the unconcealed delight of both Presidents fired a volley (blank!) with their muskets trained straight at a gaggle of newsmen and newswomen!

Customarily, the President is briefed by protocol officers before a state dinner. Sometimes these briefings are oral, but the ramifications of the Mount Vernon dinner were so complex that a sheaf of notes had been typed and the President had stuffed them in his pocket. Some of the notes, he thought, were vastly amusing.

When you go by Mount Vernon, taps will be sounded. Everyone should rise and stand at attention. This is the traditional salute to George Washington given by every government vessel. "The Star-Spangled Banner" is also played now. (It is very impressive!)

The two Presidents will have some time to kill up on the Mount Vernon "piazza" in front of the house, waiting for the guests from the *Sequoia* to arrive. It is suggested they chat with Mr. and Mrs. Wall (Director of M.V.) and Mr. and Mrs. Francis Beirne (She is the Regent General of the Mount Vernon Ladies Association) who will be standing in front of the house to greet honored guests.

It is also suggested the President will kill these some ten minutes by going through the house and showing it to the General (Ayub Khan) with Mr. Wall. They will be asked to sign the guest book in the hall.

When the last car is up, the two Kennedys and the two Pakistanis should stand in the front door of the house, in order to permit two minutes of photographs by the Press. When the Press has moved off, the little show will begin. Early in the show when you hear "Hail to the Chief," withdraw down the steps and stand in front of the four armchairs. Do not sit at the end of "Hail to the Chief" but stand through the next song, which is the salute to George Washington. The group performing is the Third Infantry Division from Fort Myer under Colonel Lee in revolutionary uniforms, accompanied by their Fife and Drum Corps. In the background is the color guard of the 50 States and 4 Territories. We have also arranged for three Pakistani sailors to carry their colors with ours, to do tribute to General Ayub. They have been rehearsing and living with Colonel Lee's men for four days.

PLEASE, Mr. President, when the colors come right towards you at the end of the ceremony and the military salute is given, put your hand over your heart.

When they all march off the field, the ceremony is over. Then the Presidential Party moves through the house out onto the porch, where they will form a receiving line. Guests will pass from this line directly into dinner.

After coffee at the table, the four Presidentials will lead their guests onto the lawns — to afford time for some to visit the House interior, others to go to the Powder Room. After about ten minutes, the concert can go on.

After the concert, everyone proceeds to the Piazza to go in cars to the Pier, all four in the Presidential Party (plus the Begum's husband) return on the *Honey Fitz.*

The day after the lovely party, reporters pressed Pierre Salinger, the President's press secretary, with their usual sticky questions about cost. This despite the fact that two syndicated columnists (one man and one woman), the White House correspondent for a major network, two out-of-town correspondents and a top-rating magazine writer had been invited to Mount Vernon and apparently enjoyed themselves thoroughly. "Since some discussion has arisen in the press about the cost of this dinner," said Salinger, opening his daily press conference, "I shall make a short statement with respect to the State Dinner.

"This dinner was carried out under a plan which has been initiated by Mrs. Kennedy since she has been in the White House," he continued, "and a substantial — in fact the bulk of the special items for the dinner were donated by public-spirited citizens as a way of helping the White House in extending welcome to President Ayub Khan.

"For example, the tents, the decorations, the music, were all donated — and the only costs involved were the costs of the food, which came within the normal State Department allocation for such entertainment —

"It would be impossible, under our budget, to entertain at State Dinners or to put on a function such as was put on last night — without the help of these public-spirited citizens —"

Reporters, like terriers, interrupted: "Ever?" "Why?"

"— Because of the cost involved." Salinger then itemized some of the gifts:" "— The National Symphony Orchestra provided the after-dinner music and paid the construction costs of the stand on which they were seated, Lester Lanin contributed a trio which played during the dinner; Tiffany & Co. of New York provided the decorations and John Vanderherschen Inc. of Philadelphia, the tent.

"I think Mrs. Kennedy will continue her policy of calling from time to time on various people for assistance in having our country put its best foot forward — in meeting some of the famous people who come to visit us." Pierre Salinger waved his cigar and turned to another question, another subject.

"The King of Afghanistan Is Coming"

To make any state dinner a success required a staggering amount of work and organization. The following is an exchange of memos between Mrs. Kennedy and Miss Nancy Tuckerman re arrangements for the state dinner honoring the King and Queen of Afghanistan. (Mrs. Kennedy would not be present as she was expecting a baby in September — Miss Tuckerman, her former roommate at Miss Porter's School in Farmington, had succeeded Tish Baldridge as social secretary in June 1963.)

June 1963. Mrs. Kennedy to Nancy Tuckerman.

I see the King of Afghanistan is coming September 5th. It should be hot enough then to have outside entertainment. — Perfect for him would be the exact same tattoo on the lawn we had for (President) Bourguiba of Tunisia — all the military bands, bagpipes etc.

Just check the weather to see what those days — Sept. 5–8 have been like the last few years. If rainy & it looks too risky — look through files for suggested State Entertainments & see what else you can come up with — & make sure this is one dinner that stays small — & does not overflow into Blue Room — we can have long Presidential table — not U-shaped — & round ones in State Dining Room & I think there can be about 115 or more — you can check. — If you have tattoo JFK & King & Queen & other ranking guests should sit on Blue Room balcony — others on driveway & stone entrance below.

Memo from Miss Tuckerman to Mrs. Kennedy July 1, 1963. [Mrs. Kennedy corrected and made suggestions in handwriting on the margins of the memo.]

As you know I was quite opposed to any military review for the Sept. 8th dinner due to the fact it meant repeating what had been done before. [Margin note from Mrs. Kennedy:

The tattoo was always one of our favorites — & would like to do it again with fireworks. It would be much more spectacular & we won't have a chance to do outdoors things until spring & then you always have the rain threat — so do this — if the odds on weather are *over- whelmingly* favorable — get reports on last year's —]

Miss Tuckerman continued:

The West family & I went to the Marine barracks on Fri. night & were completely carried away by their drill. We wished you could have been there for it is quite spectacular. After it was over Mr. West & I discussed having the Marines at the White House & it was then that Mr. West said, "Why not have dinner in the Rose Garden?" I thought it was a marvelous idea & something which would make the evening quite different — We worked it out this way:

Cocktails East Garden with music.
Dinner in Rose Garden with Strolling Strings under Colonnade.
After-dinner guests will assemble outdoors for show.
Marine Drill.
Fireworks by fountain on South Lawn.
Marines who have made exit behind shrubbery will play "Taps."

We should have no more than, say, 120 [Mrs. Kennedy notes — even less — as JFK always adds people at the end] people in for, in the event of rain, it would have to be moved to the State Dining

Room. Also if it rains we would have champagne & music in the East Room.

Mrs. Kennedy in a follow-up memo to Miss Tuckerman:

Your idea is great but 4 things —

1. If you have cocktails in East Garden (they had better have it finished by then) where will JFK appear for "Hail to the Chief" receiving line? This must be imposing. I suppose they could follow flags out of Diplomatic Reception Room & start "Ruffles & Flourishes" in the driveway. But if it can't be done with great panache in the garden — it better be in the East Room — Where would they pose for photogs — usual place — or out on drive — I don't want a lot of photogs milling about guests — maybe at the outside door of Dip. Rec. Room. Also there must be no cars cluttering the driveway.

2. Do the Marines have any bands? Or just silent drill? If Mr. West says it's OK — fine — I loved the Army Drum & Bugle Corps before — & the Pipers — but all Marines is OK — if it is good. Then you must ask the head of Marines to dinner.

3. Have Strolling Strings just come out at dessert as usual (Air Force — other ones are available) & stand all around Colonnade — as well as mingling — Have JFK's office & Cabinet Room lighted (if this looks well — you decide) If Marine band plays during dinner — they could be on the Blue Room porch.

4. See that the hall outside flower room has children's bicycles removed — & perhaps some Mimosa trees — anyway much more green trees in it — orange trees etc. ask Mrs. Mellon to help you on this — get Mr. West to ask her.

On July 6, more than two months before the state dinner, Mrs. Kennedy wrote a succeeding memo to Nancy Tuckerman:

This is a final memo. I have discussed it with JFK.

1. He definitely wants tattoo & fireworks — try to have them do the flag of Afghanistan not the King's face as it might not be recognized.

2. Use all the best parts of the Marine Drill but do add the Bagpipes & Drum & Bugle Corps. They add so much — Bagpipes come so romantically out of trees at early part of show — Drum & Bugle — is smashing near finale.

3. I don't think you should have cocktails in East Garden — as so many people will be coming in White House for the first time & that way they will never see State Rooms — & it makes an all outdoor evening — so do receiving line as usual in East Room — then dinner &

Strolling Strings outside — & get someone to ask King & Queen if they would like to go upstairs before tattoo — you can take her to my room.

July 10, 1963. Miss Tuckerman to Mrs. Kennedy.

I am not going to bother you with all the details but Mr. West & I are working out the arrangements, and he is contacting Mrs. Mellon about the garden lighting, flowers etc.

I am listing a few items you should know about, or be interested in:

1. After receiving line guests will go downstairs & out Diplomatic Reception Room (makes prettier entrance & Charles [Charles Fickler, then the head butler] needs hall outside Flower Room for serving tables).

2. Guests will arrive at front portico probably, so they won't see Rose Garden on arrival or preliminary activities on South Lawn.

3. We will ask the 4 military heads of the Services, if possible, since their men will be participating in the evening. [Here, Mrs. Kennedy notes — "but NOT their aides"]

4. Angie [Duke] and I think it would be best to have Black Tie since the evening is outdoors & also it could be fairly hot at that time of year. Weather reports are excellent.

At the end of the memo Mrs. Kennedy penciled: "Fine. Sounds marvelous. JBK."

Shortly afterwards, when all the details for the dinner to be given in honor of the King and Queen of Afghanistan had been worked out to the satisfaction of both President and Mrs. Kennedy, Nancy outlined the schedule in final detail:

North West driveway will be lined with Marines. [Note: King, Queen & their entourage entered by the North West Portico from Pennsylvania Avenue.]

2. Guests will arrive via the South West Gate. Fife & Drum Corps will be playing outside, near entrance to Diplomatic Reception Room.

3. Receiving line and cocktails will take place in East Room.

4. Dinner will be served in Rose Garden with Marine Band playing during dinner at the East end of the Garden.

5. Special lighting is being arranged by Mrs. Mellon. The President's office & Cabinet Room will be lighted.

6. Strolling Strings will play on roof of Colonnade (We rehearsed this & it appears very effective.)

7. Champagne will be served after dinner on the Ground Floor. Navy Band will play there.

Military Program on South Lawn.

The President, the King & Queen of Afghanistan, & a number of other officials will be seated on the South Portico, outside the Blue Room. The other guests will sit in 2 rows on the driveway.

Air Force Bagpipers, Drum & Bugle Corps. Silent Drill Platoon. Fireworks — by South Lawn fountain (approximately 10 minutes). Taps.

This exchange of memos merely outlined the arrangements necessary for such an elaborate entertainment. The military element was complicated to maneuver since even a trace of favoritism among the Armed Services had to be avoided assiduously. The fireworks too posed an unusual problem. Hitherto fireworks had only been set off on the Fourth of July, although there was no city regulation forbidding them. The display had been clocked for ten minutes with an elaborate finale which would flash both Afghan and American flags. But in the middle of dinner President Kennedy asked to have the program time shortened by half. It was. Easily. The fancy rockets, Roman Candles, Flower Pots and other dazzlers, were all shot off at once. The racket was terrifying. The White House switchboard was flooded with calls. Citizens asked anxiously whether it was an atomic attack or merely bombs exploding. Even the imperturbable Secret Service agents did a double take when the explosions started.

Since Mrs. Kennedy was in Hyannis Port, her sister-in-law, Mrs. Sargent Shriver, was hostess at this first dinner planned in the Rose Garden. The usual infallible sources had predicted "excellent" weather, but it rained in the afternoon. The final decision on whether to set the tables outside or in the State Dining Room had to be made two hours in advance. Though the weather did clear, the grass remained damp and the dinner was served inside. Later, the guests went outside to watch the military drills and the fireworks.

The Shah and Empress of Iran with President and Mrs. Kennedy at the Iranian Embassy during the state visit of the Shah in 1962.

The King and Queen of Afghanistan arrive by helicopter on the White House Lawn to be met by President Kennedy and his sister Eunice Shriver. Mrs. Kennedy, expecting her third child, Patrick, was unable to be present, so Mrs. Shriver acted as substitute hostess.

A Tidal Wave of Affection and Curiosity

In 1969, when Mrs. Kennedy's mail settled down from inaugural exuberance to a steady, unflagging flow, she received between 250 and 300 letters every day in the year. A tidal wave of affection and curiosity, this figure did not include around thirty thousand greeting cards (actually twice the 1961 total) sent to the First Lady and her children during the fortnight before Christmas, or the tens of thousands of holiday good wishes addressed jointly to the President and his wife. Neither did it include an astonishing variety of gifts posted to Mrs. Kennedy, Caroline and baby John, from admirers all over the globe. And besides all this, wedding invitations and stork cards arrived by the dozens.

Each week about fifteen hundred of the letters were written to Mrs. Kennedy by young people; they came from every state in the Union and many foreign countries as well. Often these communications began or ended with unexpected salutations.

> Your Majesty
> Respected Madam
> Dear Sister Jacqueline Kennedy
> Dear Madam President
> Chère Madame Jacqueline
> Yours very affectionately
> à bientôt
> With respects
> Love
> A Friend
> Vôtre devoué
> Dios y Patria! Attentamente

ncy Tuckerman, social secretary to
s. Kennedy during her final year in
the White House.

President Kennedy proposes a toast at a private dinner party the Kennedys gave in honor of Mrs. Kennedy's sister Princess Stanilaus Radziwill. In the background are blow-ups of Prince Radziwill and his "look-alike," fashion designer Oleg Cassini.

With all our love to your whole family
    from us all
Thank you for listening
Mrs. Kennedy, I think you're BEAUTIFUL!

In between formal beginnings and easier endings the substance of these letters ran the gamut of pathos, humor, "gimmes" and a delight in Mrs. Kennedy and anything she undertook. About 40 percent of the total consisted of fan mail — often from youngsters and teenagers — expressing admiration and asking for nothing except, perhaps, a photograph or an autograph. "Gimmes" accounted for another 30 percent. Usually these were not requests for direct financial assistance, since this type of plea is usually the prerogative of a parent, but instead queries about jobs, or the transfer of service boyfriends to nearer posts and an amazing number of forward young Americans asking brashly for an invitation to stay overnight in the White House. There were hundreds of requests for specific items like eyeglasses, orthopedic braces, pets, artists' material, and, once or twice, for a piano. Many asked for information needed in preparing school papers. Some of the "gimme" letters were, of course, real hardship cases for which harassed parents sought Mrs. Kennedy's assistance in substantial form, such as underwriting an operation. More often what was really wanted was a morale booster, a personal note or a photograph from the First Lady.

Fashion, etiquette, interior décor, the newly aroused interest in antiques, added another 10 percent to the total. The remaining 20 percent was an intriguing miscellany: proffered political opinions; gratuitous advice; ingenuous offers of personal service — such as baby-sitting with Caroline; youth-wants-to-know questions about government, some with a funny personal slant; many gifts from piggy banks and small, self-earned funds contributed by surprisingly young children who had been impressed by Mrs. Kennedy's TV tour of the White House; scores of polite thank-you notes written after the White House concerts for children; and uncountable requests for recipes, either personal favorites of Mrs. Kennedy or delicacies prepared for White House entertainments.

The letters Mrs. Kennedy received from adults were more sedate but equally varied. They included many requests for assistance relating to military personnel and a heavy load of mail concerned with educational, medical and child problems. The White House Restoration project attracted tremendous attention, while Mrs. Kennedy's known interest in history and less publicized interest in landscaping drew requests from all over the world for help in registering ancient houses and landmarks as Historic Monuments and from local communities seeking advice in solving their landscaping problems.

Though it seemed humanly impossible, every letter written to Mrs. Kennedy (with the exception of hopelessly illegible communications) was answered. Even the thirty thousand greeting cards were opened and individual senders listed.

The First Lady's mail was handled in a large, unadorned room across the corridor from the offices of her personal staff in the East Wing of the White House. The regular mail-room staff was headed by Tom McCoy, the chief "sorter," and Hortense Burton, who was responsible for queries requiring especially complex replies; and extra help was recruited from other White House sources during the holidays and similar rush periods. (This same staff packaged the hundreds of gifts Mrs. Kennedy distributed when she visited hospitals, children's homes and other charitable institutions. In addition they wrapped personal presents to her overwhelming number of relatives and personal friends. There were so many children given gifts that at Christmastime the toy-filled room looked like an offshoot of Santa Claus's workshop, not a sober business office in the White House.)

The incoming mail envelopes were slit efficiently by an electric cutter, then Tom McCoy swiftly scanned each letter and sorted them into a wide variety of categories. Obviously, Mrs. Kennedy did not have time to read all her mail but she did see a daily "comprehensive sampling" made up from the random choice of one out of every half-dozen or so unsolicited letters, which were placed in a folder. Other letters of special interest or human appeal were selected, while Mrs. Kennedy herself was concerned with almost any problem relating to schoolchildren and their mothers.

Tish Baldridge and afterwards her successor, Nancy Tuckerman, answered most of the notes from children as well as handling Mrs. Kennedy's official correspondence. Many of the letters from adults were passed on to appropriate government agencies. Requests for military personnel assistance were forwarded to the Department of Defense; HEW, the Department of Health, Education and Welfare, dealt with queries about educational, medical and PTA problems; and the White House curator fielded questions pertaining to his bailiwick. Correspondence on cultural matters, which were too technical for the Social Office to cope with, was first acknowledged and then passed on to August Heckscher, the Special Consultant on Art to President Kennedy. A large percentage of these letters were from individual artists or distinguished musical groups offering to perform at the White House; or from students engaged in writing reports on government undertakings in art; or, perhaps, from a variety of cultural associations who periodically brought Mrs. Kennedy up to date on their activities.

With the exception of Mrs. Franklin D. Roosevelt, recent First Ladies had not been fluent in any foreign language and the State Department had handled the modest amount of mail they received from abroad. Mrs. Kennedy, however, spoke flawless French and was at ease in Spanish and Italian. She was partially of French descent and had lived in France as a student. So, inevitably, she attracted an unusual number of letters not only from France but from other countries where French was the lingua franca. To handle this overseas enthusiasm in a more personal way, a secretary who was bi-lingual in French and English was added to Mrs. Kennedy's staff. The State Department, anxious to keep a finger on the pulse of foreign public opinion, reluctantly agreed to this impingement but continued to deal with the First Lady's considerable correspondence from other countries.

Gifts to the Kennedys were handled meticulously, in a three-way routine. When any small item such as a handkerchief or a trifle of handiwork was enclosed in a letter or greeting card, the sender was listed and received a printed note of thanks. Presents which arrived in parcels were opened and listed in similar fashion, but those whose value was estimated to be over fifteen dollars were returned. The less costly gifts were kept, the giver thanked and eventually they were sent to local hospitals, orphan asylums and homes for children. These special Kennedy fans liked to send the First Lady books, phonograph records and clothing. Caroline was showered with dolls and toy horses while John's public preferred to give him stuffed animals and mechanical toys. Occasionally, a donor would write, describing his intended gift and sounding out Mrs. Kennedy on its acceptability.

This thoughtfulness brought an unusually quick reaction from the White House:

Mrs. Kennedy appreciates so very much your generous offer to present her with the very beautiful hand-crocheted bedspread which you describe. However, when I tell you that we have literally hundreds of similar offers, you will understand why we have to follow a policy discouraging the presentation of gifts.

The replies sent out in Mrs. Kennedy's name often seemed quite stodgy. But it was difficult for the person entrusted with answering to be either original or sprightly while maintaining the dignity appropriate to the White House. Nevertheless, unintentionally, some of the pompous replies were quite funny.

A twelve-year-old girl, having read of Mrs. Kennedy's trip to India and Pakistan, wrote to ask the First Lady to find her a Pakistan pen-pal.

I am writing on behalf of Mrs. Kennedy to thank you for your letter of recent date [said the reply].

Mrs. Kennedy is most appreciative of the kind thought which prompted you to write and she enjoyed hearing from you. We regret, however, that your request cannot be granted. She receives hundreds of similar requests to find a pen-pal and we know you will understand why she is unable to reply.

Another twelve-year-old girl struck a sympathetic chord when she asked how to get a job in order to earn money to buy a horse.

Although Mrs. Kennedy would like to be of assistance to you, she receives so many requests for answers to specific questions, I am sure you understand that her many duties do not leave her time to comply. — We are enclosing an autographed photograph of Mrs. Kennedy which we hope you will like.

Two boys, high school graduates, shared a bright idea which occurred almost simultaneously to hundreds of other young people throughout the United States.

. . . we will be majoring in education. We were wondering if it would be possible for us to spend a few days at the White House to learn a little bit about how our government really functions. We would much rather see how the United States is run than read about it. I feel that a trip to the White House would help prepare for when we are older and have reached the voting age.

A student, a girl aged fourteen, was more than just interested in "how the government really functions." She was planning to run the government herself and asked for a "report" on the Kennedys. Her favorite subject was the Constitution, which she was studying because she wanted to be the first Lady President of the United States, after graduating from college and law school. The reason she wished to be President was because ". . . I am so deeply interested in our country."

Both the mother and the aunt of a fifteen-year-old girl who was seriously ill wrote and asked for a message of cheer.

Mrs. Kennedy has asked me to write you a little note to say that she hopes you are now feeling a great deal better and will soon be able to be out in the wonderful spring weather with your friends. . . . We are so sorry that you have such a painful illness . . . with very best wishes for a quick and complete recovery . . .

This message worked magic.

You will never know the light in the eyes of my fifteen-year-old daughter [the mother of the girl replied] . . . as she read the letter . . . as the day it came she was very sick . . . May God bless you all very much, always . . .

Another mother asked Mrs. Kennedy to send a word of confidence to her frightened eleven-year-old daughter. The child faced open heart surgery similar to an operation on a small Greek girl whom the First Lady had brought to the United States some months before. A letter, signed by Mrs. Kennedy read:

I am so sorry that soon you will have to have an operation. The President joins me in sending all best wishes for an early and complete recovery. Little Chrysanthemis Papacotis is now enjoying herself in a normal, happy life with her family and friends, having had a similar operation. . . . Please extend also our good wishes to your mother and father. Perhaps you would like to have the photograph that is enclosed.

The child's great-grandmother thanked Mrs. Kennedy:

. . . it has helped her so much . . . your letter has made her brave . . . she is so proud of them [the letter and photograph] and she has taken them with her to the hospital for good luck . . . so I wanted you to know what a sweet thing you had done. . . .

Some of the letters were especially appealing:

During Leadville's Winter Carnival my brothers and I won a prize of five dollars in the snow sculpturing contest [wrote John (9), Jim (7), Jerry (5) and Joy (23 months)]. We would like you to use the money in your White House project. We liked your tour of the White House on TV.

An earnest admirer won for himself the golden ring, in this case an autographed photograph of Mrs. Kennedy.

Dear First Lady:
Congratulations on being First Lady. It must be a great honor. Will you please send me a big autographed picture of yourself . . . I think you are beautiful and so do my classmates. We all think you are fitting to be the best and most beautiful First Lady there ever was and will be. Best wishes throughout the years. God Bless you. I am 11 yrs. old. Truly yours . . .
P. S. I have always been a Kennedy admirer.

Occasionally an answer was short and clear. A teenager, impressed with Mrs. Kennedy's linguistic ability, asked the best way to learn a foreign language ". . . application and hard work!" was the succinct reply from a member of the First Lady's staff.

Perhaps the most gloriously confusing of all the fan mail came from a young woman living in an out-of-the-way district of Pakistan. She had not managed to see Mrs. Kennedy during her visit but had read about it. The letter itself was embellished with an imaginative drawing of clasped hands, rosebuds and a rose plant while an inner envelope was ornamented with identical clasped hands and the Pakistan flag. The letter commenced auspiciously:

Your Majesty:

I have been deeply moved to observe your picture story through *Panorama* [a picture magazine published in Pakistan by USIS]. Broadly speaking on this point, I may add, that your infinite Sagacity, Moderation, Simple Style and highly scintillating constitution has awfully charmed me, and from this time on I am feeling an uncanny intuition of Love and respect for you.

6

Private Living

Refuge from a Fishbowl Existence

Before moving to the White House the Kennedys had wanted to
find a refuge from their new fishbowl existence. Some quiet
country hideaway, secluded yet accessible, where they could relax
and the children could play without being watched by curious
tourists, was a very real necessity. But a place with these desirable
features was not easily come by. On November weekends before
John, Jr., was born, they had inspected several houses; but all
were either too expensive or unsuitably situated. Then Bill
Walton suggested Glen Ora, a four-hundred-acre estate near
Middleburg, in the heart of the Virginia hunt country and
scarcely more than an hour by car from the White House.

Bill had long been a friend of Mrs. Raymond Tartière, the
owner of Glen Ora, and her late husband. Gladys Tartière had
been married previously to Ernest Byfield, impresario of the
decoratively as well as gastronomically resplendent Pump Room
in Chicago. Raymond, her second husband, had been born in
France but had lived many years in England where he delighted
in both riding and fox hunting. He had sought out Middleburg
because the countryside and the sporting pattern of local living
suited him perfectly.

After the Tartières bought Glen Ora in 1940, they began to
transform the old, tree-shaded house with its patchwork of additions into a rather grand French country-style mansion of buff
stucco brightened with white shutters. Eventually, four other
buildings were put in order: a farmer's cottage, playhouse, guest
cottage, a modest stable and generous swimming pool. There
were gardens, lawns, woods and pastures. And as the house was
separated from the public road by an unusually long, narrow
avenue, privacy seemed assured. Bill Walton believed the place
was ideal. Since, at the time, Mrs. Kennedy was still hospitalized
after the birth of her baby, he asked Gladys Tartière for photo-

graphs and took them to the future First Lady personally. The snapshots pleased the Kennedys, so, sight unseen, and solely on the recommendation of their friend, they rented Glen Ora.

Mrs. Tartière was spending Christmas in Chicago with her family when she signed the lease. The agreement stipulated that the house, which was rented completely furnished, would be returned precisely as it had been taken. Any changes in interior décor, such as repainting or even installing fresh wallpaper, had to be changed back before the Kennedys left.

The Kennedys wished to take over on February first, ten days after the Inauguration. Mrs. Tartière, given two weeks, asked for three weeks in which to get her house ready. She had not expected to rent Glen Ora and knew many things needed attention. The exterior was in bad repair, her bedroom wallpaper was sadly faded, but there was not time to rejuvenate them. These and other untended details were to cause distress to both owner and tenants. Gladys Tartière believed that, if Mrs. Kennedy had been well enough to visit Glen Ora before moving in, the transition would have been made more easily.

The lease was scarcely signed before the Secret Service arrived to deal with their monumental security problems. The driveway, which had seemed to assure privacy, was so narrow that cars proceeding in opposite directions had to slow to a crawl in order to pass safely. A presidential cavalcade, moving at the required fast clip, could thus be seriously endangered. To avoid this bottleneck, a special heliport was built close to the main house, and a short-wave system was hooked up, which linked an agent stationed near the entrance with a central command post. Weekends, when the President was in residence, a helicopter would be kept in readiness day and night to whisk him back over the rolling Virginia fields to the White House. The agent at the new, solidly barred gates was also in contact with four guardhouses erected at strategic points on the property. In this way any vehicle en route to or from the main house could be identified immediately and, in one second flat, the avenue closed to all traffic. Adele Murphy, shuttling back and forth between the N Street house and Glen Ora, remembers vividly how she had to stop at the gate and shout out her name. Then, eerily from

President and Mrs. Kennedy relax on the terrace at Wexford, the family retreat in Atoka, Virginia. Sharing the autumn sun with them is Clipper, Mrs. Kennedy's German shepherd and her favorite among the many Kennedy dogs. Clipper was a gift to the First Lady from her father-in-law, Ambassador Joseph P. Kennedy.

somewhere in the field, a mysterious voice would boom permission to enter.

The central command post itself was set up in two parked trailers, while the complicated equipment which melded them all together was concealed in former slave quarters. Urbanus E. Baughman, then chief of the Secret Service, recalls in his memoirs, published before President Kennedy's assassination: "I had a regular arsenal installed at Middleburg — from tear gas to every conceivable kind of gun — machine guns, shotguns, carbines, armor-piercing rifles —"* In this awesome manner the Kennedys' Shangri-la was preserved against intruders!

Secret Service agents searched the main house with meticulous attention, poking into the most unlikely nooks and crannies. At last, under the attic eaves, they hit pay dirt! A cache of cartridges! Before some long-ago hunt, Raymond Tartière had shoved extra ammunition there, and forgotten it. Nevertheless the agents confiscated the lot, "just in case" Caroline should discover the attic on a rainy afternoon.

In a remarkably short time much of the Glen Ora furniture, except the dining room suite and a few living room upholstered pieces which were immediately slipcovered, was removed to the capacious White House storerooms. Then Mrs. Murphy, who had moved the Kennedy effects so many times, chaperoned some of the same N Street furniture to the new setting in Virginia and more to the White House private living quarters.

Mrs. Kennedy's decorator, Mrs. Henry Parish, had many of the walls repapered or repainted; laid wall-to-wall carpeting in the living room and children's bedrooms; and created a private bower for Caroline, done up gaily in pink-and-white flowered wallpaper, matching chintz upholstery, and crisp ruffled organdy curtains. Miraculously, three weeks after the Inauguration, the painting was done, the carpeting, new curtains and slipcovers were all in place.

Mrs. Kennedy and the President, traveling for safety in separate helicopters, arrived at their country retreat for the first time.

The Kennedys became very much attached to Glen Ora though some of their close friends considered the main house

* *Secret Service Chief* by Urbanus E. Baughman, published by Harper & Row in 1962.

quite gloomy. But they treasured it as a sure refuge from the relentless exposure of the world's most publicized job. It was one spot where Caroline and John could frolic safe from even a prying telescopic lens; where the First Lady could hack casually on a favored mount; where the President could lounge in well-worn clothes and later, without straining his bad back, whack a golf ball on the one-hole course his wife had had built for his birthday.

The sole discordant note was that the extensive refurbishing had been expensive. President Kennedy disliked spending money unless he considered it essential: he was surprised and annoyed. Though it was scarcely Mrs. Tartière's fault, the first time the President was introduced to his landlady he complained, "Your house cost me a lot of money!"

This was not an ingratiating opening remark, and Gladys Tartière, in turn, was surprised and annoyed. The following year when Clark Clifford, the handsome and persuasive Kennedy lawyer, suggested that President Kennedy would like to renew his two-year lease and might even like to purchase the property, Mrs. Tartière unequivocally refused. It was after this that the Kennedys, searching for a substitute retreat, bought thirty-nine acres, less than twenty miles distant, on isolated Rattlesnake Mountain. Here they built a house which Mrs. Kennedy herself designed. She named the place Wexford after the native Kennedy county in Ireland.

One day, shortly after the foundations had been dug but little other building progress made, President Kennedy took Charles Bartlett to see the site. The President, who passionately loved the sea, was dubious about being closed in by mountains. As he looked out over the brown grass on the surrounding hillsides, he turned to Bartlett with a shrug: "Imagine my ending up in a place like this!" he exclaimed. After the house was finished, the President spent precisely four weekends at Wexford.

*Mrs. Kennedy rides Sardar with John as Caroline rides
alongside on Macaroni.*

"Brave Enough to Build a Brick Wall"

When the children first arrived at the White House after the Inauguration, Mrs. Kennedy set about making their lives as everyday as possible. She was determined to devote as much time to them as she had in the past. She felt her children would develop happy natures if they were kept out of the public eye, protected from being spoiled by well-meaning individuals, and could continue to see their young friends in the greatest possible privacy. In any family, the First Lady believed, wherever and under whatever circumstances they lived, as long as the father was the central figure of authority and the mother provided love and guidance, children had a better than average chance of turning out successfully.

Because so many official duties, from the elaborate reception of state visitors to the complex restoration project, had to be coped with, it was difficult to keep a regular schedule. But Mrs. Kennedy managed her time skillfully and gave more of herself to Caroline and baby John than many ordinarily busy mothers. That first year, when John was a baby, she gave him both his morning and evening bottles and he stayed on her bed for a while after breakfast. Then Mrs. Kennedy, dressed in slacks and sweaters, took him outdoors and pushed his pram around the grounds. Later, when he was mobile, John would play on the lawn with the dogs while his mother tramped briskly around and around the driveway or batted a tennis ball for exercise. ("I could work better at my desk," Mrs. Kennedy explained, "after I had some exercise.") On her way back to the house she invariably walked past her husband's office and almost always he called her in.

When Caroline's play-group became a real school, she carried a box lunch to her classes in the third floor Solarium. John had his midday meal at twelve-thirty and most days his mother ate with him. She never tired of a cup of hot soup and the same grilled cheese sandwich which she had favored since her teens. Afterwards, she would "put John in" for his nap and, when the President came "home" at one-thirty or two, she sat beside him until he finished luncheon and he, too, took a brief nap.

In between times Mrs. Kennedy did her paper work. She worked in the West Hall sitting room at her small Empire desk. The papers accumulated relentlessly and finally the President suggested she move to the more secluded Treaty Room. Here, the folders were stacked on a larger desk where she could flip through them easily, make telephone calls and summon a secretary for dictation. But Mrs. Kennedy continued to be "so terrible at dictating" that her many letters were more often written longhand.

Caroline was geared to longer naps so she could stay up later to be with her father. When both children were awake, Mrs. Kennedy might "do" something with them in the afternoon. Their young friends would be invited in to play, or perhaps she would take them to a small park in Georgetown.

When John grew up a bit he had supper with his sister at six. By then Mrs. Kennedy was usually done with afternoon appointments and joined them. Sometimes, as a special treat, she would let them bathe in her bathroom or, if the occasion merited something extra, she would delight them with a bubble bath.

While she dressed for supper, they would tumble about her room and on most evenings they stayed up until their father returned "home." After leaving his office the President always swam in the White House Pool and there changed into evening clothes before coming upstairs. Then, relaxed, sipping a drink in his room, he would devote a quarter of an hour or more to his children, sometimes roughhousing, sometimes reading them Western stories, sometimes just having fun. Their nurse would bundle them off to bed, and a little later, on their way to dine, the President and the First Lady would stop in to kiss Caroline and John goodnight.

Winter weekends, which were always spent at Glen Ora, were strictly family affairs.

By the autumn of 1962, when Mrs. Kennedy was about to start

John hurries after his father as the President, deep in thought, heads toward his office in the West Wing of the White House.

The First Lady pushes John
in his pram around the White
House grounds.

Mrs. Kennedy accompanies
Caroline, John, and their n
Maud Shaw up the hill tow
Wexford, their new house i
Atoka, Virginia, in October
1963.

her third year in the White House, she evolved a personal schedule which she hoped to follow. It was posted to her offices in the East Wing and to the Chief Usher's office.

Mrs. Kennedy's Schedule for this winter when the children return
October 30th, 1962

8:00	Breakfast
8:30	Play with John
9:00	Take Caroline up to school
9:00–10:00	Exercise
10:00–12:30	Work at desk. All folders should be sent from your office to be on my desk by 10:00. *No other folders to come over all day long!*
12:30	Lunch
3:15	Take children out
5:30	Bring children back
6:30– 7:00	Play and read with Caroline
7:30	Guests asked for dinner
8:00	Eat

If I stick to this vaguely — I will get lots more accomplished.
Tell switchboard no calls from anyone 8:00–9:00 A.M. and 6:30–7:00 P.M.
Please don't call me. I'll call you! during day — except 10:00 — 12:30 work period. Phone ringing and folders arriving make it impossible to work long enough on anything.
When I have hair done, make appointment for 4:30 — so I will always be free 6:30 for Caroline.

In a letter to Palm Beach before the Inauguration, Mr. West, the Chief Usher, had suggested a likely spot for a children's playground would be under the trees near the South West entrance. Before long Mr. West received a memo from Mrs. Kennedy, enlivened by mini-sketches of her ideas for the playground. It should include (*a*) wire cages for both rabbits and guinea pigs, (*b*) a tunnel of wooden barrels which turned a sharp corner (for crawling through). (*c*) a tree house platform reached by a small ladder, (*d*) a swing, (*e*) a snow fence atop a tiny mound and an enclosure where lambs might be kept.

The flaw in this otherwise splendid plan became only too apparent by spring. The trees and shrubbery were sparse and offered little protection. As the White House enclave was fenced by iron bars set far apart, enterprising sightseers, queueing for the White House tour, could photograph as well as watch the children at play. As the weather bettered, the lensmen increased in numbers and enthusiasm. Finally, Mrs. Kennedy made a complete survey and, in still another memo to the obliging Mr. West, drew a rough outline of the playground and indicated a spot on the iron fence with an X. "If you stand in the children's playground — you will see that lots of people can take photographs from the place marked X," she wrote. "Could you have some more trees planted — or, perhaps rhododendrons? It must be a solid wall — invisible through." Then underneath the sketch was a plaintive query, "Who will be the first President brave enough to build a brick wall?"

Blissfully Unimpressed

The autumn of 1960, before the Kennedys went to the White House, Caroline Kennedy, then three, had joined a play-group. There were nine other little friends and they met twice a week for supervised play at the house of one or another of the members. The play-group had started when most of the children were scarcely a year old, and their mothers, who enjoyed the sessions as much as the youngsters, became fast friends. After the 1960 election, when Mrs. Kennedy invited the play-group to meet at the White House, the other mothers were hesitant. The play-group was such a simple thing that the White House atmosphere might prove too grand. But they accepted and the nine mothers formed such a fiercely loyal band that not even the most ingenious reporter ever discovered the children's names or the most inconsequential detail of their activities.

By March 1961, Mrs. Anthony Hass, founder of the play-group, had engaged a teacher, bought the requisite furnishings and a playroom was installed in the third-floor Solarium. It was a cooperative venture, perhaps the only such one ever to have functioned in the White House; at each meeting two of the mothers took their turn helping the teacher. The cozy atmosphere remained the same, and the children were so young the change of scene meant nothing to them. Nor did they feel that Caroline's father, who sometimes appeared when they were playing on the lawn at recess, was in any way different from their own.

But though the children were blissfully unimpressed by their surroundings, the public was well aware of their presence in the White House. Stories about the play-group, though vague in particulars, had appeared in newspapers throughout the country. In the Washington area, scores of mothers requested admission for their youngsters, others asked to view the children at play, while a surprising number of publishers and toy manufacturers wished to donate their products and, of course, be given recognition for their gifts. Tish Baldridge countered eager mothers with a polite note: "Mrs. Kennedy was most interested to read of your young son, X, of whom you must be very proud. However, we cannot grant your request in that Caroline's play-group is not a school in any sense of the word. It is merely a small, informal group of her friends who meet to play together under supervision."

By the spring of 1962 the children had outgrown the play-group: they were ready for nursery school. Mrs. Kennedy interviewed a number of prospects and engaged young Alice Grimes to organize a more advanced curriculum. A Sarah Lawrence graduate who had been teaching kindergarten classes at the Brearley School in New York City, Miss Grimes was given carte blanche with the sole proviso that everything should be "the best."

The original play-group children were of slightly varying ages and, according to the new teacher, should be in two different groups. To make it the "real school" situation which Alice wanted, each group had to be added to, and eventually there were ten in a nursery school class and another ten in kinder-

Indians in full regalia pay visit to Caroline and her schoolmates in the White House school.

Caroline and friends in the playground Mrs. Kennedy had built near the Southwest Entrance.

garten. This arrangement was planned originally for a single year, but it proved so successful that Mrs. Kennedy asked Alice to continue the following winter with a kindergarten and first grade.

Because of the larger enrollment, Alice added an assistant and two part-time teachers. One taught music, the second rhythm; courses planned to make the youngsters aware of music and to develop their motor control. Later, Jacqueline Provoost Hirsh, who was to give President Kennedy French lessons, taught the younger pupils too.

Though Alice's program was called "Reading Readiness, an Introduction to Phonetics," the curriculum was strictly her own. The program was well planned and covered "everything," but of course there were many extras. Educational movies were shown in the White House theater. Indian chiefs who came to town for the Congress of American Indians paid a call in their tribal regalia. One morning thirty-four little Korean orphans, who spoke no English, sang "Rudolph, the Red-nosed Reindeer" in perfect American. Sometimes the children were invited down to the State Rooms to meet famous guests and their greatest thrill was shaking hands with the astronauts. They took field trips through museums and made a special expedition to the National Gallery of Art when the Mona Lisa was on loan. Because of Caroline these outings were always chaperoned by Secret Service agents, but Alice Grimes is convinced that the President's daughter was seldom recognized.

Many private citizens were quick to inquire what the school was costing them in taxes. The school was on a regular tuition basis which was paid entirely by the parents. The equipment was strictly regulation and all gifts were refused because Alice found there was always a string attached. Hundreds of interested persons asked for the list of books used in the school, but Alice never gave it out. There were also many letters scolding about integration. But some time previously, five-year-old Avery Hatcher, son of the assistant press secretary to the President, who was a Negro, had joined the group. (Avery quickly became very popular and, according to his father, Andy Hatcher, "had himself a ball.")

Alice made a real effort to capture a "school" feeling. She paid no special attention to Caroline, though she was always careful to tell the little girl to go "home" instead of "downstairs." The other pupils were transported in family car pools. The second year, when they brought their own lunches, they assembled in the glass-enclosed area outside the Flower Room and waited before going upstairs until Caroline arrived with her father, whom they greeted with a "good morning, Mr. President."

Though the school was kept out of the public eye, it did make the headlines once, literally with a "bang." In October 1962, Ben Bella, Premier of Algeria, was the first state guest to arrive on the White House lawn by helicopter.

There was an elaborate welcoming ceremony with a military detachment presenting arms smartly and the traditional nineteen gun salute accorded to a chief of state. Since this was a historic occasion, the children were allowed to watch from the balcony outside the Solarium. It was exciting to see the helicopters land, hear the crisp commands and the big guns booming. One little boy, standing at the end of the line, was carried away. He mimicked the officer's voice and with great relish boom-boomed after each salvo. Where the children were standing the acoustics were such that Alice Grimes could not hear the voices below. Therefore she believed that her enthusiastic but disturbing little pupil also was unheard. But his every syllable had echoed loud and clear, and participating dignitaries found it difficult to keep straight faces during the impressive ceremony.

After President Kennedy's assassination, the school continued for a few weeks in the White House. Then it met in the British embassy until the end of the school year.

"Please Do Not Disturb the Puppies"

Every presidential family had lavished affection on pets. Thomas Jefferson owned a mockingbird which perched on his shoulder and hopped upstairs behind him to bed. John Quincy Adams

John and Caroline, resplendent in Hallowe'en costumes, surprise their father in his office. Afterwards their mother took them out on a trick-or-treat expedition. The children rang the doorbells of various family friends.

The Kennedys celebrate Christmas in Palm Beach with Prince and Princess Radziwill and their children, Christina and Anthony. Provie's son is included in this portrait, still in his king's costume from a Christmas play the children had performed.

raised silkworms; Lincoln's son Tad kept a pair of goats; while each of Ulysses S. Grant's two boys owned a Shetland pony. Surprisingly, Mrs. Coolidge's favorite was a collared raccoon called Rebecca. But until the Kennedys came to the White House, Theodore Roosevelt's children had held the record for owning the greatest variety of creatures. Stars in their private zoo were a real, live black bear; a pony named Algonquin, which Quentin, the youngest, took upstairs in the elevator to his half-sister Alice's room to cheer her when she had measles; and, of course, Alice's own snake Spinach.

The Kennedy children, being younger, made up in number what their pets lacked in Roosevelt exotica. That last summer of 1963, counting Pushinka's puppies, there were nine dogs at Squaw Island, off Hyannis Port, where the Kennedys had rented a house. Among the minor Kennedy beasts were Billie and Debbie, a pair of hamster escape artists who, after frantic search, were usually retrieved from the President's bathroom. Caroline named the canary Robin; her two lovebirds Maybell and Blue-bell; while her almost mature cat was called Tom Kitten, after the Beatrix Potter character. Tom Kitten found White House living too confusing and soon took up residence in more placid surroundings as a paid boarder with Mrs. Kennedy's secretary. There, from time to time, both the First Lady and Caroline called to make sure Tom Kitten wasn't homesick.

For a brief period a waddle of ducks quacked around the White House. "I wanted something the children would love on the White House lawn," Mrs. Kennedy explained, "so we acquired the ducks." The First Lady had chicken wire painted black, tethered between the bars of the White House fence and comfortable pens built for them. But the ducks were very naughty indeed. They gobbled every tulip bud on the plants fringing the South Pool, and each day Charlie, the Welsh terrier, chased them hilariously while the infuriated gardeners, in turn, chased Charlie. Charlie, a devil-may-care character, had lived with the Kennedys quite a while. When the ducks were banished, he turned from bird-chasing to romance and became the father of Pushinka's puppies.

Pushinka was a daughter of the first dog astronaut to orbit the world and had been given to Mrs. Kennedy by Khrushchev, after

*The Kennedys pose on the porch of their summer house on
Squaw Island.*

*The family dogs were not left behind in Washington when
the Kennedy family headed to Squaw Island off Hyannis
Port for a summer vacation in 1963.*

Caroline commandeers her father's lap on board the Presidential yacht Honey Fitz.

they had met in Vienna in the late spring of 1961. Though, when Pushinka arrived from Moscow, she was billed as "No Breed," this label did not give her a social inferiority complex. Almost immediately she attracted tremendous personal attention. She pleased President Kennedy by learning to climb the ladder up to the children's tree house and to skid down the slide on the other side. She gave birth to Charlie's puppies in the men's locker room, in a wooden box which Trapes Bryant, a White House electrician, had made for her. But the locker room was used by all the men of the White House work staff, and seemed scarcely an appropriate setting for the happy mother and her many callers. So Irvin Williams, the White House horticulturist, obligingly moved out of his office to make room for the new family.*

An increasing number of well-wishers dropped in to Mr. Williams's office to admire the puppies and they became very fretful. Mrs. Kennedy tacked a sign on the door which read "Please Do Not Disturb the Puppies," but people still continued to intrude; and one evening, returning from a swim in the White House pool, the President himself stopped by. He asked Trapes Bryant what they ate, when they would open their eyes, and things like that, before noticing his wife's polite sign. When he learned that the puppies were being bothered by so many visitors, the President borrowed Bryant's pen and wrote in capitals under Mrs. Kennedy's lettering a stern KEEP OUT.

Bryant, who worked on the afternoon shift, came early on his own time to care for the dogs. He originated the idea of taking the dogs to the South Portico when the President's helicopter set down. He would hold up one or more of the family pets so that President Kennedy could pat them without stooping. Often the President would walk directly from his whirlybird and ask Bryant about their health and behavior. Besides Charlie, Pushinka and their family, the Kennedy pack now included Clipper, a police dog which Ambassador Kennedy had given his daughter-in-law; an Irish wolfhound which Caroline called Wolf; and finally a cocker spaniel, Shannon, a fresh Irish immigrant who became the President's favorite.

When the veterinarian indicated the puppies were sturdy enough to travel, President Kennedy asked Bryant to escort them

* Williams now owns Pushinka.

to Hyannis Port. "Take them all," the President said, "to surprise the children."

They went by plane, and when the children were out, he deposited all nine dogs on the front lawn. They were romping energetically when Caroline and John, thrilled and very much surprised, returned home. Bryant had been asked to dog-sit for a weekend, but the President rented him a car and a nearby motel room, so he remained a month with his charges.

Four puppies had proved too many, and it was decided to hold a contest, the winners to be the two children who wrote the most convincing letters explaining why they wanted a Pushinka pup. Some five thousand letters were received, and, out of a sampling of ten, Mrs. Kennedy chose a ten-year-old girl and a nine-year-old boy.

There were other pets too. Mrs. Kennedy hoped to keep some Irish deer on the White House lawn. The gift of Eamon de Valera, these were such shy things that she was finally convinced so public a place would never do and they were detoured directly from plane to zoo. The President of Ireland also sent John a tiny pony called Leprechaun, but most famous of all was Caroline's piebald pony Macaroni. He was soon immortalized in a song titled "My Pony, Macaroni" written by a New York pianist-composer and then picked up by the United States Navy Band. The Navy musicians played it, complete with whinnies and hoofbeats, often and successfully. Macaroni was a flexible little horse. Caroline rode him, and he pulled a small sleigh around the White House grounds when there was sufficient snow. He was stabled in a maintenance shed near the old tennis courts and traveled in a blue trailer to Glen Ora and occasionally to Camp David, the presidential hideaway near Gettysburg. Inevitably, each year, some congressman inquired whether Macaroni was costing the taxpayer money. He wasn't. His hay and oats came from Glen Ora, as did his trailer and a stableboy.

"A Casual Sort of Grandeur"

The Kennedys' private life in the White House has been described in two different ways, by an outsider looking in and an insider also looking in. Both were right in their own different ways.

A sophisticated British journalist, familiar with American mores, quoted a certain prime minister who, for obvious reasons, preferred to remain nameless. "They certainly have acquired something we have lost — " the Prime Minister mused — "a casual sort of grandeur about their evenings, always at the end of the day's business, the promise of parties, and pretty women, and music and beautiful clothes and champagne, and all that —" The Prime Minister concluded, "I must say there is something very 18th century about your new young man, an aristocratic touch there that reminds me, more than of anyone else, of Charles James Fox." (Fox was one of the most fascinating and complex characters in British political history, a brilliant orator and one of the early liberals.)

The insider was Dave Powers, the most earthy member of the Kennedy Irish Mafia, who was the President's devoted shadow. "Once you were behind the sliding door — it was a completely private life — you might trip over John-John's toys or Caroline's tricycle. It was so cosy. Here she was at home — a mother, a wife," he continued sentimentally, "and the First Lady provided it all. She was marvelous at arranging their private life as a place where John Fitzgerald Kennedy could relax and get away from all the commotion — and where, in the Oval Room, he could see people without the formality of down below."

When they had no official engagements, Mrs. Kennedy planned their evenings solely for her husband's relaxation and pleasure, and, as the anonymous Prime Minister put it so aptly, there was always a casual sort of grandeur about them. This ambiance was partly because of the setting itself, not only the White House, but the private rooms which had been done over in such exquisite taste, the lovely food and the cachet of Mrs. Kennedy's presence. There was an indefinable excitement in being invited to dine with the President and his wife in their private domain, a sense of special intimacy which set their guests apart from and a cut above those who attended the more obvious entertainments in the State Rooms below.

Mrs. Kennedy made her planning seem effortless. But it was not. "We usually had guests for dinner," she said, "sometimes just two people." Most often the guests were not invited until the late afternoon. The President was seldom sure in the morning what his mood would be that evening. Perhaps he would want no one to dine and, instead, would go over his papers and get to bed early. Or perhaps he might like someone to "cheer him up." "I would check with Mrs. Lincoln in the afternoon," Mrs. Kennedy continued, "and ask her to find out whom he wanted that evening — and then have her call them." As this did not give guests much notice, they usually invited on these evenings their oldest and closest friends — the Charles Bartletts, the Benjamin Bradlees, the Ormsby-Gores, Bill Walton.

"It was great fun to go to the White House to dinner," said Charles Bartlett, "you'd arrive about seven forty-five and go up to the Oval Room. JFK would have finished his exercises and his swim. In the beginning, the swimming pool was a great novelty to his friends, and they often would take a swim, too. You'd feel fine as you sat in the Oval Room with a drink. The President, who always wore his blue suit, would sit in the rocking chair by the fire. Then you'd go in to dinner and afterwards to the room at the end of the hall — which was very cosy. Sometimes they'd play the phonograph and then, usually about ten P.M., JFK would say, 'I've some reading to do before I go to bed.' And that would be it. Sometimes, though, an aide would appear with an envelope marked 'For the President's Eyes Only' and, as he tore it open, he would wince a bit, because it was more likely to be bad news than good."

"About once every ten days I tried to plan a dinner ahead for him," Mrs. Kennedy recalled, "about eight people — very informal — but I thought it was good for him to see new faces." The First Lady asked people to these dinners whom she didn't feel she could invite at the last minute. "These guests wouldn't stay very long after coffee," she concluded, "and we would usually go to bed about eleven."

She chose a wide variety of people, all of them stimulating: sometimes they were diplomats, occasionally businessmen with outside interests. They might have André Mayer down from New York, or the Dick Goodwins, Jean Seberg, Romain Gary, or the "Chip" Bohlens, if they were back from his embassy in Paris. It was at one of these small gatherings that Greta Garbo, conspiring with the Kennedys, pretended not to recognize the President's school roommate and good friend Lemoyne Billings, who had bragged about their meeting the previous summer on the Riviera. But the most publicized of these unpublicized dinners occurred one weekend when it was too foggy for the helicopter to take off to Glen Ora. The Kennedys remained in Washington and one of their last-minute invitations was extended to Carol Channing, her husband Charles Lowe and a number of other stars who happened to be in town. Mrs. Joseph P. Kennedy was visiting her son but did not join the party. Lowe, a history enthusiast, was offered a tour of the private rooms by the President and wanted, most of all, to see the Lincoln Bed. They paused outside the Lincoln Bedroom while the President, finger to lips, opened the door a crack and peeked in. He closed it with great caution and whispered, "Sorry! The tour's off! Mother's IN the Lincoln Bed!"

Louis XVI Elegance

The Oval Room, the President's Dining Room and the Treaty Room were the three second-floor rooms in which the Kennedys did most of their private entertaining. They were beautiful rooms, individual in inspiration; and Mrs. Kennedy achieved each of the trio by entirely different means.

The transformation of the pallid Monroe Room into the gay and intriguing Treaty Room was a personal tour de force. Mrs. Kennedy rejuvenated and wittily combined furniture rescued from government storage rooms, grotesquely outsized historic paintings, and framed facsimiles of United States diplomatic treaties, all within the confines of the flamboyant Victorian era.

The President's Dining Room, which had been a sitting room before Mrs. Kennedy remodeled the second-floor private quarters, became a showplace of the dignified American Federal period through gifts from a handful of wealthy Kennedy friends and White House enthusiasts. The Oval Room, an integral part of the White House architectural plan, was furnished and redecorated through the generosity of a single donor who, uninterested in public recognition, wished only to offer a charming retreat for the private pleasure of the First Family.

When the Kennedys came to the White House, the Oval Room contained two TV sets and a few pieces of furniture; but refurbished, it became the First Lady's favorite. It was a large room, grand yet practical since it served as their best drawing room and the place preferred by the President for his most important conferences. Fortunately, the changes were not undertaken piecemeal but as an entity under the close supervision of Mrs. Kennedy, the guidance of experts, and the carte blanche collaboration of Mr. and Mrs. John Loeb.

This elegant redoing of the Oval Room came about almost accidentally. It was obvious, when Mrs. Kennedy's White House Fine Arts Committee was being set up, that its membership should be politically bipartisan. An outstanding Republican member, interested in the arts, was indicated. Mrs. Henry Parish, the decorator, suggested Mr. Loeb, the head of an outstanding New York investment firm. Though Mrs. Loeb was a niece of the late Democratic Senator Herbert Lehman of New York, her husband was then a confirmed Republican. They were both connoisseurs of fine furniture and had assembled an admired collection of Impressionist paintings. Mr. Loeb was unable to be present at the first committee meeting. But when Mrs. Kennedy, whom he had never met, wired him, John Loeb came to the second. He was captivated by the First Lady's earnestness of purpose and charm.

In the spring of 1961 Mr. and Mrs. Loeb came to Washington and dined upstairs with the President and Mrs. Kennedy. Eager to contribute to the White House Restoration, they were permitted to make a survey of the private as well as the public rooms. They decided that the Oval Room was not only the most attractive but the room that would be most rewarding to redo. They offered to redecorate and refurnish it completely.

Mrs. Kennedy wrote them a letter immediately:

Dear Mr. and Mrs. Loeb: — You cannot imagine how touched and appreciative I am that you want to help with our Oval Room. It is not a public room — so that makes you both so much more patriotic — to wish to help in a room which thousands of tourists will not see except in photographs.

It is my favorite room in the White House — the one where I think the heart of the White House is — where the President receives all the Heads of State who visit him — where the honor guard is formed to march downstairs to "Hail to the Chief" — All ceremonies and all the private talks that really matter happen in that room — and it has the most beautiful proportions of any in the White House —

It has always been so ghastly and so neglected — Every future President would be so happy to have it a room he could be proud of —

This was the first in a flock of letters exchanged, consulting on the furnishings and reporting on progress. Mrs. Kennedy's enthusiastic letters were lengthy as always and sometimes totaled four pages, each side covered with her handwriting. Once, realizing this fact, she wrote: "Forgive me this endless letter. I think I must get larger writing paper."

Since the Oval Room was private, historic furnishings were not sought. "I think it would be rather appropriate to have it Louis XVI which Presidents Madison and Jefferson both loved & had in the White House —" Mrs. Kennedy had written Mr. and Mrs. Loeb. So it was redecorated in eighteenth-century style with the Louis XVI furnishings which best suited its high ceiling and ample size.

Slowly, the beautiful furnishings were found; some of the most notable were discoveries of Mrs. Charles Wrightsman, a recognized authority on eighteenth-century French furniture and a prime mover in the White House Restoration. "I have combed Paris and have collected photographs of the things I like best. Everything is so expensive and pretty things are so rare it is depressing," Jayne Wrightsman wrote to Mrs. Parish. "I found a set of furniture stamped J. LeLarge consisting of a canapé and six side chairs. The model is charming and they would completely furnish the room. It would be more simple than gold chairs but I think it might be very chic and in some ways more practical. At present the chairs are badly painted and they must be completely re-painted. The set would go extremely well in the room as it is simple and of a lovely quality and not too fragile for our needs."

Mrs. Wrightsman had photographs and scale drawings of the "discoveries" sent to Mrs. Kennedy. The authenticity of the furniture was verified by experts, then the set was reserved for Mrs. Kennedy and John Loeb's decision. Set aside, too, then sent to the White House were bronze candelabra strung with chains of rock crystal beads; handsome gilded bronze andirons; and, a wonderful find, a spinach-green marble mantelpiece ornamented with a very American eagle carved in white marble.

Mrs. Kennedy, who supervised everything right down to the precise placing of a Chamberlain-Worcester ashtray, traced a number of designs for the elaborately looped yellow draperies and rejected several samples as "not crisp enough" for the paler silk undercurtains which she eventually obtained. The sofas were upholstered in gold silk taffeta, the pillows in gold silk brocade, and of the ten side chairs, four were covered in brown. "— ten makes too many in yellow — gives a suite-look which I hate," she noted to the decorator. "I rather like them brown — so let's try it — as it's just 4 side chairs & if it is a mistake, I'll re-do it myself."

Mrs. Kennedy rushed the workmen impatiently. Finally, when it was done, she wrote Mr. Loeb how much the President appreciated the lovely room. "I never dreamt anything so perfect could happen. A million, million thanks! Shall we have a little statue of you on the mantelpiece?"

Superb American Federal

In the Kennedy scheme for private living those invited to dine with them upstairs without fanfare sipped their apéritifs in the Oval Room and sat down to table in the President's Dining Room; and afterwards, the men repaired to the Treaty Room for coffee and cigars. These were such different rooms: the Louis XVI elegance of the Oval Room, the Treaty Room, a dream of Victorian furbelows, while the President's Dining Room was superb American Federal.

The "new look" of the President's Dining Room was not completed until the autumn of 1962; before then, furniture from the N Street house filled it. Several of the "new" antiques, pieces fashioned by eighteenth-century Maryland cabinetmakers, had been drawn to White House attention through letters from the owners, while others had been bought directly from dealers.

Historically speaking the most interesting piece in the room is one of the few objects known to have been saved when the White House was burned in 1814. A small wooden case with brass rail handles, it had been designed as a portable medicine cabinet and was presumably a possession of the Madisons. It had been looted by a British soldier and belatedly returned by one of his descendants in 1939. (The case is on permanent loan to the White House by the National Archives.)

The mantelpiece, too, was of unusual historic interest. It had been made by a Philadelphia artist in 1817. A center plaque depicted the Battle of Lake Erie, with Perry's immortal words "We have met the enemy and they are ours" carved on a fluted marble riband above the battle scene, and busts of Washington and Franklin adorning the plinths of the flanking columns.

The most conventional pieces included a serving table attributed to John Shaw, the famous Annapolis cabinetmaker; a hunt board with drawer pulls made of silver; and a very special sideboard inlaid with a satinwood American eagle, which had Daniel Webster's initials carved inside a drawer.

There were extravagantly looped silk curtains in two tones of blue which were copied from an early nineteenth-century design book and a Waterford crystal chandelier, which is perhaps the most traveled object in the White House. This shining fixture was purchased in London and given "anonymously" to President Truman by the late Chester Dale, a famed collector of modern art. In 1948 the chandelier hung in the Red Room; then for a decade, from 1952–1962, it lighted the Blue Room. Briefly, in 1963, it was moved to the Green Room, until finally that same year Mrs. Kennedy anchored it, possibly permanently, in the President's Dining Room. (It still hangs there.)

The pedestal dining table and the accompanying side chairs were Sheraton in style. Most of the chairs had rectangular backs with a center slat carved in a knot of tracery and were copies of the originals. Many of the antique chairs were soon relegated to the sidelines, because President Kennedy, never a placid "sitter," broke or cracked so many of them.

Mrs. Kennedy liked to have the oval table set with white place mats embroidered in white and, from dinner to dinner, she changed the china services. Perhaps her favorite was the purple-bordered china that had been ordered during the Lincoln administration. She had found the plates "stacked underneath great shelves" in a White House basement closet. Mrs. Kennedy recognized the distinctively colored border and had the china brought upstairs to the President's Dining Room. There was enough of the set still intact to serve eight to ten people. That same evening the Lincoln plates were used at a private dinner given by President and Mrs. Kennedy for Senator and Mrs. Albert Gore of Tennessee. Later, several other similarly incomplete sets of presidential china were transferred to the new upstairs dining room where they were used constantly and much admired. On the side tables Mrs. Kennedy often placed pieces of old silver which President Andrew Jackson had bought from Baron de Tuyll, a czarist minister, when he returned to St. Petersburg from Washington.

But all these delightful pieces of mahogany, silver and crystal were really incidental to the magnificent scenic wallpaper which covered the walls of the President's Dining Room. The background of sky, clouds, woods, lawns, rivers, lakes, waterfalls was similar to that of the scenic paper which now embellishes the walls of the Diplomatic Reception Room at the south entrance. Both had been made by Jean Zuber of Alsace in the early part of the nineteenth century — but with an important difference in subject matter. The Diplomatic Reception Room paper portrayed "Scenic America," in other words, what Europeans of the period imagined America looked like. The President's Dining Room paper portrayed four lively vignettes of the American Revolution. These compositions had been superimposed on the original background at a later date, in 1852–1853. They showed, in faithful detail, Lafayette commanding French troops in the capture of a redoubt on Wechawk Hill; Washington in command at the Battle of Niagara Falls; the Capitulation of the English General Cornwallis at Yorktown; and the Triumphal Entry of General Washington into Boston.

This striking wallpaper, displayed in the window of a London antique shop, had first attracted the attention of a niece and namesake of the American-born Viscountess Astor, the former Nancy Langhorne of Virginia. The younger Nancy had written to Mrs. Parish, Mrs. Kennedy's decorator. In turn Henry du Pont sent the curator of Winterthur, his famous museum, to inspect the paper. Mrs. Charles Wrightsman, a constant donor to the White House, had the paper photographed while she was in London en route to Paris. The photographs were sent to Lorraine Pearce, the first White House curator. Finally, there were so many letters and cables that "l'affaire" of the scenic paper became hopelessly confused. Mr. Stanley Pratt, the London antique dealer, understandably bewildered and believing the White House did not want the Jean Zuber paper, sold it to an Italian, a Dr. Goffi of Rome.

Eventually the matter was straightened out to everyone's satisfaction except, perhaps, that of Dr. Goffi, who gallantly relinquished his purchase on learning that it was truly wanted for the White House. There were just thirty-two strips of this unique paper, not quite enough to cover the high walls of the President's Dining Room. Then, a minor miracle occurred. A New England lady offered several pieces of Zuber clouds and sky to the White

House. Mrs. Vincent Astor, who had originally offered to purchase the paper, not only did so but also paid the not inconsiderable bill for the complicated installation. Now, the "Scenes of Revolutionary America" is considered one of the real treasures of the White House.

A Dream of Victorian Furbelows

Some time after the settling-in period, when Mrs. Kennedy's Restoration had taken hold, one of her most fascinating projects was creating the Treaty Room. At minimal expense, using furniture almost entirely retrieved from the White House storerooms, she was to conjure a most useful retreat where, in a pleasingly opulent atmosphere, the President might conduct necessary business in privacy; and where masculine guests, invited to dine upstairs in the Kennedy family quarters, could retire comfortably for after-dinner coffee and cigars.

"I do think every room should have a purpose," Mrs. Kennedy explained, "this can be a sitting room — my husband has so many meetings up here in this part of the house. All the men who wait to see him now sit in the hall with the baby carriages going by them. They could sit here [i.e. the newly redone Treaty Room] and talk while waiting for him."

Before President Theodore Roosevelt had banished offices from the private apartments, this sizable space had served in turn as office then Cabinet Room through the latter part of the nineteenth century. An inscription on the mantelpiece read: "This room was first used for meetings of the Cabinet during the administration of President [Andrew] Johnson and continued to be so used until the year 1902. Here the treaty of peace with Spain was signed." Theodore Roosevelt had changed the workroom into a study, and in 1929 Mrs. Hoover transformed it into a parlor. She called it the Monroe Room because in it were copies she had commissioned of three pieces of furniture preserved in the fifth President's Virginia law offices. It was not a cheerful room.

From Palm Beach, using the Chief Usher's photographs before she moved in, Mrs. Kennedy had described it to her decorator. "This is now a sitting room in which no one sits — and that sofa is where Monroe died — We could make it a cosy sitting room — and take that sofa out of it."

"The sitting room in which no one sits" was renamed when Mrs. Kennedy realized that, most probably, a number of international treaties had been signed within its confines. On one wall hung an immense oil by Theobald Chartran of *The Signing of the Peace Protocol Between Spain and the United States in 1898.* Though the actual treaty which ended the Spanish-American War was finalized in Paris,* the recording of this preliminary diplomatic contract or "Peace Protocol" was of special interest to the First Lady. For not only did the canvas portray President McKinley and other notables of the era, but the painstaking background detail proved conclusively that the ceremony had taken place in what was still called the Monroe Room.

When Mrs. Kennedy decided that the Monroe Room was to be transformed into the Treaty Room, her inquiring mind went to work at top speed. Immediately she enlisted Mr. West to help research her idea. "Mr. West. I was talking about treaties — in the Treaty Room. a) They should all be the ones that were signed in that room — that would be [Andrew] Johnson — T.R. isn't that right? Or did J. Q. Adams use that office and sign treaties there? Is there any way of finding out which were signed in the office — when the room was that — & which when Cabinet Room — probably not. So I think Treaty of Peace with Spain was obviously signed in this room. [Mrs. Kennedy was misinformed: only the preliminary protocol papers were signed there.] We should have Johnson — T.R. — & lots more treaties of 1864–1902. We could put them up on the walls also. b) When the name of treaty is printed on mat — I think date should be printed also — as it is too complicated to read treaty to find out. c) Can this be *rushed* so we'll have them before Mexico. Thank you." (The Kennedys were scheduled to make a state visit to Mexico.)

The National Archives obligingly "rushed" a number of original treaties to the White House, but the risk was too great and

* Both the mantelpiece inscription and, later, Mrs. Kennedy, were in error.

soon the priceless papers were replaced with specially framed facsimiles. The United States had participated in all kinds of treaties during that Victorian period; some were signed in the Cabinet Room; a few in pre-Johnson times when the room had been Lincoln's office; another few, ratified overseas. But President Kennedy made the Treaty Room his own when, in August 1963, the most significant concord of modern times was concluded. In that original and stimulating room, which was so particularly Jacqueline Kennedy's own creation, John Fitzgerald Kennedy, underscoring his wife's sense of history, penned his signature to the Nuclear Test Ban Treaty. Though Mrs. Kennedy had hoped to have the document signed on either General Grant's desk or Cabinet table, so many dignitaries participated in the ceremony that the smaller antiques had to be replaced with the Kennedys' own Louis XVI desk.

"Pulling the Treaty Room together" was a historical jigsaw puzzle. Before Mrs. Kennedy was satisfied, the portraits of three Presidents of the United States were hung and, in addition to the "Peace Protocol" painting, two other enormous, fantastically detailed canvases covered different walls. There was rugged old Zachary Taylor, a portrait from a famous collection of Early American paintings; a likeness of General Grant, painted from life when he was President; and Andrew Johnson, Lincoln's successor, whose portrait had hung in the Red Room until Mrs. Kennedy, finding an old photograph of the "Cabinet Room," returned the picture to its historic place.

One of the giant paintings, *The Peacemakers,* romantically portrays Lincoln, Generals Sherman and Grant, and Admiral David Porter on the warship *River Queen,* anchored off the mouth of a Virginia river. The scene was set toward the end of the Civil War and the four leaders were thought to be discussing not only the terms of military surrender but the means of Southern reconstruction as well. This remarkable painting was executed by G. F. A. Healy, a sensitive yet prolific artist, who was responsible for the gentle and contemplative portrait of Lincoln which ornaments the State Dining Room.

The third tremendous oil, one of the most beguiling in the White House, records a reception given by Lincoln in honor of General Grant on the occasion of his being named commander-in-chief of the Union Armies. Francis B. Carpenter, a New York artist, had been engaged to paint a colossal historical mural for the Capitol and was invited to the Lincoln reception. Here he busily sketched all the important people and later dovetailed these staccato impressions into a staggering whole. In recent years, historical experts have scrutinized the canvas relentlessly and identified at least 90 percent of those present at the huge gathering. Prominent in the crowd are all Lincoln's Cabinet members and, slumped in a corner seat surrounded by doting, hoopskirted ladies, is octogenarian General Winfield Scott, hero of the Mexican War of 1848.

Most of the period furnishings which Mrs. Kennedy installed in the Treaty Room were identified from old photographs or older engravings. Many pieces were rescued from White House warehouses in a state of shocking disrepair. "— practically all the furniture in this room we found so battered that there were cries of disbelief when I brought them home —" Mrs. Kennedy told an audience of millions in her televised tour of the White House, "— but when this room is finished you'll see how impressive it will be."

There were heart-backed chairs ordered by General Grant for the State Dining Room and later used in the private dining room of Rutherford B. Hayes, his successor. There was a Grant sofa, and General Grant's desk and famous Cabinet table which was equipped with a drawer for every member of the Cabinet. Grant locked them with a single key after meetings. Later, Mrs. Grant's own desk was donated to the White House and Mrs. Kennedy placed upon it an ornate malachite and marble clock which the General had bought for five hundred dollars in 1869 and which, eighty-six years afterwards, another General-President, Dwight Eisenhower, had had repaired.

A suitable wall covering had been difficult to decide upon. Finally, the picture-hung walls were covered with green "flocked" paper bordered in magenta, black and touches of green. This design had been copied from a room in the Peterson house across the street from Ford's Theatre, where the mortally wounded Lincoln had been carried that tragic night. The plum-colored velvet curtains, with scrolled edges and tasseled tiebacks, draped over lace inner curtains, were duplicates of those found in Victorian period drawings.

The upholstering, done in appropriate yet comparatively inexpensive red and green velvet, was undertaken by White House staff workmen. Among the quaint memorabilia placed in the Treaty Room is President Grant's tortoise-shell wastebasket. Several generations of family had cherished this curious object which once dangled from a drawer knob on the General's desk but now hangs demurely over the arm of a Victorian armchair.

As ultimate fillip, an overwhelmingly ornate chandelier, one of three bought by President Grant for the East Room in 1873, was installed. This chandelier has an amusing history. Theodore Roosevelt, the widely accepted story goes, was so disturbed by the tinkling of the myriad crystal prisms that he dispatched one of the trio to the Capitol office of the Vice-President with the gleeful message: "To keep the Vice-President awake!" Some time later the three noisy chandeliers were purchased by the United States Capitol, where they hung until Mrs. Kennedy tracked them down. One still tinkles in the Senate Appropriations Room, another in the Ceremonial office of the Vice-President. With the acquiescence of the then Vice-President Lyndon B. Johnson and the Senate Majority and Minority Leaders, Mrs. Kennedy retrieved the third from the Senate Connecting Corridor. On indefinite loan to the White House, the once annoying noisemaker now hangs placidly in the Treaty Room.

The offending sofa on which Mrs. Kennedy had been told President Monroe died was transferred to the East Hall, and a more "of-the-period" horsehair covering replaced the mauve brocade. The sofa itself had been given to the White House during the Eisenhower administration by descendants of the fifth President. It had never been associated definitely with Monroe's demise. He had died in New York, conventionally, it is presumed, in bed. There is no proof that he expired on this exceedingly uncomfortable couch.

Mrs. Kennedy believed it important to keep the Monroe memorabilia together. She had found, on one of her explorations, a circular, marble-topped Empire table and a china fruit basket, both bought by Monroe. These she grouped in an alcove of the wide East Hall, together with the sofa, the furniture Mrs. Hoover had ordered, and several engravings of the period. A brief description of both the antique pieces and the reproductions was placed nearby, and this area is known as the Monroe Hall.

7

Travel

A Sea of Admirers

It was Paris, June 2, 1961. At the Palais de Chaillot, several hundred members of the French Diplomatic Press Association and the Anglo-American Press Association of Paris had joined forces at a luncheon to honor a former member of their profession. Except for the head table guests, only journalists were invited and neither General de Gaulle nor any high-ranking member of his government was present. The luncheon was unusually satisfying: Saumon glacé au vin du Rhin; Koulibiac de turbot côte d'Emeraude; Coeurs d'artichaut La Fayette; Parfait Francillon — all delightfully sluiced with champagne. The coffee had been served when the guest of honor started his speech. He was, of course, John Fitzgerald Kennedy, once a young newsman, now the President of the United States, and his audience settled back in comfortable anticipation.

The President began conventionally enough: "Mr. Secretary of State, Ambassador Alphand, Ambassador Bonnet, Ambassador Gavin, Monsieur Redmond, ladies and gentlemen —" Then the President paused and lowered his voice to a more serious tone: "I do not think it entirely inappropriate to introduce myself to this audience. I am the man who accompanied Jacqueline Kennedy to Paris, and I have enjoyed it!" The President, flashing an enormous smile, paused again. There was a moment of absolute, startled stillness. Then, like a thunderclap, the audience simultaneously roared with laughter and applauded frantically.

President Kennedy's remark made headlines — and it underscored what "le tout Paris" had made abundantly clear: Jacqueline Kennedy was the stellar attraction.

The Paris chief of police had estimated the welcoming crowds lining the city streets as greater than those recorded at visits by Eisenhower or Khrushchev. He "guessed" diplomatically, "the desire to see Mrs. Kennedy swelled the crowds." As she rode from

June 1961: President de Gaulle welcomes Mrs. Kennedy as President Kennedy looks on. Madame de Gaulle is behind the First Lady.

*Escorted by President de Gaulle, Mrs. Kennedy attends the
dinner given in honor of the Kennedys at Versailles.*

Soviet Premier Nikita Khru-shchev converses with Mrs. Kennedy at an Austrian state concert given in Vienna.

During her visit to Karachi, Mrs. Kennedy met Bashir Ahmed, the Pakistani camel driver who had come to the United States the preceding year as the guest of Vice-President Johnson. The First Lady presented Bashir with a letter from the Vice-President and gave presents to his family; then she and her sister Princess Radziwill ventured a ride on Bashir's camel.

USIS PHOTO

Orly airport seated in a limousine beside Mme de Gaulle, the Paris crowds had shrieked "Jacquiii!" Next day, driving about the city, the bubble-top which her hosts provided was stopped dead time after time by jostling admirers. As she set out for a state dinner with her husband, she was photographed smiling in such a charming, startled way that the caption read: "En route to the Elysée, President Kennedy looks tenderly at 'Jackie' who seems overwhelmed by her Paris reception . . ." Even when she was pictured with her distinguished host, the press descriptions were sentimental. Before the glittering dinner in the Hall of Mirrors at Versailles cameramen snapped the General helping Mrs. Kennedy to her seat at the magnificent table: "Attentive, almost fatherly, de Gaulle shows 'Jackie' to her place before last night's dinner."

In Vienna, several days later, when Mrs. Kennedy and Mme Khrushchev were luncheon guests of the Austrian president's daughter, thousands jammed the square in front of the Pallavicini Palace, calling for "Jackeee." The French are volatile people and the Viennese notably warmhearted, so perhaps the enthusiasm was to be expected. But when she arrived in conservative England there was no longer any doubt that Mrs. Kennedy had become a world figure in her own right. The Kennedys had come on an unofficial visit to attend the christening of the First Lady's niece. Yet airport crowds put up with dismal weather to shrill her name. In London, while the usually resourceful British bobbies did manage to control traffic around the President's car, they sometimes were forced to leave Mrs. Kennedy's limousine temporarily stranded in a sea of admirers.

This unsought recognition was nebulous yet, paradoxically, since it had been sparked by the reflection of her personality, it was real. Now, wherever she went she would inescapably be viewed as a symbol of her country. (The following year, when Mrs. Kennedy visited India and Pakistan, thousands of her new fans, in all seriousness, called her the Amerika Maharani — the Queen of America.) She had been First Lady scarcely four months and had not expected — not did she at first realize — that her triumph in Paris and throughout Europe would also make her a fantastic political asset to her husband at home.

Later, a politician urging her presence at a series of political gatherings was to say, "It would help a great deal if Mrs. Kennedy came. She had captured the imagination of the nation and particularly the women." He explained, "She had come to stand for culture, beauty, fashion . . ." In a more informal way, a newspaper vendor in St. Louis would sum up Mrs. Kennedy's pulling power. Charles Bartlett, on a journalistic assignment in the Missouri city, learned from a newspaper headline that Mrs. Kennedy was to join her husband on the final trip to Texas. As he was about to take the newspaper off the stand, the old newsman smiled, "Now everything's going to be great," he said chattily to Bartlett. "This is a girl with a lot of savvy!"

Though Mrs. Kennedy had the obvious advantages of being young and lovely looking, the facility of speaking fluent French, plus a catchy nickname, she had achieved success abroad as she had, perhaps less dramatically, at home; by being her natural self and by her "savvy" in paying meticulous attention to every detail concerning her trip. Her manners were not only perfect but unshakable. She had an inquiring mind, and she knew just what she wanted to see and do. She was warm, friendly, curious and not afraid to show her feelings. She planned carefully to be appropriately dressed for each engagement, and if necessary would cheerfully undertake the tedious process of changing her clothes several times a day.

In Paris, Mrs. Kennedy charmed the Parisians by taking time to view an exhibition of Impressionist paintings with the Minister of Culture. Then, unexpectedly, she delighted all the French by naming as favorite a nude, dramatically painted by Manet. She made an excursion to Malmaison, the plaisance of Napoleon's Josephine, to admire the handsome Empire furnishings, which were in key, both in period and in elegance, with her plans for White House Restoration. Mrs. Kennedy gave a television interview in perfect French; and as the first wife of a visiting United States President to preside at a formal press conference, she kept it just that. In the dignified American embassy, she greeted each feminine member of the Gallic Fourth Estate personally, and in their own tongue. She exclaimed in unaffected delight when the Mayor of Paris presented her with the tiniest of gold watches. She flattered everyone in France by her Parisian-designed gown and coiffure at the historic Versailles gala — and by visibly beguiling the discriminating General de Gaulle.

In Vienna, Mrs. Kennedy appealed to the people by her excitement when she watched breathlessly the incomparable Lippizaner horses mincing through their complex, set-to-music maneuvers. But diplomats were impressed because Nikita Khrushchev was so openly intrigued. Before greeting President Kennedy at the state banquet in Schoenbrunn Palace, the Soviet Chairman asked permission to shake hands with the American First Lady. He exclaimed, "It's beautiful!" as he eyed Mrs. Kennedy's gown; and, resisting all other entanglements, he insisted on sitting on a sofa next to the First Lady while they sipped after-dinner coffee.

On her own, Mrs. Kennedy was to make a single, semiofficial trip to India and Pakistan; and she accompanied her husband on all except the final state visit. The joint journeyings of President and Mrs. Kennedy included Canada, France and Austria, Venezuela and Colombia, and Mexico. In the early summer of 1963, as she was to have a baby, Mrs. Kennedy remained home. President Kennedy, accompanied in relays by sisters and his sister-in-law, Princess Radziwill, flew to Ireland, West Germany and Italy.

The preliminary planning for each state visit, and for Mrs. Kennedy's solo trip as well, was unbelievably complicated. Tish Baldridge, in a rare moment of leisure, once sat down and tallied all the items of baggage and arrangements that had to be dealt with in order to insure a successful visit. Incredibly, they added up to 439! Mrs. Kennedy's social secretary was in a good position to know, for she not only synchronized the home planning, but for several of the trips acted as "advance man," sent ahead to check that everything was laid on properly and in split-second working order.

Every minute of the journey was accounted for. Long in advance, the places Mrs. Kennedy was to visit were determined. In Washington, the White House found out what the host government would like her to see and do, and conversely, what her own government wanted *her* to do. Paris, for instance, presented no problem. Mrs. Kennedy's predilections in art and eighteenth-century French history were well known. But her most absorbing interest was children. In every country Mrs. Kennedy visited a children's hospital. She always carried baskets full of treats for the small patients. And American candy bars and giant lollypops were high on the list among the magic 439!

But in Paris, instead of a hospital, the First Lady visited the Ecole de Puériculture, a free dispensary for young children and a training school where highly qualified nurses were taught the care of incubator babies. Mrs. Kennedy herself had had three premature babies and would have a fourth. Their care was a subject close to her heart. So instead of sweets, her gift to the shabby little dispensary was the gay redecorating and furnishing of a waiting room.

Mrs. Kennedy put a great deal of thought into the selection of imaginative presents to be given on her trips abroad. For Pope John XXIII's desk, she commissioned the design of an exquisite, velvet-lined vermeil box as a receptacle for letters. To the Institute for the Protection of Children in Mexico she bought a set of four washable wall panels colored with an all-over design of toys and animals to brighten the nursery; and for the First Lady of Mexico, a vermeil bureau set. In India, she presented to Mrs. Gandhi a Children's Carnival of Art for the youngsters of her country. A play and art center for children between four and twelve, it was set up so that children could play and paint, while parents and teachers looked on without being seen. For General and Mme de Gaulle, Mrs. Kennedy's gift was a framed watercolor titled *Boulevard des Capucines,* painted by an American artist, Maurice Brazil Prendergast, who had studied in Paris at the end of the nineteenth century.

The transportation and delivery of these often cumbersome gifts were included in Tish's list of 439, as well as scores of signed photographs, and smaller objects like signed silver bowls for lesser officials, silver pen and pencil sets for their children and a cowboy suit for the five-year-old son of a special Maharana, reputedly a direct descendant of the sun.

And what else? Checking of such everyday items as food preferences, room temperature, staff facilities, doctors, writing paper, calling cards, useful telephone numbers, lists of local dignitaries due for thank-you notes. More? transportation schedules were checked and rechecked, and in countries where tummy trouble

While on a state visit to Mexico with her husband, the First Lady greets costumed schoolchildren who presented her with roses.

While in New Delhi, Mrs. Kennedy visits Bal Sahyog, an institution for needy children. With her are Mrs. Indira Gandhi and Mrs. John Kenneth Galbraith, wife of the U.S. Ambassador to India.

President Kennedy receives a tumultuous reception in Galway, Ireland. Mrs. Kennedy, expecting the birth of Patrick, was unable to accompany him on this trip.

was rife, a supply of American or European bottled water was included.

Perhaps the most unusual of the 439 items bobbed up only in India: it was an elephant-mounting platform built especially for Mrs. Kennedy. Elephants, in their native countries, are usually mounted from a *machan,* an open, stepladder-like platform. There had been no complication when foreign ladies climbed aboard an outsize pachyderm until the advent of short skirts. When Mrs. Kennedy was scheduled to ride in a howdah atop one of the gorgeously bedizened elephants at Amber, an abandoned Moghul city maintained as a tourist attraction, the visit of Queen Elizabeth the previous year was suddenly recalled. For this occasion Her Majesty had worn a safari outfit — bush jacket *and* trousers. But Mrs. Kennedy was to wear a summer dress. Then and there the local authorities and those responsible for Mrs. Kennedy's visit agreed the everyday peek-a-boo equipment would not be dignified. So a high, solid platform, covered with cloth and decorated with marigold garlands was erected. Then, assisted by the steadying hand of Ambassador Galbraith, the First Lady stepped aboard her mount at howdah level!

In addition to the 439 items which insured the official success of foreign visits, Mrs. Kennedy added a few for her own personal purposes. In advance she wrote a stack of postcards which she asked Mr. West to stamp with real stamps and deliver personally to Caroline and John each day. From the Carlyle Hotel, before leaving New York, her memo read: "I have numbered these cards. Could you give one each day to the children — in order of numbers — and put stamps on them first as they want to believe it was mailed — Could you send some of them to Florida — 2 or 3 each — and put stamps on them first as they want to believe it was mailed — seal them. Thanks." From India where Air India had presented her with two very young tiger cubs, she replenished the stock of postcards. "Dear Mr. West, Could you put stamps on these and give them to the children each day in their numbered order —

"If you read Caroline's No. 4 you will be delighted to learn that I am bringing home 2 baby tiger cubs — to keep in a cage at the White House for a couple of months — then give them to the zoo. Could you find out what kind of cage to make for them and

*Mrs. Kennedy is greeted by Prime Minister Nehru during
her visit to India.*

*President Ayub Khan of Pakistan escorts the First Lady in a state landau as
they arrive at the stadium for the spectacular Lahore Horse and Cattle Show.*

if they can be outside — unless they're wanted in the Flower Room!" Thanks JBK." (Unfortunately, but perhaps fortunately for Mr. West, both cubs died a few days later.)

President Kennedy set great store by his visit to Ireland. Though this was the one major trip on which Mrs. Kennedy could not go, she wished to make every detail perfect for him. The First Lady took an active part in the planning and was especially solicitous that the social amenities be properly handled. In 1963 she spelled out her instructions in a longer than usual memo to the Social Office.

MEMO TO SOCIAL OFFICE:

I would like each present to be labelled — as to contents — city it is for — person it is for — date JFK expects to be in that city and give it.

I would also like Mrs. Lincoln given a list — Have duplicates of the list made —

Will these presents travel with JFK — or will they be sent on ahead to the Embassy in each place? I think they should be sent ahead — if it isn't too late — as it is always such a rush getting the baggage — and someone in each Embassy who you must contact — must be responsible for getting them to Mrs. Lincoln — some JFK will want to give in person — others for children, etc. will have to be delivered. There should be someone *over there* — who can cope with getting them delivered the proper way.

Mrs. Lincoln will also decide which of the presents and little souvenirs JFK gets — to bring home — could someone *over there* make a list of *everything* from State presents to little booties which should be acknowledged. Mrs. Lincoln will do her best to keep a list — but no one actually on the trip can do it properly as in some cities they will just be there a few hours —

One thing I told Mrs. Lincoln your office will do is acknowledge the presents when they come home. JFK's office is much too busy. So she will give you a list when she gets back — and you should get a batch of JFK's writing paper and prepare the letters for his signature. You will know how to thank for booties.

However, on the letters to Presidents, Prime Ministers and Mayors, you should check with JFK first as he may be writing them longer letters himself — just make sure his letters include a couple of sentences thanking for the presents. Discuss this with Mrs. Lincoln or maybe you should speak to Kenny as he will be on the trip and know what to say about each place visited. JBK.

Far in advance of each official trip Jacqueline Kennedy would plan her wardrobe with Provie. This was more difficult than it might seem, as the First Lady's engagements were so numerous and varied in character that a complete change of costume was frequently necessary three or four times in a day. Usually there were nine different items to be laid out for each such change: a hat, coat, dress, shoes, stockings, handbag, gloves, jewelry and underwear. Since the overall effect would always be subjected to passionate public scrutiny, at least eight of the nine items had to be assembled with this very much in mind. As the wardrobe plan gradually formalized, Provie listed each outfit and the accompanying accessories in a big ledgerlike book, which was seldom out of her sight.

Logistically, the most complicated trip was Mrs. Kennedy's personal journey to India and Pakistan in the spring of 1962. The adventure had been suggested by a close Kennedy friend, Kenneth Galbraith, the United States Ambassador to India. Galbraith persuaded Mrs. Kennedy that she could make a semi-private, cultural visit. But once the First Lady had accepted, her program in both countries became so alarmingly complicated that she shortened the trip by ten days. "No one could be interested in me *that* long!" she told Galbraith.

The trip commenced conventionally in Rome with an audience with Pope John XXIII. But when Mrs. Kennedy reached the Indian subcontinent her schedule zigzagged through a dizzy maze of state dinners, luncheons, tented lawn parties; ceremonies at the mausoleums of Gandhi and Jinnah; inspections and gift-giving in children's hospitals; boating down the Ganges; a moonlight look at the Taj Mahal; a sunset reception in the Shalimar water gardens; watching performances of tribal sword dancers; snake charmers; and a plethora of unusual athletic events — jumping with the crack New Delhi mounted guard, riding ornately painted elephants and a tassel-strung camel; driving in an open landau pulled by six glistening black horses to inaugurate a Pakistani livestock show; and next day, by contrast, riding in a diminutive pony trap with President Ayub Khan holding reins while a beturbaned dwarf groom stood proudly in the rumble behind.

A galaxy of costume changes and special outfits were imperative to meet even the minimum sartorial demands of these exotic happenings. Many of Mrs. Kennedy's informal frocks had been bought in past years and several of her evening gowns had been worn at White House dinners. Nevertheless, they all appeared dazzlingly new to the throngs who came to see her.

Each morning, afternoon and every evening, Mrs. Kennedy appeared exquisitely gowned. A squad of sixty-two journalists and cameramen covered the trip. The cameras seldom ceased clicking; and the newswomen, who reported everything Mrs. Kennedy said, did and wore, and were often given to feline comments, were now too impressed to be other than complimentary.

This shining perfection, however, was not done with mirrors but by efficient organization and hard work. The luggage logistics which Provie handled were staggering. The two-day stopover in Rome had been easy. But four trunks had been sent ahead to India, and once in New Delhi a trunk was packed and sent ahead to Pakistan and another to Jaipur, the capital of Rajastan State. Here, as an accommodating political gesture, Mrs. Kennedy was scheduled to be an overnight guest of the Rajastan Governor, who represented a liberal party; and then to "vacation" two days, sheltered from the press and without public engagements, in the pink palace of the glamorous Maharajah and Maharani of Jaipur, who were conservatives. To dispatch these trunks to their separate destinations, Provie had been required to unpack everything and then repack the contents in separate suitcases geared for shorter stops.

A single valise was prepared meticulously to carry everything needed for the next scheduled event. Wherever Mrs. Kennedy went, a car was always waiting to whisk Provie and this special bag ahead so that any costume change would be laid out for her when she arrived. Occasionally, the First Lady would choose to substitute one dress for another. Then Provie might have to delve to the bottom of a trunk for a handbag or other vital articles. Packing was made even more difficult on one-night stands, as the suitcases were picked up at 7 A.M. and therefore had to be ready the previous night.

Provie herself always carried Mrs. Kennedy's jewelry and briefcase. The briefcase contained a variety of small things:

writing paper; information about places on the itinerary; and list after list, with brief profiles attached, of the important and interesting people Mrs. Kennedy would meet. These she studied on planes, on trains, and undoubtedly in her room at night.

8

The Restoration

"The Sacred Cow"

Mrs. Kennedy had seldom gone to the White House even when her husband was a member of Congress. But she did attend a single evening reception and several of the traditional annual luncheons given for Senate wives by every First Lady. "The White House always looked so sad," she commented. Her tour with Mrs. Eisenhower had not changed her impression. "I always loved beautiful houses; all the time I was in Europe I had gone out of my way to see so many. So I suppose that when I knew I would be living there [i.e. the White House] it wasn't a matter of wanting to restore it or not, it was something that had to be done just as one had to do something about the food."

Her initial step as First Lady-to-be was to ask the Library of Congress to lend her everything in their files pertaining to the Executive Mansion. There were about forty books in all and a great many articles which, through the years, had been published in magazines and art reviews. After her son was born, she took these to Palm Beach. There she not only managed to read them all but to retain almost every detail with remarkable precision. Later, on several occasions, the First Lady was able to identify furniture discovered in government warehouses or tucked away in some unexpected White House nook, because she recognized it from sketches or photographs in some old publication. Gradually, from this intensive study, Mrs. Kennedy evolved a special attitude toward the White House. "Everything in the White House must have a reason for being there," she explained. "It would be a sacrilege merely to 'redecorate' — a word I hate — It must be *restored* and that has nothing to do with decoration. That is a question of scholarship."

The future First Lady discussed her still uncertain plans with Mrs. Charles Wrightsman, a Palm Beach neighbor. Jayne Wrightsman, who shuttled back and forth from Paris to her magnificently furnished Palm Beach villa or even more splendidly accoutered New York apartment, was a much respected connoisseur of eighteenth-century French furniture and painting. She was delighted with Jacqueline Kennedy's ideas. Both Mrs. Wrightsman and her husband, who was taken into their confidence, agreed to help. But before any plans could be formulated, the complete approval of the President-elect had to be obtained.

The President-elect approved of his wife's plans but nevertheless was wary of public reaction. He turned to Clark Clifford for advice. Clifford had made his first Washington success as adviser and attorney for President Truman and had therefore enjoyed considerable White House exposure. Currently, Clark Clifford was not only a Kennedy friend and personal lawyer, but also was in command of the important transition arrangements between the Republican administration of Eisenhower and the Kennedy administration takeover for the Democrats. His advice to Jack Kennedy was both clear and succinct. "The White House is a sacred cow of the American people and woe to any President who touches it." He based this dictum in part upon his intimate recollection of the country-wide commotion caused when President Truman added a second-floor balcony to the South Portico of the White House. Any attempt to change the White House, he was convinced, would antagonize the nation.

At this moment of uncertainty, Charles Wrightsman made what proved to be a most discerning suggestion. Henry Francis du Pont, creator and owner of the prestigious Winterthur Museum near Wilmington, Delaware, was a close friend of the Wrightsmans'. Mr. du Pont was also acknowledged as the supreme authority on 1640–1840 period American furniture and decorative objects. Charles Wrightsman was convinced it would insure national approval for any restoration project if his friend could be persuaded to head a White House committee and to accept responsibility for the ultimate result. The Wrightsmans broached the subject with diplomatic finesse to Harry du Pont who, somewhat reluctantly, accepted.

Mrs. Kennedy had never met either Mr. du Pont or Ruth, his wife. The du Ponts wintered at Boca Grande, in Florida, and when they invited Mrs. Kennedy and Mrs. Wrightsman for luncheon, Mr. Wrightsman chartered a small plane to fly the two ladies from Palm Beach. Their host had suggested they bring bathing suits and, in the same informal spirit, they dressed in slacks and smart pullovers. On arrival in Boca Grande they were dismayed to discover that the du Ponts had arranged a sizable luncheon party and that the feminine guests without exception wore not only summer frocks but stylish hats as well!

Despite this sartorial gaffe, the meeting was a great success. Mrs. Wrightsman had taken care to brief Mr. du Pont on the future First Lady's capabilities: "— she has a tremendous sense of organization," Jayne had said, "— is never lazy, never wastes a minute, makes a note of everything — and she has a wonderful gift for cozy arrangement." Mrs. Kennedy had brought with her a selection of the Congressional Library books as well as complete documentation on White House history. Together they explored the possibilities of a White House Restoration and carefully mapped plans for what was to become the Fine Arts Committee for the White House. Predictably Mr. du Pont was impressed with Mrs. Kennedy's organizational ability as well as her knowledge and obvious flair for what she wished to undertake. Though he was usually extremely chary of being quoted, Mr. du Pont admitted to Mrs. Wrightsman that he was "captivated" by the future First Lady.

Mrs. Kennedy was openly enthusiastic. "I didn't know or care what Mr. du Pont's politics were," she explained. "Without him on the committee I didn't think we would accomplish much — and with him I knew there would be no criticism. The day he agreed to be Chairman was the biggest red letter day of all."

A few days after the Inauguration, President Kennedy, anxious to make sure his wife was not plunging rashly into an impossible commitment, invited Clark Clifford to a leisurely luncheon *à trois* with the First Lady. They discussed first the mechanical details of running the White House. Clifford then recalled the Mansion had been gutted during the 1948–1952 Renovation and that President Truman, who had sponsored this drastic reconstruction, had told him the new interior was "inferior" and even "tacky." Funds for redecorating the haphazardly furnished but now sturdy building had been grossly inadequate, a fact which the history-conscious Harry Truman had deplored. Mrs. Kennedy told Clifford of her desire to "make the White House the most perfect house in the United States" and outlined her idea of launching a guidebook to pay for this perfection. Clifford, well aware that the First Lady now was backed by impressive people and irrevocably determined to carry out her plans, agreed to organize the legal work for whatever committees she would deem necessary.

On February 23, 1961, scarcely a month after Jacqueline Kennedy had become First Lady, the Fine Arts Committee for the White House was established. The purpose of this committee, as the initial White House press release stated rather uncertainly, was to "locate authentic furniture of the date of the building of the White House (1802) and the raising of the funds to purchase this furniture as gifts for the White House." Almost immediately, however, the committee adopted a broader approach to the project. It was felt that the restoration should reflect the whole history of the presidency of the United States as represented by furnishings both historically appropriate and of museum quality. It was unfortunate that a second press release announcing this decision was not issued immediately.

The confused wording of the first White House press release inspired *Life* to a quick follow-up: in the March 3 issue an editorial was published titled "Forward to 1802." The editorial quoted David Finley's endorsement of furnishing the White House according to a historical theme: but *Life* disagreed with this premise of a one-period décor and suggested that too much had been happening in the Executive Mansion *since* 1802. *Life* then outlined amusingly what they thought should be restored to the White House. (Some of the items thus enumerated actually were returned to the White House: Mrs. Kennedy "restored" the Victorian chairs Lincoln used, and the typewriter on which Woodrow Wilson had tapped his 1917 Declaration of War was given back by the sons of President Wilson's doctor.) The editorial ended with a gay query: "Since when did the New Frontier end in 1802?"

The *Life* editorial triggered a barrage of additional press comment. The First Lady was besieged with requests for both personal interviews and appointments to photograph her restoration activities. To clarify her conception of the White House

Restoration and explain to the public her basic reasons for carrying it out, Mrs. Kennedy decided to cooperate with *Life*. The interview, illustrated with handsome photographs, was painstakingly prepared and appeared in the September 1 issue, six months after the editorial.

Though Mrs. Kennedy related fascinating stories about the adventures involved in her efforts to restore the White House in the interview, her definition of what the Mansion represented and her reasoning on how its restoration should be undertaken were brief and to the point. "— the White House does and must continue to represent the living, evolving character of the Executive Branch of the National Government. Its occupants have been persons of widely different geographical, social and economic backgrounds, and accordingly of different cultural and intellectual tastes — it would therefore be highly inadvisable, even if it were possible, to fix on a single style of decorating and furnishings for a building that ought to reflect the whole history of the Presidency. This," she continued, "should put to rest the fears of people who think we might restore the building to its earliest period, leaving all that came after; or fill it with French furniture; or hang modern pictures all over it — and paint it whatever color we like. The White House belongs to our past and no one who cares about our past would treat it that way —"

Mrs. Kennedy became honorary chairman of the Fine Arts Committee for the White House, and Mr. du Pont was chairman. There were fourteen committee members, all of them expert in the fields of painting and the decorative arts. Since the majority had more than sufficient means to acquire the most costly possessions, their contacts with owners and dealers in superlative antiques were invaluable.

There were eight women on the Fine Arts Committee for the White House:

Mrs. C. Douglas Dillon and her husband, the Secretary of the Treasury, were to set the period for the newly glowing Red Room with a gift of historically priceless American Empire furniture.

Mrs. Charles W. Engelhard, wife of the chairman and president of the Engelhard Industries of Newark, New Jersey, took a warm personal interest in the White House. The magnificent Engelhard contributions would include necessities such as handsome Lowestoft ashtrays; the cheerful redecoration of the Family Dining Room (which the First Lady had found so gloomy) ; and the major pieces of rare Federal furniture which would add great elegance to the President's Dining Room, created by the Kennedys in their living quarters.

Mrs. Henry Ford II was to involve the Ford Motor Company in the White House. In February 1962 the company presented a portrait of Alexander Hamilton by John Trumbull, which had been bought from the Edsel Ford estate some years previously. Mrs. Kennedy, on accepting the painting, thought it appropriate to hang the likeness of the first Secretary of the Treasury in the Red Room which Douglas Dillon, the current incumbent, had so handsomely furnished.

Mrs. Albert Lasker, though best known through the Mary and Albert Lasker Foundation for her work in medical research and psychiatry, had been active in professional art circles during a previous marriage. She had assembled a famed collection of paintings which spanned the years from Corot through Picasso. Imaginative as well as generous, Mary Lasker was to donate, often anonymously, a galaxy of treasures to the White House. Among them would be a Savonnerie rug for the Blue Room; a sofa which had belonged to Daniel Webster; a pair of Baltimore inlaid card tables fine enough to grace the Green Room; a bust of George Washington in the manner of Houdon. And, quite apart from the restoration project, Mary Lasker would make a personal gift to President Kennedy of a bright modern painting which he placed in his private cabin in *Air Force One.*

Mrs. Henry Parish, Mrs. Kennedy's decorator, worked tirelessly on the restoration project from its inception and was responsible for some of its basic ideas. Mrs. Parish and her husband would present a Victorian settee and two side chairs which had been given in 1862 as a wedding present to Mr. and Mrs. John de Witt by President and Mrs. Abraham Lincoln.

Mrs. George Henry Warren had a more extensive practical knowledge of restoration problems than any other committee member. Mrs. Warren, alone, had initiated the action which saved historic Newport from certain obliteration. She had raised countless thousands of dollars toward this end and had interested people all over the world in her successful methods of preservation. She had served as president of the Preservation Society of Newport County for fifteen years. Specifically, for the White House, she was to persuade a group of her Newport friends to contribute to the purchase of a handsome marble bust, attributed to Houdon, of Comte d'Estaing, a comrade-in-arms of General Lafayette.

Mrs. Paul Mellon, wife of the president of the National Gallery of Art, daughter-in-law of its founder, and a noted horticulturist in her own right, was to play a specially intimate role in the White House rejuvenation. Mrs. Mellon was to redesign the President's Rose Garden and transform the drooping East Garden into the charming Jacqueline Kennedy Garden, which was completed after Mrs. Kennedy had left the White House. Mrs. Mellon also set up what was to become an admired White House feature, the "Flemish" type of flower arrangements which Mrs. Kennedy preferred. She supervised the rehabilitation of government-owned greenhouses to supply the White House with plants, shrubs and the less exotic flowers. Beside this individual contribution, Mr. and Mrs. Mellon were to make an outstanding historic gift: a much sought-after portrait of President Thomas Jefferson by Rembrandt Peale. Mrs. Mellon was also to urge her parents, the Gerard Lamberts of Princeton, to donate a portrait of President Andrew Jackson, painted in 1819 by John Wesley Jarvis. Mr. Lambert was a direct descendant of the artist and eventually the painting would have been inherited by Mrs. Mellon. On the more frivolous side, the Mellons ordered twenty-four bamboo-embossed vermeil bowls. Flower-filled, they would center the small circular tables which Mrs. Kennedy originated to accommodate more guests and make dinners gayer and more informal.

Mrs. Charles Wrightsman, who had been so largely responsible for Mr. du Pont's participation, was to become, in a way, the practical inspiration for the restoration project. She gave unstintingly of her time, taste and expertise, in New York, Paris and on special trips to Washington. She personally would underwrite many of the unseen heavy expenditures on which the success of the restoration depended. Each of her known contributions, like the beautiful bronze-gilt French chenets which were to be placed in the Blue Room fireplace, would be of museum quality.

There were six masculine members of the Fine Arts Committee for the White House:

Charles Francis Adams, a Boston businessman, chairman of the board of the Raytheon Company, was active in many educational and philanthropic projects. But more important to the Fine Arts Committee for the White House, Mr. Adams was a direct descendant of two Presidents. He was a great-great-grandson of John Quincy Adams and a great-great-great-grandson of the second President of the United States, John Adams, the first occupant of the White House. Adams was to give seven armchairs and six side chairs, all especially handsome reproductions of the original Bellangé furniture which President Monroe had ordered in 1817 from Paris for what is now the Blue Room. As Miss Catherine Bohlen of Villanova, Pennsylvania, had given an original Bellangé armchair, and Mrs. Kennedy was to retrieve the original Bellangé pier table from storage, the suite of furniture now would tally numerically with the original Monroe order.

Leroy Davis was a collector who specialized and lectured on American paintings and antique furniture. He was president of the Davis Galleries in New York and of APF, a firm which specialized in framing American paintings. Some of the White House paintings and others which were to be donated were badly framed, so as his personal contribution, Mr. Davis provided many handsome and suitable frames.

David Finley had been director of the National Gallery of Art from its founding until his retirement in 1956. He then became chairman of the Commission of Fine Arts which passed on questions of art and architecture in the capital and also chairman of the board of trustees of the National Trust for Historic Preservation. Mr. Finley was donor of an eighteenth-century American walnut highchest, the first gift made to Mrs. Kennedy's restoration project.

John L. Loeb, the New York investment banker and collector of superb Impressionist paintings, was to redecorate and refurnish in entirety the lovely Oval Room.

Gerald Shea, a former associate of Joseph P. Kennedy, was chairman of the Acquisitions Committee of the Society for the Preservation of Long Island Antiquities.

John Walker was director of the National Gallery of Art and a trustee of the American Academy in Rome, the American Federation of Arts and the National Trust for Historic Preservation.

The second in the series of committees involved in the restoration was a Special Advisory Group composed of museum presidents and curators. Mr. du Pont outlined its purpose in a letter, dated March 29, 1961, addressed to members of the Fine Arts Committee:

In talking with Mrs. Kennedy about the way in which the Fine Arts Committee for the White House may best fulfill its task — we thought it would be well to invite a small group of people knowledgeable in the fields of fine arts, decorative arts, and cultural history to serve as advisors to the committee.

In selecting this group, we had two principal thoughts in mind. First, to find those whose training and present positions equip them to supplement the knowledge and experience of the members of our Committee; and second, to assure nationwide representation.

— I am sure you will agree that we are fortunate in securing the assistance of such a distinguished group to act as a scholarly resource for our Committee, and each of them, I know, will do whatever work we may request of him.

On November 21, 1961, James Fosburgh of New York accepted the chairmanship of a Special Committee for White House Paintings. The Special Committee, an adjunct of the Fine Arts Committee, was appointed to acquire a permanent White House collection of the works of eighteenth- and nineteenth-century American painters. Fosburgh, an artist in his own right, gave lectures on American art and had been a member of the Frick Collection staff for over twenty years. The members of Fosburgh's Special Committee were well-known patrons of art who resided in important cities throughout the country. They hoped to expand the meager White House collection to include "landscapes and still lifes in keeping with the history and tradition of the President's House and to replace certain non-historic paintings of Presidents with those which were actually painted from life."

James T. Babb, the Librarian of Yale University, was asked to form a Library Committee the following May. When President and Mrs. Kennedy had come to the White House, the small downstairs library contained little more than Agatha Christie and similar paperback "who-dun-its." The Kennedys decided to assemble a working library of old and new American classics (even Louisa May Alcott's *Little Women* was to be included) with presidential history predominating. Their basic idea was to

At the first meeting of the Special Committee on Paintings for the White House, Mrs. Kennedy chats with James Fosburgh, the committee chairman, and Henry du Pont.

James Roe Ketchum, the third White House curator, posed in the Lincoln Room.

acquire books which would be "most essential to the understanding of our National experience." Library Committee Chairman James Babb found that the library had shelf space for only 2,600 volumes, a space inadequate to cover in depth a subject of such vast proportion. Therefore, his choice had to be most selective. The Yale Librarian's main reference was the 1960 Library of Congress *Guide to the Study of the United States of America*. To winnow this voluminous list Babb asked the assistance of three presidential historians: Lyman H. Butterfield of Harvard, editor of the Adams Papers; Julian P. Boyd of Princeton, editor of the Jefferson Papers; and Arthur Schlesinger, Jr., of Harvard, who was now associated with the White House.

The White House Library became a real working library. There were few old or rare volumes included, and most of the books were donated by authors or publishers and those persons who became interested in the undertaking.

However, there is one particularly interesting volume which is rarely available in the library. This is the Appointment Book of President Lincoln, from March 5 to 27, 1861. It is the first record book used at the White House after Abraham Lincoln was inaugurated, and in it his secretaries John Hay and John Nicolay note briefly the day-to-day presidential activities. A gift from the then Vice-President and Mrs. Lyndon B. Johnson, the book is catalogued as Documentary Material and is on display from time to time in both the Lincoln Room and in the showcases containing White House memorabilia which Mrs. Kennedy arranged along the gallery through which tourists enter.

On November 3, 1963, two years and nine months after she initiated the restoration of the White House, the First Lady was to write Clark Clifford a summary of her achievement: "— the White House is as it should be — it is all I ever dreamed for it — there are only a few things left to be done — I know we are in the red — but after this year we will not be —" Her remaining trio of projects were the golden draperies for the East Room, which she had ordered but which, as they took two years to weave, were hung during the Johnson administration; chair upholstery and draperies for the State Dining Room; and what Mrs. Kennedy described as "a decent pair of chandeliers for the ground floor where the tourists come in." Less than three weeks after Mrs. Kennedy had dispatched this letter, she was no longer the First Lady.

Story of a Great Heritage

On November 17, 1952, the Washington *Times-Herald*'s Inquiring Camera Girl, Jacqueline Bouvier, had made the front page with a story titled "Mamie's Namesake, 10, Glad Uncle Ike Will Be President." The versatile young columnist illustrated her interview with four smart little pen and ink drawings.

The editor had assigned Jacqueline to record the reactions of Mrs. Eisenhower's namesake and niece to having her uncle in the White House. The ten-year-old Mamie Moore, approached as she walked home from school, was unaware that she was talking to a newswoman and made unselfconscious, childishly amusing replies. Soon after the story was published, Jacqueline, conscience-stricken by the deception, wrote an earnest letter of apology to little Mamie's mother.

Though the incident was unfortunate and out of character from Jacqueline's point of view, it brought oddly prophetic results. *New York Times* man Arthur Krock enjoyed the piece and alerted Bess Furman, a *Times* staff member and the author of a book on the White House. The following day she wrote to her young colleague Miss Bouvier:

Arthur Krock called my attention to your charming story and drawings on Mamie Eisenhower's namesake. I told him it would make an excellent first chapter for a children's book — though trying to write anything original about the White House is like asking for the moon — but I believe if you could carry little Mamie through the Inaugural and a few White House visits to her aunt — and perhaps a children's party — it would make a fine addition to White House lore. — I think there would be real value to your sketches if you could add a few lines to make them look like White House interiors — if you could get hold of my book, *White House Profile,* on page 93 you will find a charming sketch of the Hayes family — and now, with photography, only the stiffest and most stilted White House interiors are ever shown —

Someone inside with a little girl and a sketchbook could certainly freshen up the scene — Good luck to your typewriter and pencil —

Two days later, from Merrywood, the lovely place in Virginia where her stepfather, Hugh D. Auchincloss, and her mother lived, Jacqueline replied in a burst of enthusiasm:

— It was so kind of you to take the trouble of writing me. I can't tell you how happy I was to get your letter — . That is the most wonderful idea — the children's book — I know something like that would go over so wonderfully — if I could only do it the right way — it is such a lovely idea I would hate to mangle it — I've ordered your book — and I would so love to meet you — I'm so in love with all your world now — I think I look up to newspaper people — the way you join movie star fan clubs when you're ten years old —

Jacqueline Bouvier never went to the White House with little Mamie, but she did read Bess Furman's book with attention. It sharpened her interest in the White House and provided answers to some of the things she had wanted to know. For when she was eleven her mother had taken her there for the first time and even then her inquiring mind had been frustrated. There had been no one person to answer her questions. Not a booklet or a fact sheet was provided to explain what she had seen or to explain historically what she had not seen but would like to have known. She had never forgotten.

John Walker, director of the National Gallery of Art, was an old family friend of the Auchinclosses, and soon after the Inauguration Mrs. Kennedy called upon him for advice. As they toured the White House together, so he could absorb the overall effect of its dreariness, the new First Lady commented wryly that living there was like being imprisoned in the Lubianka. To emphasize her point, she indicated a drab lithograph; but when Walker turned the picture over to discover its origin, they had perhaps their only real laugh: on the back was printed "Loan from the National Gallery of Art"!

Mrs. Kennedy told her friend that she planned to accomplish just two things: "To make the White House the most beautiful 'house' and a point of pilgrimage to all Americans"; and to provide a guidebook as souvenir of a White House visit. The First Lady envisioned no ordinary brochure, but a real book of superlative standards. Walker consented to help Mrs. Kennedy, and some months later, when the project was well along, she wrote him: "— I agree with you, too, this must be scholarly — and not talk down to the public — then they will learn from it — and I have never seen a case, in politics or books, when talking down did any good — it just bores people —

"This book shall be something the White House Historical Association will always be proud of — and that historians will admire — It shall be something which Berenson, Uncle Lefty and Arthur Schlesinger would want to read —" (These three men whose intellectual attainments Mrs. Kennedy admired, were Bernard Berenson, the famed art critic; Wilmarth Lewis, her stepfather's brother-in-law, an expert on Walpole; and historian Schlesinger who was a member of President Kennedy's staff.)

The production of a White House guidebook entailed many problems and so much work that it was not published until July 1962. There were at the outset two basic difficulties to overcome. First, before the photograph of a valuable donation could be reproduced in a permanent guidebook, legislation had to be enacted by Congress to prevent the object being removed by any future President. (Legislation to cover this contingency was passed in September 1961.) Second, government publications cannot be copyrighted: their contents must, by law, remain in the public domain. For this reason the guidebook could not be produced under government aegis. Instead, a publishing agency was needed which could copyright the material and turn all profits over to the White House. Mrs. Kennedy knew that there were hundreds, perhaps even thousands, of national historical associations scattered throughout the country, and that most of them published booklets whose sales contributed to the maintenance of the special historic site involved.

Consequently, on November 3, 1961, the White House Historical Association was chartered as a nonprofit organization in the District of Columbia. Directors were named, an office was established, and its *raison d'être* was stated as: "to enhance understanding, appreciation and the enjoyment of the Executive Mansion. Its purpose is primarily educational. Income from the sale of this booklet will be used to publish other materials about the White House, as well as for the acquisition of historic furnishings and other objects for the Executive Mansion." The booklet was to be titled *The White House: an Historic Guide.*

Mrs. Kennedy and those associated with the White House discussed the guidebook format constantly during the early months of 1962. Conrad Wirth, then director of the National Park Service (which benefits substantially from the sale of tourist booklets) , was present at these sessions. Wirth was also a trustee of the National Geographic Society, and he suggested that Dr. Melville Bell Grosvenor might be of assistance. Dr. Grosvenor, president and editor of the National Geographic Society, proved to be invaluable. Immediately he placed not only the printing and engraving facilities of his organization at the disposition of Mrs. Kennedy but also the services of his photographers and writers.

Dr. Grosvenor's staff prepared a guidebook dummy, complete with text and glossy photographs. The First Lady, however, had definite ideas about the guidebook makeup, and the dummy projected the *National Geographic* image too closely to be acceptable. During the months since the guidebook idea was first conceived, the Fine Arts Committee had engaged Mrs. John N. Pearce as curator — the first in White House history. Now Lorraine Pearce was set to work on the guidebook, writing the text in the style Mrs. Kennedy preferred. The First Lady then rearranged and painstakingly edited the manuscript until it was very close to the high standards she herself had set.

Finally, when the *National Geographic* lensmen arrived to take the requisite pictures, Mrs. Kennedy, who had been a casual photographer during her brief newspaper career as "The Inquiring Camera Girl," supervised the camera angles to obtain the effects she wanted.

The White House: an Historic Guide went to press in May and June. The first edition, some 250,000 copies, was placed on sale July 4, 1962. Seven and a half years later, when the ninth edition of the White House guidebook was issued, over 2,500,000 copies had been sold.

The formal presentation of the first copy took place on June 28, 1962, in the Fish Room at the White House. (The Fish Room is the reception room outside the Office of the President. The room derives its curious name from the Franklin Delano Roosevelt era. President Roosevelt liked to stand his tropical fish aquaria along the walls and hang his finny catches — stuffed and mounted, that is — above them.) Guests at the ceremony included those who had been actively involved in the venture. Before giving the first copy to Mrs. Kennedy and the second to the President, Dr. Grosvenor made a brief speech: "Every line, every picture represents your own particular attention," he said to the First Lady. "The happy results reflect your desire to bring to the public the story of our great heritage, the President's House."

David Finley added, "Mrs. Kennedy has been the inspiration for its publication — her knowledge of history, her good judgment and her impeccable taste are evident in every page." Then President Kennedy, after thanking those who had participated in the creation of the guidebook, turned toward Mrs. Kennedy: "— my warmest congratulations and appreciation to my wife."

To launch the guidebook John Walker borrowed forty thousand dollars from a member of the Mellon family, and one of the many historical associations lent an additional five thousand dollars. Happily, the guidebook was such an immediate success that not a penny was needed and both sums were returned. *The White House: an Historic Guide* deserved success. It was, and in each succeeding edition continues to be, a beautiful book. The format has remained the same.

The front and back covers were brilliantly colored aerial photographs of the White House taken from both north and south approaches. The porticoed President's House spread cake-icing white on dappled lawns where fountains jetted under pale blue skies. The end papers, actually the first and the last two facing pages, reproduced an écru-colored map of Washington, copied from the original L'Enfant plan;* and at the back was a drawing based on an aerial photograph of the President's Park, some eighteen-plus acres which surround the White House. The trees planted by many past chief executives were indicated on the drawing by letters. An American elm, selected by John Quincy Adams (son of John Adams, the first White House occupant), was the most venerable; the grandiflora magnolias, which Andrew Jackson crowded close to the Mansion, were easily identified; while the newest trees shown in the guidebook were a black walnut and three varieties of oak, all four set down by Dwight D. Eisenhower.†

On the first of 132 pages of illustrated text was a foreword by the First Lady, typewritten on White House stationery:

This guidebook is for all of the people who visit the White House each year.

It was planned — at first — for the children. It seemed such a shame that they should have nothing to take away with them, to help sort out the impressions received on an often crowded visit. It was hoped that they would go over the book at home and read more about the Presidents who interested them most. Its purpose was to stimulate their sense of history and their pride in their country.

But as research went on and so many little-known facts were gleaned from forgotten papers, it was decided to make it a book that could be of profit to adults and scholars also.

On the theory that it never hurts a child to read something that may be above his head, and that books written down for children often do not awaken a dormant curiosity, this guidebook took its present form.

I hope our young visitors will vindicate this theory, find pleasure in the book, and know that they were its inspiration.

To their elders, may it remind you that many First Families loved this house — and that each and every one left something of themselves behind in it — as you do now by the effort you have made to come here.

Jacqueline Kennedy

* Pierre de L'Enfant, a French architect, was invited by George Washington to make a city plan for the new capital of the United States.

† The trees President Kennedy chose were planted on April 6, 1961, but they missed being recorded in the first edition of the guidebook. There was a Pacific Pride apple tree sent from the State of Washington, and a number of soulangeana magnolias were placed strategically in the Rose Garden.

The guidebook contained all, and more than, Jacqueline Bouvier could have wished to know on that first long-ago visit to the White House. The contents included a brief history of how a permanent President's House came to be created; how it was burned by the British; and how, soon afterwards, it was rebuilt and refurnished. A chapter devoted to "The Changing White House" showed, in drawings and photographs, exterior alterations both projected and realized. They ranged from the absurd to the extravagant: from a Victorian doghouse built for a pet of President Benjamin Harrison; to a suggestion made in 1948 that the unsound condition of the Mansion warranted demolition and the erection of a modern structure.

A sketch of "Life in the White House" as it was lived by so many differing First Families preceded a march of chapters on "Great Paintings," "Great Furniture" and the fine collections of china, vermeil, and *bronze-doré*. The remainder of the book was a "Guide to the Rooms." Sixteen were listed, and they included not only the State Rooms, which were shown on White House tours, but rooms of equal fascination which were not on public exhibition.

The illustrations were superb. In the 132 pages there were 197 photographs, drawings and reproductions of paintings, prints and even ancient newspaper cartoons. Some of the old drawings showed the State Rooms grotesquely decorated in their furbelowed Victorian and "Mississippi Steamboat" worst. The new photographs, in glowing color, not only depicted a sumptuous double-page spread of the gold-and-white State Dining Room with small tables set up for 120 guests, but also enchanting minutiae, mostly small White House treasures, like a blue basket-weave design teacup and saucer made by Dagoty of Paris for President Madison; a sugar bowl of Chinese export porcelain with both handles missing, part of a service presented to Martha Washington (the broken handles have since been replaced with ones copied from a similar piece of porcelain); an amusing "Lighthouse Clock" inset with a medallion of Lafayette, made by Simon Willard of Roxbury, Massachusetts; and such earthy souvenirs as the "signature marks" made by the masons who constructed the President's House. These cabalistic-looking characters, cut into soft sandstone, were discovered in various parts of the Executive Mansion during the 1948–1952 Renovation. President Truman, a history enthusiast, had the "signatures" gathered together and set above the mantelpiece in the old Ground Floor Kitchen, which now serves as an office for the White House curator.

Among the guidebook memorabilia of the great and near-great who have lived in the President's House, there was only a single photograph of the First Lady whose imagination, persistence and unceasing hard work had made the guidebook possible. She was not photographed alone. Mrs. Kennedy was seated among her guests in the East Room after a dinner honoring the Governor of Puerto Rico and Señora Muñoz Marín. Pablo Casals, the famed Spanish cellist, self-exiled from Spain and a resident of Puerto Rico, had just finished playing. He was standing, bow in hand, acknowledging the applause of President and Mrs. Kennedy and their distinguished guests.

Beside the problem of bringing the guidebook into being, there had been the question of whether it was in keeping with White House dignity to sell it within such revered walls. Mrs. Kennedy had been most tactful. "Just let me try it for a little while," she said. "If there are protests — we will sell it in book stores or somewhere else."

At first a desk was placed in the East Foyer on the ground floor where the tourists entered. In charge of the sales was one or another of the young secretaries from the brand-new White House Historical Association office. The guidebook then sold for a dollar in paperback and in hardcover for two dollars and fifty cents.

To Mrs. Kennedy's delight, statistics soon showed that 20 percent, or one out of five persons to tour the White House, bought the guidebook. Eighteen percent settled for the dollar book while 2 percent preferred the more elaborate version. The production costs of the paperback fluctuated between forty and sixty cents, and all profit went toward either acquisitions or underwriting White House Historical Association expenses.

As the sales mounted, President Kennedy, more than ever impressed with the business acumen of his wife, one day exclaimed in genuine amazement, "Jackie! You're making more a year than I am!"

The First Lady lost no chance to sell a guidebook. When a member of President Kennedy's staff, who had initially opposed salesmanship within the White House walls, was completely won around, he suggested that perhaps additional books could be sold to tourists *on the way out*. Mrs. Kennedy immediately wrote a memo to Mr. West. As usual, the First Lady was bursting with practical ideas and anxious to tally every penny taken in.

Mr. West.

The President tells me that one of his staff (who was against selling guides in the beginning) now says lots more could be sold on way out — but timidly says this is your province & doesn't dare mention it — which is rather sweet —

I agree & we can use the $. Would you have a table set up in entrance hall 9–12 during public tours —where guards sit — I suggest 3 bridge or wooden tables (like I have by bookcase in West Hall) in a row — or a trestle table — a long plank of wood on 2 supports. This could be stacked away when not in use — it could be covered with a piece of red felt same color as ground floor screen — So it won't look awful — Or could you keep desk by that window — flush with wall & pull it out at right angles to wall when selling is going on — If it is not too large — You and curator decide which looks best —

Another idea for a table — one panel of the screen — rectangular — not with curved top — with brass studs — just laid across 2 columns — painted black — at the right height — single ones carpenter shop could make —

This may be a nuisance & now we can discourage it eventually but let us start at once with any table available until you get the right one (Use old kneehole desk that was in 2nd floor hall under Eisenhower to start with — just leave it there all day flush with the wall) as every penny is needed — do let me know as soon as you start this & how much we sell —

Guidebook sales increased with the number of tourists, and the number of tourists grew as the White House became more beautiful. Less than a million visitors had been attracted to the White House in 1960. The following year, after Mrs. Kennedy had announced her plans for the restoration program, the total increased by several hundred thousand. The final year of her residence in the White House almost two million tourists would inspect what the First Lady had accomplished.

As impressive new acquisitions were announced, and rooms were restored and readied for public inspection, the guidebook had to be updated. Supervising changes in text and layout added to the already heavy workload Mrs. Kennedy had undertaken. She estimated casually that besides the accepted obligations of merely being the wife of the President of the United States, her schedule now included such extras as writing, longhand, about twenty letters daily; inviting prospective donors to tea — and afterwards touring the White House with them; determining policy matters with members of her various committees; and deciding on materials and other ornamentation for the rooms which were to be redone.

On January 25, 1963, when the guidebook had been on sale only eighteen months, some $58,988.43 from this source had been contributed to the Fine Arts Committee for the White House, and additional funds had been expended in maintaining the White House Historical Association.

At the end of the calendar year 1969, the White House guidebook had grown from 132 pages to 156 pages and was about to go into a ninth edition. Nearly 2,500,000 copies had been sold, not only in the White House but also in some fifty National Parks, forty nonprofit museums and art galleries, and at the National Geographic Society headquarters in Washington. Over $580,000 had been contributed to the White House Restoration program and the White House Historical Association financed as well.

Public Law 87–286

From the day Mr. du Pont accepted the chairmanship of the Fine Arts Committee for the White House, Mrs. Kennedy worked unremittingly on the technical and legislative details which would make her restoration project permanent and therefore attractive to the would-be donor of major historic *objets d'art*.

When Mrs. Kennedy came to the President's House, except for a few outstanding pieces, the furniture consisted of a mélange of pathetic, unsalable castoffs from many past administrations and, even in the State Rooms, blatant reproductions ordered during the Truman Renovation in 1948.

Before 1925, the authority to accept donations for the White House had been as confused as their permanent retention was uncertain. Until the Coolidge administration, gifts were presented through the incumbent President or his First Lady, who, if they chose, could relinquish them to the Executive Mansion on their departure. However, the line between a personal present and an official gift was hard to define and depended solely on the individual interpretation of the presidential couple. There was no assurance that a donation left in the White House would remain there indefinitely, either, because the incoming chief executive and his wife could readily dispose of furnishings they found displeasing, regardless of their origin. Sometimes unwanted objects were banished to government warehouses. Sometimes they were sold at public auction, and the money thus obtained contributed to the purchase of replacements more in tune with the new incumbent's personal taste.

These well-publicized sales, staged at local auction rooms, attracted many affluent buyers. At the most famous pre-Civil War auction, sanctioned by bachelor President James Buchanan (1857–1861), many of the fine purchases made by President Monroe (1809–1817) were dispersed. Among the treasures sold was the unique set of gilded Bellangé chairs, ordered especially from Paris by the fifth President (Monroe) for what is now the Blue Room. (Three of the original dozen chairs were returned as gifts after Mrs. Kennedy's public plea for historic White House furniture.)

President Chester A. Arthur, in 1882, was responsible for the most notorious sale of all. No less than twenty-four wagonloads of White House furnishings were carted off to auction. A Washington newspaper humorist described the mountain of miscellaneous goods as "— so complete that it included the rat-trap that caught the rat that ate the suit that had been worn by Mr. Lincoln."

Elegant Chester Arthur, a widower, on his unexpected succession to the Presidency,* found the Executive Mansion so "shabby" that he refused to move in until he felt certain it could be extensively refurbished. The new President offered to pay for this embellishment out of his own pocket and called in Louis Comfort Tiffany to redecorate the Mansion in the then emerging "art nouveau" style. The total effect was a grand scale conversation piece; and the outstanding Tiffany creation, an extravagant stained-glass screen which sealed off the Cross Hall and the State Rooms from the draughty north entrance foyer, invited virulent criticism.

Twenty years later the controversial screen and other remnants of Chester Arthur's expensive effort to make the White House contemporary were swept away in a classically oriented renovation undertaken by President Theodore Roosevelt.

Mrs. Coolidge and her successor, Mrs. Hoover, took the first steps to stem the tide of vanishing White House possessions. They tried, too, to arouse public interest in the acquisition of historic furniture. The inevitable committee was formed to achieve these ends, and during the Coolidge days legislation was passed to permit the acceptance of gifts to the White House. But in the 1920s it was difficult to publicize ideas effectively since television and mass-circulation picture magazines were not available to capture the interest of the country as a whole.

On February 25, 1925, Congress took the initial step toward making the acceptance of quality gifts for the White House official. The independent office of director of Public Buildings and Public Parks of the National Capital was created, and a Joint Resolution passed two days later, provided "that with a view to conserving in the White House the best specimens of the Early American furniture and furnishings, and for the purpose of maintaining the interior of the White House in keeping with its original design, the officer in charge of public buildings and grounds is hereby authorized and directed, with the approval of the President, to accept donations of furniture and furnishings for use in the White House."

---

* Arthur succeeded James Garfield who was shot in the Washington railroad station three months after his Inauguration. Garfield died at his Elberon, New Jersey, home on September 19, 1881.

The new director of Public Buildings and Public Parks was the first government official to be accorded the responsibility of accepting gifts for the White House. To facilitate this task, the Joint Resolution also authorized him to appoint, with the approval of the President, a committee to evaluate such donations as might be offered.

In 1934 the Office of Public Buildings and Public Parks was absorbed by the National Park Service, which was under the Department of the Interior. The director of this service then assumed the authority to accept White House gifts, "all such articles thus donated," the mandate emphasized, "to become the property of the United States and to be accounted for as such."

The committee for evaluation which had been appointed with the approval of President Coolidge in 1925 continued as an adjunct to the director of the National Park Service until the Truman Renovation in 1948. The following year, 1949, President Truman appointed a Committee for the Renovation of the Executive Mansion. As the White House would remain closed during the four years it underwent reconstruction, the "evaluation" committee became defunct. Nevertheless, two members, Mrs. Dwight Davis and David Finley, were appointed as "advisers in interior decoration" to the Renovation Committee. When, in 1952, the Executive Mansion was again ready for occupancy, the Renovation Committee was dissolved. But David Finley and members of the Commission of Fine Arts, of which he was chairman, remained as advisers for White House acquisitions throughout both Eisenhower administrations.

While these maneuvers concerned with the acceptance of White House donations were focused in the right direction, actually very little of practical substance had been spelled out. A concise statement was needed which would provide a machinery not only to confirm the historic and artistic merit of gifts which Mrs. Kennedy's Fine Arts Committee would propose, but also to make it impossible in any way to dispose of furnishings thus authenticated. The legal angles of the problem were meticulously analyzed for Mrs. Kennedy by Nicholas de B. Katzenbach, the Deputy Attorney General. It was obvious that congressional legislation would be necessary to resolve them.

The member of Congress best equipped to be helpful about

these problems was Senator Clinton P. Anderson of New Mexico. Among other important committee memberships, Senator Anderson was chairman of the Senate Interior and Insular Affairs Committee, which dealt, in part, with matters pertaining to the Department of the Interior and its subsidiary bureau, the National Park Service, which in turn administered the National Park System, nominally charged with White House care. In addition to this influential congressional connection, Clinton Anderson was the senior of two senators then regents of the Smithsonian Institution. Therefore, he was experienced in the possibilities as well as the complexities of grandiose museum administration.

When Mrs. Kennedy invited Senator Anderson to "tea," he accepted with some reluctance. Many years previously he had determined to avoid getting "mixed up" with women in cultural matters in which he, as senator, was involved. Nevertheless, if possible, he wanted to be helpful.

Without delay, the First Lady plunged into her subject: how best to preserve the White House and its possessions. The Senator, tall glass in hand, listened. Later he recalled that Mrs. Kennedy had told him about finding "a set of dishes over a hundred years old" in the White House basement. "They were obviously an historic treasure," she had continued, "yet no one had known about them." The Senator then remembered that, at the time of the Lincoln assassination, enemies had bundled many of the dead President's effects into the White House basement, too, and some of these historically priceless relics had disappeared. Clinton Anderson added that, in his opinion, a President had the right to use such White House furnishings as he wished but definitely did not have the right to dispose of those which did not suit his taste. Senator Anderson believed the most effective means of preserving the collections and permanently safeguarding the acquisitions which Mrs. Kennedy anticipated would be to establish the White House as a National Monument. A National Monument, he said, could be created by both a Presidential Proclamation and by congressional legislation, while an Historic Site could be defined only by Congress. The Senator found the First Lady ". . . friendly, nice and a genuinely sincere person. She was so enthusiastic," he concluded, "I felt she would do a good job!"

"I can't let this gal down," he decided later and explained, "sometimes in politics one agrees to do something — and never does it — but *this* was different."

Setting up the legislation proved complicated. Since the White House was involved, Senator Anderson had to "touch base with everyone — to keep people from getting their noses out of joint." And though his powers of persuasion were notable, they failed in one striking instance. President Kennedy admitted he enjoyed living in the White House, but balked at the idea of making a National Monument (in reality a museum) of what was now his home.

Nevertheless on August 15, 1961, Anderson introduced Senate Bill No. 2422 whose purpose was "to establish the White House as a National Monument." Shortly afterwards a bill introduced earlier in the House of Representatives by Representative J. T. Rutherford of Texas was amended to be identical in content with the Anderson legislation. In their original wording, the Anderson and Rutherford bills were not passed, but their basic intent was to be realized in slightly different form.

The most interesting aspect of the Anderson Bill was an arrangement which the Senator, Mrs. Kennedy and her advisers had worked out to retain indefinitely past, present and future White House acquisitions. In its completed form the plan had been read to and accepted by Dr. Leonard Carmichael, the secretary of the Smithsonian Institution. This clause reads:

> — that articles of furniture, fixtures and decorative objects of the White House, when declared by the President to be of historic and artistic interest, together with such similar articles, fixtures and objects as are acquired by the White House in the future, when similarly so declared, shall be considered thereafter to be inalienable and as the property of the White House; that such an article, fixture, and object when not in use or on display in the White House, shall be transferred by direction of the President as a loan to the Smithsonian Institution, for its care, study, and storage or exhibition; and that such articles, fixtures and objects shall be returned to the White House from the Smithsonian Institution on notice by the President.

Meanwhile, quite apart from President Kennedy's aversion to transforming the Executive Mansion into a National Monument, there were other considerations for the good of the White House and the success of the First Lady's restoration project, which needed legislative support.

By this time Mrs. Kennedy knew that the most feasible way to publish her projected guidebook was through a specially set-up historical association. Legislation passed in the 1940's had authorized the National Park System to organize a series of "nonprofit, cooperating associations" through which guidebooks and other educational material could be published and sold at the many (currently 272) parks and historic sites which they maintained. But there was no word in any legislation which definitely linked the Executive Mansion with the National Park System. In order to avail herself legally of the convenience of creating a White House Historical Association, the status of the White House itself had to be clarified and its identity with the National Park System more closely established.

And, since the White House was not to be established as a National Monument after all, the preservation of the museum character of the State Rooms needed to be defined, and the private living quarters and executive office areas delineated. To this end both the Anderson and Rutherford bills were amended, and the resulting Act was approved by Congress on September 22, 1961 and became Public Law 87-286.

The Act commenced:

Be it enacted by the Senate and House of Representatives of the United States of America in Congress Assembled, That all of that portion of Reservation numbered 1* in the city of Washington, District of Columbia, which is within the President's park enclosure, comprising eighteen and seven one-hundredths acres, shall continue to be known as the White House and shall be administered pursuant to the Act of August 25, 1916 [the "organic" Act which created the National Park Service] and Acts supplementary thereto and amendatory thereof. In carrying out this Act primary attention shall be given to the preservation and interpretation of the museum character of the principal corridor on the ground floor and the principal public rooms on the first floor of the White House but nothing done under this Act shall conflict with the administration of the Executive Offices of the President or with the use and occupancy of the build-

* The first of seventeen plots of land called "Reservations" which made up the original area of the District of Columbia.

ings and grounds as the home of the President and his family and for his official purposes.

The clause in Senator Anderson's original bill which provided storage in the Smithsonian for objects not in use or on display in the White House was included verbatim in the final Act. A third and final clause provided that the security of the White House would continue to be provided by the White House Police and the United States Secret Service.

Strange Harvest of Gifts

The first meeting of the Fine Arts Committee for the White House was held at teatime in the Red Room on February 21, 1961. Mrs. Kennedy presided. Of the Committee proper, five ladies—Mmes Dillon, Englehard, Parish, Warren, and Wrightsman — were present; also Charles Francis Adams, David Finley and John Walker. Clark Clifford, prepared to advise on legal problems that might arise, was seated informally at a card table. Tish Baldridge sat at one side, pencil poised to record the proceedings; and as Mr. du Pont was unable to attend, Mrs. Englehard took notes too, and later sent him a "confidential report" of the session.

As they arrived, each committee member was given a memorandum prepared jointly by Mrs. Kennedy and Mrs. Parish. This memorandum listed the "items" which they considered most needed in the White House. Some of these could replace "unfit" furniture, others might fill in where both furniture and decorative objects were lacking.

When everyone was seated and tea had been served, Mrs. Kennedy welcomed her guests and then made a brief speech. She "felt strongly" that as soon as possible committee members "should start looking for furniture, rugs and bibelots," as donations to the White House. Clark Clifford quickly spoke up in support of the First Lady, explaining in his urbane manner that such gifts were completely tax-deductible, as were checks sent in lieu of specific articles.

There ensued a lively discussion about how donors might be approached, and what guidelines should be set up for the acceptance of anticipated gifts. It was agreed that committee members would write individual letters to specially selected friends. "Every assurance can be given the donor that his gift will be permanently part of the White House," Mrs. Engelhard wrote in her report to Mr. du Pont. But since no legislation had as yet been formulated to guarantee the permanency of gifts, this statement was qualified in a somewhat hazy manner. "If the next President should dislike a specific article, the donor can designate a museum to which it can be transferred at such time."

The basic guidelines for gift acceptance were uncomplicated. All furnishings were to be eighteenth or nineteenth century. Preferably, furniture for the State Rooms was to be American, although it was subsequently decided to make an exception in the case of any of the outstanding French pieces which Monroe had bought for the White House. Each gift offered was to be accompanied by a photograph and an authentication signed by at least one recognized expert in antiques. Once accepted, gifts would be numbered and catalogued immediately. If a gift proved unacceptable, to avoid offending personal friends of individual committee members, it was to be refused in the name of the Committee by David Finley — whose name carried added prestige as he was also chairman of the Commission of Fine Arts.

Mrs. Engelhard concluded her report on a cheerful note: "Mrs. Kennedy was extremely gracious and patient with her Committee, and the meeting went off with enthusiasm and optimism for our success."

Nevertheless no date was set for a second meeting. It was thought best "to wait and see how people responded to our requests."

(At this moment no one, not even in that group of ultra-sophisticated men and women, entertained even the slightest suspicion that within a few weeks an almost unbelievable sixty to

At the opening of the Treaty Room, which Mrs. Kennedy had renamed and redecorated, the First Lady stands with Senator Dirksen, Vice-President Johnson, and Senator and Mrs. Mansfield.

seventy-five thousand letters would sweep into the White House. This torrent of letters was written, not by personal friends of the committee members, but by excited citizens from every state in the Union, offering to give or sell to the White House just about anything of presumed presidential interest: from a spittoon once supposedly owned by President Andrew Jackson, to a bust of George Washington which the owner conservatively valued at two hundred thousand dollars!)

After the meeting ended, committee members inspected the White House from the third floor to the basement. Mrs. Engelhard, commenting tactfully on the tour, wrote to Mr. du Pont: ". . . there is still room for improvement."

Mr. du Pont replied promptly. From Boca Grande he addressed a joint letter to Mrs. Kennedy and to members of the Committee. The chairman approved the procedure for accepting gifts; to avoid duplicating appeals, he suggested it might be useful to establish a clearinghouse for the names of prospective donors; a printed letterhead for committee correspondence should be obtained. It would save time and effort, Mr. du Pont continued, if a printed list, similar to Mrs. Kennedy's memorandum, could be made up of "what is needed" in each of the State Rooms and included in every personal letter. In a modest "P.S." the chairman concluded, "I would like the opportunity of checking the terminology on the list of items needed in the official rooms — before it is printed."

Since many members of the Committee shared the same circle of friends, a clearinghouse for names was a practical idea. Mrs. Wrightsman took over this responsibility, and a list of "items" needed for the state rooms was compiled and checked by the chairman.

On April 10, 1961, Mrs. Kennedy sent a short note to members of her Committee:

Dear _____:

Enclosed is a copy of a suggested form letter to be sent to all possible donors.

Obviously, it is too formal in many cases, when you are writing to close friends. So change it as you wish, but I wanted you to have it, as it describes the procedure for sending data and donations.

In a few days I will send you our stationery and then you can start writing your letters.

Sincerely,

s/ Jacqueline Kennedy

A month previously, from Boca Grande, Mr. du Pont had written to his friend and committee member, Mrs. George Henry Warren: " . . . I am going to the White House on April 27 to make a thorough survey." Mrs. Kennedy had invited him to luncheon, and her other guests included Mr. and Mrs. Wrightsman; John Walker, the director of the National Gallery of Art; John Sweeney, the director of Mr. du Pont's Winterthur Museum; and Janet Felton, a friend of Mrs. Kennedy's, who had been persuaded to come to Washington and take over as secretary to the Fine Arts Committee for the White House.

Mr. du Pont arrived punctually and brought with him a great mass of glowing flowers from his famed Winterthur gardens. The luncheon was served upstairs in the private living quarters, in the new President's Dining Room, still not completely decorated. Afterwards, they made a "thorough survey" of the White House, Mr. du Pont being spared only the drab third-floor guest rooms. A shy man, who seldom revealed his emotions, the chairman seemed visibly shaken by the enormity of the task he had undertaken. Janet Felton walked beside him, pad in hand, ready to jot down his suggestions.

The first of what would become hundreds of suggestions was to rehang both curtains and heavy draperies *inside,* instead of *outside,* the handsome moldings which framed the tall windows in the State Rooms. As they inspected each piece of furniture, Mr. du Pont told the true story of how Mrs. Franklin D. Roosevelt, to facilitate cleaning the floors and avoid soiling the draperies, had them all scissored off a foot from the floor. "She didn't care *how* they looked," the chairman emphasized, "as long as they were clean."

Mr. du Pont pointed out, in their progress through the State Rooms, that though there were a few good antique pieces, none were right either in period or proportion to the early nineteenth-century, high-ceilinged rooms. They had finished with both the Red and the Blue Rooms when, at the entrance to the Green

312

Room, Mr. du Pont paused. He had noticed two Baltimore card tables, graceful in form and exquisitely inlaid. He sighed with relief. "Those," he said, "are the only pieces in the room which are both correct in proportion and of the period! I'd like to know who gave them —"

An inventory of the Green Room contents was consulted and, to Mr. du Pont's obvious delight, the pair of tables had been presented to the White House by his sister, Mrs. Louise du Pont Crowninshield!

During the first months in the White House, Mrs. Kennedy had roughly checked through a list of some 26,000 items which were either in the White House or in government storage. The preparation of an annual White House inventory* was a mandatory government regulation; but far more difficult and time-consuming for the White House staff members involved was handling the thousands of packages, cases and crates which began arriving almost immediately after the First Lady had announced her plans for restoring the Executive Mansion. Many donors, of course, followed the suggestion of first mailing a photograph; but a large percentage apparently just packed up the objects they wished to send to the White House and shipped them directly to Washington.

At first the letters were sent to Mrs. Parish's New York office, but soon her staff was unable to cope with the volume. Then the White House assumed responsibility for the whole operation, and three outsize basement storerooms were made available for the influx of parcels.

As standard operating procedure, everything addressed to the White House, from a postcard to possibly a grand piano, is automatically rerouted to the adjoining Executive Office Building for a thorough security check. When the initial overwhelming load of mail was brought across to the White House, Tish Baldridge valiantly tried to deal with the crisis. Immediately she composed a "thank-you" note which was dispatched to everyone who had either written a letter or sent an offering to Mrs. Kennedy's project. As the tempo of arriving gifts increased, her polite

---

* An inventory, unlike a catalogue, merely lists each object tersely: "6 forks, 6 spoons, 6 knives," while a catalogue describes the origin or provenance and any other pertinent facts.

gesture proved inadequate, and eventually some ten different form letters were evolved to cover various contingencies: acceptances, refusals, and possible acquisitions. The confusion was such that two months elapsed before this unexpected "happening" could be efficiently organized.

What did the people want to give or sell to their President's House? Really, everything: chairs especially; old washstands; hooked rugs; beds of all sizes, styles and conditions; oil lamps; ridiculous things like fancy chamber pots; cobblers' benches; crocheted afghans and antique patchwork quilts; old guns and pistols; mustache cups; pressed glass bottles; Victorian whatnots; samplers and framed pressed flowers or shells; prints, paintings of every size and variety; and, of course, an Andrew Jackson spittoon, which proved authentic.

Meanwhile this strange harvest of gifts was carefully sorted and listed. Ultimately, over 95 percent of the offerings had to be declined, either because they were "inappropriate" for the White House or because similar items had already been accepted. Even objects obviously without value could not be disposed of; and everything which had been refused had to be repacked, heavily insured, then sent back. The insurance was a necessary precaution since the receipt served as sure proof of return. Later, should the donor be in a less generous mood, he would be unable to bill the White House for appropriating his treasure. This complicated turnaround of unpacking and repacking added a tremendous burden on the hard-working White House staff.

The relatively small number of articles which appeared from their photographs to be appropriate and of sufficiently high quality to meet the new White House standards were, when possible, inspected for authenticity by a member of the Advisory Committee. Prospective donors who could not arrange to have their offerings examined at home shipped them directly to the White House. Then, there was the ticklish question of appraisal. How much was the piece of furniture — or the bibelot — worth, either to the donor as an income tax deduction, or to the seller? Since both committee members and members of the White House staff were forbidden by law to make appraisals, when necessary they referred donors and sellers to reputable antique dealers.

The prices which owners sometimes placed arbitrarily on anything they wanted to sell to the White House were too ridiculous to be believed. The Andrew Jackson spittoon was an amusing example. A photograph of this handsome receptacle was mailed by its owner from a Florida trailer camp. (Research was to reveal that Andrew Jackson had ordered twenty such monogrammed spittoons, at a total cost of $250, as adornments for the East Room.) The owner requested succinctly: "$2,000 net — after taxes." The bust of Washington was another, not as amusing, example. This *objet d'art* was worth possibly a few hundred dollars. Yet the price demanded was two hundred thousand dollars! Occasionally, Janet Felton, for the Committee, would write the owner of what, from a photograph, appeared to be an attractive antique piece. She would ask for additional documentation — and the cost. Almost invariably the asking price was astronomical, and the inquiry was dropped.

Though completely unpublicized, a cautious policy was pursued in accepting donations. As a precaution, because gifts given in support of the restoration program were so closely associated with the First Lady, the Justice Department undertook a careful study of the situation. It was difficult to make ironclad rules, but there were several pitfalls to be avoided. Was the prospective donor involved in some way with the United States government and therefore might he expect some favor in return for an extravagant gift? Was an expensive gift offered, its value perhaps overestimated, because the donor planned to take an exaggerated tax deduction?

For cash gifts, a number of relevant factors were set down for consideration before acceptance.

1. The size of the gift, particularly in relation to the capacity of the donor to give this amount.
2. The extent to which the donor was or could be readily identified from other activities with an interest in philanthropy or art or history.
3. The extent to which there was common knowledge that the donor had financial interests which might be importantly affected by government action or inaction.

Gifts of furniture or art were easier to make a decision about. Family pieces or pieces from collections lacked the same public associations as cash. Yet cash difficulties could not be bypassed by having furniture purchased, then donated. It was suggested that Mrs. Kennedy be disassociated as much as possible from the solicitation of funds and that contributions by more than one person be encouraged to purchase particular *objets d'art*.

Fortunately, because the Committee was thus forewarned, there were no untoward incidents relating to the restoration project; though James Fosburgh, chairman of the Special Committee on White House Paintings, on several occasions had to return a painting because the gift itself was out of line with the tax deduction the owner planned to obtain.

There were, of course, a number of suitable and valuable items among the "possible" 5 percent. The most interesting of these were forwarded to Mr. du Pont for consideration. And, after all the preliminaries had been settled, the final decision for acceptance or purchase was made by Mrs. Kennedy and Mr. du Pont.

"A Wonderful Job"

Two weeks after the first meeting of the Fine Arts Committee, Mrs. Kennedy wrote a newsletter to the members. In it she detailed the various decisions made during her second visit, on March 6, to Mr. and Mrs. du Pont at Boca Grande. One item read: "A curator for the White House is being sought, preferably one trained at Winterthur. Before we announce his appointment, I will let you know his name." (A specially trained person, who knew about the furnishings and how to care for them, had never been employed at the White House.)

Mrs. Kennedy kept her word. It was still March when the identity of the first curator in White House history was disclosed. Surprisingly, "he" turned out to be a "she": a young, outgoing brunette who was singularly well prepared for her taxing new job. She was Lorraine Pearce, though she preferred to be called by her married name, Mrs. John Newton Pearce. Her husband was with the National Trust for Historic Preservation; they had a small child, and recently had moved to Washington.

As a student at City College in New York, Lorraine had been the first undergraduate to be offered a Fulbright Scholarship. (Fulbright Scholarships are granted for postgraduate study.) As a Fulbright Scholar at Strasbourg, in France, she concentrated on modern French and German history. Afterwards Lorraine returned to earn a master's degree in Early American Culture in a course co-sponsored by the University of Delaware and the Winterthur Museum. She met John Pearce, and while he completed his studies at Winterthur, Lorraine became a member of the Museum staff.

One evening in early March 1961, in the Pearces' small house on Capitol Hill, the telephone rang. It was Charles Montgomery, the director of Winterthur and the former boss of Mrs. Pearce.

"Lorraine," he asked without preamble, "are you having another baby?"

"No," she replied. "Why?"

Montgomery continued, "Then I have a wonderful job for you!"

There was only a single difficulty. Since there never had been a White House curator, no provision had been made in the budget for a curatorial salary. This stumbling-block, however, was bypassed discreetly. The great, sprawling Smithsonian Institution, which is congressionally funded, has, in addition, private funds used for many special purposes, including the salaries of some top officials who do not belong to Civil Service. The new curator was recompensed from this source.

Lorraine's work as White House curator was generally defined: to take physical care of the furnishings and decorative objects in the Executive Mansion; to have the facts of their documentation readily accessible; to supervise their arrangement and interpretation; to be helpful as well as knowledgeable in finding and judging acquisitions.

Actually, her task was far more strenuous than it might look from this description. She had, first, to familiarize herself with the White House, its contents, its history. She had to acquaint herself with public reaction, to know what the public hoped for and wanted of the White House. She spent long hours poring over selections of the "acclamatory" mail which had been received at the Executive Mansion after the foundation of the Fine Arts Committee had been announced. Sometimes accompanied by Mrs. Kennedy, sometimes with Janet Felton or on her own, she searched the vast White House cellars, the closets and other storerooms. When she found odd pieces of tarnished silver or vermeil, her Winterthur training had prepared her to recognize the hallmarks. When she discovered stray pieces of china, she could identify them. Eventually, she could often relate articles to each other to create an "incomplete" whole set. Later, she went through the giant government warehouse at Fort Washington. Here she rescued badly damaged historic furniture: numerous old pieces, unrecognizable except to an expert, with peeling varnish and paint and their upholstery in shreds; and an authentic Lincoln chair, with a missing leg!

Part of the curator's assignment was to handle public relations. Lorraine might be summoned from her other work to "show people around," or to give special tours to important people and possible donors, when the First Lady was unable to do so. She was also in charge of special members of the press: editors of art magazines and cultural publications planning to write about the White House.

Once she had settled into her job, Lorraine was given the added responsibility of selecting the objects which would serve as illustrations in the First Lady's projected guidebook. And, tucked away in a private room in the Executive Office Building, she wrote the basic text which Mrs. Kennedy was to rearrange and edit.

"She was brilliant and full of energy and charm," Mrs. Kennedy said. "She was as excited as a hunting dog, wanting to find out everything. She knew her field absolutely, and we were incredibly indebted to her."

It became apparent, almost immediately after Lorraine Pearce arrived, that she would have to have an assistant. The restoration project was widening in scope and a trained registrar was needed if the new acquisitions were to be catalogued adequately. Lorraine wrote to friends in various universities, and in September of 1961 William Elder became the first White House registrar.

A young man with an "impeccable eye" for judging antique furnishings, Bill Elder had concentrated on American art in graduate work at the University of Pennsylvania, and he specialized in Baltimore furniture. In personality he was the exact opposite of Mrs. Pearce. "Very quiet and shy," Mrs. Kennedy described him, "a wonderful, kind man and a dedicated scholar." He, too, knew his field thoroughly, the First Lady said.

In the late summer of 1962, when Lorraine Pearce decided to return to private life, Bill Elder became the curator. But the public relations aspect of his White House work, Mrs. Kennedy realized, was not compatible with his scholarly nature. "He would have been wonderful as a curator doing research in a cloistered place," she commented half-seriously. Two months before President Kennedy's death, when Elder accepted a position more suited to his temperament at the Baltimore Museum of Art, the First Lady said regretfully, "The museum there was really so lucky to get him."

On October 21, 1963, just thirty-two days before President Kennedy was assassinated, Mrs. Kennedy summoned James Ketchum to the Treaty Room. She asked him if he would take over from Bill Elder as White House curator. Ketchum was twenty-four but looked older: he was tall and sturdy, wore glasses and talked in a deep, booming voice. (Afterwards, the First Lady allowed the press to guess that he was twenty-eight.)

Jim replied vehemently that he could not take the job, he was too young and, besides, he had no real experience.

Mrs. Kennedy looked him straight in the eye. "They said Jack was too young!"

Jim mumbled again that he couldn't accept, he was only twenty-four and too inexperienced.

The First Lady, eyes unflinching, gazed steadily at Jim. "But at least you could try!" she said calmly. Meekly Ketchum agreed that he could. He murmured, under his breath, "But I shall always feel like the 'Man Who Came to Dinner'!"*

James Ketchum was twenty when he came to Washington from

* George S. Kaufman and Moss Hart's play in which a guest accidentally breaks his leg after dinner and remains in his host's house for weeks.

near Rochester, New York, to study for a law degree at Georgetown University. Because he had always taken a keen interest in
history, Jim became interested, too, in antiques; and since he was
a small boy he had enjoyed accompanying his father to country
auctions near his upstate New York home. So it was natural he
should turn to history — and antiques — to earn extra money
while he studied law. He found a job with the National Park
Service which administers the Custis-Lee Mansion, a white-pil-
lared house on the hill above Arlington National Cemetery,
where General Robert E. Lee lived for thirty pre-Civil War
years. The exhibits in the Mansion, which is open to the public,
had never been catalogued, and Jim was set to work putting
pertinent information in order. It was not a challenging job, and
before long the Park Service director, recognizing Ketchum's
ability, suggested he apply at the White House where help was
needed for the restoration project. Jim soon became so enthralled
by the White House that he abandoned his law courses, and
when Bill Elder was promoted to curator in August 1962, he
succeeded as registrar.

Mrs. Kennedy had selected Ketchum in the same instinctive
way she had chosen Anne Lincoln as housekeeper. He was
intelligent and on her wavelength, and with these assets she was
sure he could succeed in almost any job. The First Lady explained her reasoning: "— when you wake up and find yourself
in the White House, you must do everything at once. You don't
have the leisure, the absence of pressure, of criticism, that you
would have in your own house. You can't do it all by yourself —
just as the President can't. So you must pick the people you know
are qualified for each field and tell them what you wish — and
supervise it all, as nothing is ever any good without overall
unified supervision of the person who is putting all this in
motion."

Jim Ketchum, as Mrs. Kennedy had foreseen, was not handi-
capped by his youth. He had been employed in the White House
for two years and was at home there. He was a "quick study" and
adept at public relations. Jim carried through the difficult days
following President Kennedy's death with unobtrusive tact. Four
months later, on March 4, 1964, the legislation which Mrs.
Kennedy had initiated came into being through an Executive

Order, signed by President Johnson, which provided for a curator of the White House and also established a Committee for the Preservation of the White House. The post of White House curator was now official and the duties defined. "There shall be in the White House a Curator of the White House. The Curator shall assist in the preservation and protection of the articles of furniture, fixtures, and decorative objects used or displayed in the principal corridor on the ground floor and the principal public rooms on the first floor of the White House and in such other areas in the White House as the President may designate." The curator, as a member of the White House Preservation Committee, was also to report to the President and make recommendations as to the furnishings used or displayed in the museum area of the White House, which would be "best suited to enhance the historic and artistic values of the White House."

It was an impressive position for a man who had not as yet reached the quarter-century mark.

Selecting in Advance

After the first round of letters requesting either cash donations or gifts of appropriate and valuable furnishings, it became apparent to Mrs. Kennedy and her committee members that their approach was not sufficiently appealing. A more effective method would have to be evolved. The Committee, wishing to avoid a national fund-raising drive, had purposely written only to those known to "care" about antique furnishings and paintings. But, in the beginning, many in even this select group refused to make a gift unless their name was physically attached to it; yet this was obviously impossible except when a plaque could be fastened onto the frame of a painting.

Mrs. Kennedy realized that most people wanted to give something permanent "to show their descendants, perhaps, as a source of pride for having given something to the White House collection." Hopefully, she added, if the Committee could somehow make this possible, it would be a way to start people giving. They had found, however, that very few collectors of great Americana were willing to part with any treasured piece in their collections and, conversely, very few of these collectors had pieces which were really needed in the White House.

So, to encourage giving, instead of asking for money (when either a token check might be sent or the plea ignored entirely) the Committee first found objects which were wanted badly, then sent a list, with prices attached, to prospective contributors. The response was so generous, it was clear that most donors preferred to have a gift listed in the White House catalogue beside their name, rather than the near-anonymity of a cash donation. This manner of offering was time-saving too, as the authentication of every object was taken care of in advance.

The idea of this preprepared giving came about gradually, not all at once. Mrs. Douglas Dillon and her husband, the Secretary of the Treasury, were determined to contribute what was most needed, and had found a pair of large and extremely rare bookcases for the private upstairs hall. Mrs. Kennedy, however, because they "cared so much," wished them to give something "spectacular" which could be seen and appreciated by the public. The First Lady had already decided to restore the Red Room in American Empire. As red was a favored color of this period, it seemed appropriate for the room to be redone in an American version of the French style. Several exceptional pieces of this period had been found; so Mrs. Kennedy asked the Dillons if they would be interested in donating them. The Secretary and his wife were enthusiastic. Shortly afterwards, when other equally impressive objects were offered, the Dillons presented them too, and this distinguished group formed the focal point of the Red Room refurnishing.

In this same generous vein the Charles Engelhards completely refurbished the Family Dining Room which adjoined the State Dining Room. They not only gave the handsome Federal furniture but also the rug and elaborate curtains; they underwrote, as well, such "unseen" items as the complicated, expensive process necessary to paint in subtle shading the walls and unusually high ceiling of this elegant room. Some time afterwards, when Edward Troye's superb equestrian portrait of Brigadier General John Hartwell Cocke of Bremo came on the market, the Engelhards acquired it for "their" room. The General, mounted on his horse Roebuck and accoutered in the ornate uniform worn during the War of 1812, fitted superbly into the Federal décor.

Though the Dillon and Engelhard gestures were magnificent, it was the acquisition of individual items which firmly established the system of selecting in advance. Unexpectedly a desk which had belonged to Daniel Webster was offered. It was historically unique, expensive, and in immediate danger of being bought before the White House could get a chance at it. There were no adequate funds available, so Mrs. Albert Lasker, politely alerted, purchased it immediately. "Mary Lasker was always so sweet about things which were badly needed," Mrs. Kennedy commented appreciatively. Then there was the less immediate but even more difficult problem of acquiring the exactly right rug for each of the State Rooms. Beautiful rugs and carpets were not only costly but perishable too. "You couldn't find people who would give something like that," said the First Lady, "a rug or a carpet cannot be a permanent gift —" But a perfect rug was needed desperately to finish both the Red and the Blue Rooms. Mary Lasker presented the exquisite Savonnerie rug which had been selected (perhaps too optimistically) for the Blue Room. André Meyer, president of the Bank of France and a firm Kennedy friend, gave an equally unusual Savonnerie rug for the Red Room. (These fragile old rugs were made to be admired rather than walked on, unfortunately. By the time the Kennedys left the White House, too many guests at too many receptions had damaged them badly. Copies were woven in Puerto Rico, and now the antique rugs are put down only on special occasions such as state dinners.)

The Fine Arts Committee for the White House issued its first progress report to the nation on July 4, 1961, by announcing the gifts, loans and discoveries made in White House furnishings. The Committee proudly added that, since its founding four months previously, it had secured furniture which had belonged to George Washington, Abraham Lincoln, James and Dolley

Madison, James Monroe, Martin Van Buren, Nellie Custis and Daniel Webster. There were twenty-five individual donors; four major loans; and a list of the "discoveries" made by Mrs. Kennedy and Mrs. Pearce. It was a most creditable showing.

The First Lady followed up the Progress Report with a letter to the members of her Committee, outlining what had been learned during the initial four months of the restoration project. It was written with more than her usual sense of urgency:

> I am sending this letter to everyone on our Committee today. Also enclosed is a new list of things desperately needed for the White House to round out the things already acquired, so that some of the rooms will look unified by this winter.
>
> It has turned out to be impractical to ask people to donate pieces of their own furniture, except in rare cases where we know they have collected beautiful American things. We have also found that very few people want to give money without having a specific piece catalogued as their gift. Therefor, could you send to prospective donors a copy of this list? Anything they choose to give will be registered in their names. Many of the things have not yet been found, but if they wish to give, for example, the appliqués for the Green Room, we will let them know when we find them.
>
> It has been found to be more practical to have Mr. du Pont either find or approve all furniture; by keeping it under his surveillance we are assured of harmony in all the rooms. I fervently hope you will be able to raise the money to acquire some of these things by fall when we have our next meeting.

Fifty-six Million Tour the White House

That first year two comfortable sums of undesignated money *were* received by the Fine Arts Committee. Both were earned by Mrs. Kennedy. When the First Lady agreed to be interviewed by *Life,* she was aware, with all due modesty, that such a story would appreciably increase magazine sales. Mrs. Kennedy believed that the White House should profit by her efforts. "I was glad to work for the White House," she explained. "I knew that I would have to march through the rooms on all four floors; to pose again and again for photographers; and talk to a reporter for days. But, as it was for the White House, I was delighted to do it!" The financial arrangements were uncomplicated, and Mrs. Kennedy did not participate in them in any way. *Life* merely made a direct contribution to the restoration project. "They were so nice about it!" she recalled appreciatively.

Hugh Sidey, *Life*'s White House correspondent, was assigned as writer. Two staff photographers took the fourteen photographs which illustrated the eleven-page article (eight drawings relating to Executive Mansion history were also included). The cover picture of Mrs. Kennedy in a plain, two-piece white jersey dress, posed on a White House balcony with the Washington Monument soaring mistily in the background, was the work of Mark Shaw, her favored cameraman.

Though Hugh Sidey was well prepared in advance, as Mrs. Kennedy, with her usual thoroughness, had supplied him with pages of notes handwritten on yellow legal pads, the undertaking took the greater part of the early summer to put together. Sidey flew to and from Hyannis Port to consult with the First Lady, and the First Lady returned to the White House for the necessary photographic sessions. When the much-polished product was finally completed, it was titled "The First Lady Tells Her Plans for the White House," and she told them in a clear and appealing way.

Less than a month after the *Life* article had appeared, Blair Clark, the general manager of CBS News, invited Mrs. Kennedy to appear on a special hour-long television program. The purpose would be to show the basic changes made in the White House by the First Lady. There was a sound precedent for the proposed show, Mr. Clark pointed out, as in 1952 President Truman had participated in a similar program to explain his White House Renovation. Mr. Clark estimated that some sixty million people, or almost one-third of the nation at that time, might view the program, as it would be telecast at prime evening time with a repeat performance on both NBC and ABC networks scheduled for a later date.

Realistically, CBS might have preferred to have the program commercially sponsored, but approval would have had to come from the White House; so the program was sponsored by the network itself. Their Public Affairs Office guaranteed in advance that the production would be treated with the same meticulous attention whether commercially sponsored or not.

CBS was the first network to suggest an hour-long television program to Mrs. Kennedy, and, despite the work entailed, she accepted. On October 29, 1961, Blair Clark wired Mrs. Kennedy: "I am absolutely delighted at your consenting to help with the January 29th program on the restoration of the White House. Personally and for CBS I promise the best, most imaginative and scrupulous production a TV program has ever had. Best regards."

The Truman program lighting and camerawork, done in the early days of television, had been catch-as-catch-can. None of the objects to be discussed had stood out significantly. The shiny surfaces of portraits reflected light which made the paintings themselves indistinguishable. Furniture, shot from above, looked ordinary. Because television cameras cannot shoot back at windows, the rooms had been half-visible, and Mr. Truman's face had gone black when he passed one. Besides, as President Truman could not be asked to trail a long cable through the White House, he was often half-obscured by the interviewer who stood at his elbow with the microphone.

These technical difficulties had to be eradicated. Closeups of objects which Mrs. Kennedy would single out for attention were carefully lighted and photographed previous to the actual filming. Reverse angles were then shot in the major rooms, and the closeups inserted into Mrs. Kennedy's discussion. To dispel the window-blackout, a clear Polaroid plastic gel was hung between the valances and windows in many of the rooms. Charles Collingwood, who had been selected to interview the First Lady, was kept off camera as much as possible, and Mrs. Kennedy concealed a cableless microphone and a small transmitter in the bodice of her two-piece maroon wool dress.

Added to these and many additional technical problems were the important questions of what White House rooms were to be

President Kennedy dedicates the replica of the State Dining Room mantel-piece originally installed by President Theodore Roosevelt. Mrs. Alice Roosevelt Longworth, Theodore Roosevelt's daughter, attended the ceremony with Mrs. Kennedy, John J. Powers of the Marble Industry Board of New York, and Edwin B. Olson of Steinmann, Cain and White, the donors of the mantelpiece.

Mrs. Kennedy inspects the State Dining Room before the filming of her famous television tour of the White House. The table is set with the Monroe vermeil surtout de table and the Morgantown glassware. The sensitive Healy portrait of Lincoln hangs over the fireplace.

shown, what objects discussed; the choice of historically correct background music; and the careful research required to complete the forty-two-page script. There were also many small, seemingly inconsequential decisions to be made, such as selecting special flower arrangements to insure that they would photograph to the best advantage. All this caused understandable delays and postponed the actual taping to January 14 and 15, 1962.

Mr. Clark and CBS had been true to their promise. Even though commercially unsponsored, no television show had ever had a more "imaginative and scrupulous production."

On January 13 President Kennedy decided to participate in the program. His supporting role was brief. The President came on set near the program's end when Mrs. Kennedy was explaining the still unfinished Treaty Room, which had formerly been known as the Monroe Room. President Kennedy answered two questions gracefully, and by his presence added glamour as well as official approval of his wife's plans.

A CBS crew of forty set up the equipment, manned the cameras and remained in the White House for three days. Mrs. Kennedy planned what pieces of furniture she wanted to talk about and approved almost every essential facet of the hour-long program. Fearful of being too nervous to use a prepared script, even if she had memorized it previously, the First Lady ad-libbed as she moved from room to room. The first day she rehearsed from 9:30 A.M. to 12:30 P.M. and in the afternoon from 2:30 P.M. to 6:30 P.M. During the actual taping of the program she was on set almost seven hours. Afterwards, Mrs. Kennedy taped the introduction to the program in both French and Spanish for overseas distribution.

Yet during these often onerous preparations her private life had been beset with worries. The First Lady was organizing the complicated logistics of her trip to India and Pakistan, and she was deeply concerned about the senior Mr. Kennedy's grave illness. Despite the added hazards of her shyness and her deep sense of privacy, the First Lady carried out her part with the assurance of a veteran performer. She was so pretty, so earnest in her cause that her audience was captivated.

The CBS program "A Tour of the White House with Mrs. John F. Kennedy" was telecast on Wednesday, February 14

Mrs. Kennedy opens the White House Library. James T. Babb, Librarian of Yale, had headed up the Library Committee which was responsible for acquiring suitable books for the library. Mr. Babb and his committee assembled an impressive list of 2700 volumes of American authors of every era, from George Washington to James Thurber.

1962 at 10 P.M. The joint NBC and ABC showing followed on Sunday, February 18 at 6:30 P.M. A special Nielsen analysis estimated 28.3 million "homes" as having watched the hour program for fifty minutes or more. Conservatively averaging two people to a "home," over fifty-six million citizens, truly almost a third of the nation, had followed the program over the three networks.

The morning after the telecast the White House was inundated with telegrams, cables, then mail. These communications were almost entirely laudatory. Among the many were messages from both a Democratic and a Republican congressman.

The first was sent by Carl Albert, a Democrat and a veteran congressman from Oklahoma.

Dear Mrs. Kennedy: —
We were delighted to clip the attached editorials from the Oklahoma City *Times* and *Daily Oklahoman*. This is the first time a Democrat has received such favorable treatment in these papers since the memory of man runneth out."

The second was written by Paul B. Dague, a Republican from Pennsylvania.

Dear Mrs. Kennedy: —
May I convey to you — on behalf of our entire family — our grateful appreciation of your moving description of the President's House, as presented to all of America through the medium of TV.

The graciousness with which you detailed its furnishings and background was a heart-warming experience and gave us a sense of prideful possession that has never before been ours.

Incidentally, we are the so-called "loyal opposition" — and pretty partisan at that — but your brilliant presentation compels the abandonment of all political bias and prompts these heartfelt thanks for an outstanding contribution to the history of the Nation.

I have the great honor to be
Most respectfully, —

Quality, Aesthetics and History

Late in the summer of 1961 Mrs. Kennedy decided to form a special committee to assemble a permanent collection of paintings for the White House. For the first time in history a collection of value was feasible, since legislation confirming its permanence in the White House would be passed by Congress in a matter of weeks. The Fine Arts Committee was now successfully established, and as handsome acquisitions were placed in various rooms the need for pictures of equal quality and historic significance became more painfully apparent.

The White House paintings consisted almost entirely of portraits of Presidents and a few First Ladies. There were no landscapes, no still lifes, no marines, none of the familiar American genre pictures and only a few historical scenes. And most of the portraits of Presidents and their ladies were inferior copies of lost originals — copies painted many years after the subjects were dead.

Among the portraits of the first seven Presidents, only the two Gilbert Stuarts of George Washington had been painted from life. Aside from the Stuarts, the earliest presidential portraits of any quality still remaining in the White House were those by George P. A. Healy and Eastman Johnson. Healy painted a number of Presidents, commencing with John Quincy Adams (1825–1829) and including both President John Tyler (1841–1845) and Lincoln. Though these Presidents did, at one time or another, sit for Healy, Healy had a habit of making later copies of his own work, and because of the problem of fixing the dates of these paintings, it was difficult to ascertain which were copies and which the more desirable and valuable portraits done from life. (The famous Healy portrait of Lincoln, which Mrs. Kennedy had rehung in the State Dining Room, was known to have been painted in Rome.) Eastman Johnson had painted both Grover Cleveland (1885–1889 and 1893–1897) and Benjamin Harrison (1889–1893); but thereafter, with few exceptions, the artists commissioned for presidential portraits had been mediocre. These exceptions included an elegant Sargent of Theodore Roosevelt; a decorative portrait of his wife by Theobald Chartran; and a dashing likeness of William Howard Taft by Anders Zorn.

Mrs. Kennedy faced this bleak situation with the same determination she had shown in establishing the Fine Arts Committee. But she was uncertain about whom to ask to be chairman for what was to be the "Special Committee for White House Paintings." She needed not only someone who knew paintings and where to find them, but perhaps more important, a person "admired by the people she hoped would give them." John Hay Whitney, who had recently served as Eisenhower-appointed Ambassador to Great Britain, was suggested. The First Lady knew and liked him. She wrote him a personal letter asking him to accept the chairmanship.

Later, Mrs. Kennedy realized her move had been naïve. Jock Whitney was a Republican; more important, he was the actively involved owner of the New York *Herald Tribune,* the newspaper which President Kennedy was to bar from the White House in disapproval of its editorial stance. Though chairmanship of a White House cultural committee was, of course, far removed from journalism, the First Lady came to realize that Whitney's heavy responsibilities kept him much too busy to accept. Jock Whitney, however, did solve her problem indirectly by suggesting that his wife's brother-in-law, James W. Fosburgh, be approached. The First Lady had never met Jim Fosburgh, but they had many mutual friends, and she was delighted when he accepted. He and his wife, a sister of both Mrs. Whitney and Mrs. William S. Paley, were discriminating collectors of American paintings.

It turned out to be a most felicitous choice. In the little more than two years before Mrs. Kennedy was to leave the White House, at least 150 paintings (including five life portraits of early Presidents); drawings; prints; and pieces of sculpture, all of historic interest, and conservatively valued at over two million dollars, became part of the permanent White House collection.

Mrs. Kennedy's letter to Jim Fosburgh arrived literally "out of the blue," as Fosburgh described it, and after the First Lady announced his acceptance of the chairmanship and outlined her plans for the Special Committee for White House Paintings, his hitherto smoothly organized life was to change dramatically.

"The response was extraordinary," Fosburgh said. "I received countless letters and telephone calls, from every part of the country and from people in every walk of life, offering donations of every variety." Often his doorbell rang at an unorthodox hour of the day or evening. "When I opened the door — there was someone with a picture under his arm. Or, perhaps, a picture in the back of his car. It was sad," he added, "that these generous offers had to be rejected so often!

"The excitement was all over the country," Fosburgh continued. He would call up museums in every state, talk to museum heads who were eager to listen, searching for clues to some possibly appropriate but elusive painting. "Everyone was interested and in the next two years there wasn't a painting of first-class quality and pertinent subject which we didn't get — or have offered to us." Even after that first excitement, for over two and a half years, he personally answered between twenty and twenty-five letters daily concerning the newly acquired White House paintings.

Fosburgh's first move was to select a committee. He chose exceptionally informed persons, usually friends, from the ten main art centers across the country. Mrs. Kennedy gave this group a grand title: "Committee of Art Historians and Collectors."

His next move was to prepare for the first committee meeting, scheduled for November 21 at the White House. Mrs. Kennedy had suggested that he should select a number of paintings which would be of sufficient merit to warrant being included in a permanent collection. "I didn't know what was on Mrs. Kennedy's mind," Fosburgh said, "or what she really wanted."

Painstakingly he assembled about thirty-five paintings, choosing them at art galleries and "from everybody!" Among this interesting diversity of Americana were: *Mouth of the Delaware,* an 1828 oil by Thomas Birch, the first great American marine painter; a Jasper Cropsey landscape, *A Mountain Glimpse,* painted in 1854; a Civil War maneuver, *Cannonading on the Potomac,* depicted by A. Wordsworth Thompson in October 1861, as cannon engaged in battle across the river; and a "port-hole" type painting, circa 1835, of *Niagara Falls,* by John F. Kensett, leader of the "Hudson River" school of painting. (Later Mr. and Mrs. Fosburgh presented the Kensett to the White House.)

A White House truck fetched the canvases from New York. When they arrived, Fosburgh, his wife Minnie, and Mr. West propped the paintings against the walls in the spacious State Dining Room. This would serve as an impromptu sort of gallery, where the committee members could see them easily.

At this first meeting the new Committee determined the criteria upon which gifts of painting and sculpture could be accepted. They were simple and logical. First was quality. Only the best from both the aesthetic and historic points of view would be considered. Second, acquisitions of both paintings and sculpture would be restricted to Americana. Artists would be American, the subjects they portrayed would illustrate either American life or the American scene. Portraits, preferably, would be of historic personages. Landscapes, if possible, would include some American landmark — like Niagara Falls. Other paintings would relate to the presidency and the White House. (Afterwards a few exceptions were made, to include one or two foreign paintings of United States subjects and, conversely, United States paintings of foreign subjects.) Third, no living artist would be represented, since it would be impossible to choose between different artists and different schools of painting. Fourth, the whole span of White House history should be represented in the collection and no single period stressed. Fifth and finally, as all important visitors were entertained at one time or another upstairs in the private living quarters, Mrs. Kennedy pointed out that if the paintings there were inferior, it would make the State Rooms downstairs seem like a façade.

The Committee agreed with the First Lady and by so doing greatly widened the range of possible acquisitions. The proportions of the public rooms were so vast that small pictures tended to disappear on the wide reaches of their walls. In the less grand private rooms, it would be possible to hang smaller paintings of high quality.

When the session adjourned, Mrs. Kennedy and the committee members went into the State Dining Room to view Jim Fosburgh's "exhibit." The First Lady walked slowly from picture to picture. "I *like* this —" she would say. "I like this, *too* —" One of the many paintings Mrs. Kennedy "liked" was a small still life by William Chase, whose own life had spanned from 1848 to 1916. It was called *Lettuce and Tomatoes,* a composition created with a basket of tomatoes, a head of Romaine lettuce, with a pewter pitcher and bowl in the background.

This charming still life was the first painting bought for the new, permanent collection. The purchaser, Suzette Morton Zurcher of Chicago, was a member of the Art Historians and Collectors Committee. A descendant of the famous American Indian Princess Pocahontas, she owned the Pocahontas Press which printed distinguished art books; she was also a trustee of the American Federation of Arts and an eclectic collector, her *objets d'art* ranging from classical antiquities to Picasso.

When he had borrowed the paintings, Jim Fosburgh promised the owners, "I'll have them back immediately!" He assumed that they had been returned until his friends began to call, demanding to know the whereabouts of their pictures. Fosburgh telephoned Mr. West who, with his usual aplomb, replied soothingly that seven of the paintings had already been hung, Fosburgh, amazed, then got through to Mrs. Kennedy. The First Lady acknowledged that the pictures had indeed been hung. "We'll get the money somehow," she added calmly.

The delayed return of the paintings had been due to Mrs. Kennedy's difficulties in making a selection. Happily, before too long, the seven paintings were donated, and the Birch, the Cropsey, the Thompson and the Kensett became part of the White House Collection. The remaining pictures were repacked in the White House truck and sent back to New York.

Shortly after the creation of the Special Committee for Paintings, a firm policy against loans was determined. At first, when there were so few fine paintings in the White House, loans had been welcomed. Individual loans were often accepted in the unspoken hope that they might later be donated. Unfortunately, most owners wanted their possessions returned. Then the disillusioning fact was discovered that some unscrupulous owners, once loans had been accepted and hung, withdrew the objects quickly — their value having been greatly enhanced because they had been on view in the White House.

There were other disadvantages to accepting loans. Even though some loans might be considered "permanent," the paintings involved were not bona fide White House possessions and therefore could not be included in the permanent guidebook. To maintain the dignity of the Executive Mansion, Mrs. Kennedy and her committee felt strongly that all furnishings and *objets d'art* should belong to, rather than be borrowed for, the White House. From the professional point of view, Fosburgh noted that the removal of a single painting, such as one that had been on loan, would necessitate rehanging all the others in the room. This task required infinite patience and know-how; besides, it could cause irreparable damage to the expensive fabric wall-coverings.

Loans from museums were in a different category. Museums' paintings could not be given away; and many were stored because wall space on which to hang them was lacking. Often museums loaned paintings to United States embassies, and Mrs. Kennedy thought it quite natural they should also be offered to the President's House until its own collection could be assembled. In the beginning many American paintings from important museums across the country were made available to the Executive Mansion. But in a surprisingly short time, the White House collection *was* assembled, and there was no further need for borrowed works of art.

There were, however, two private loans of magnificent paintings made to the White House. Shortly after the Inauguration the White House walls were brightened by a group of portraits of the first five Presidents, all painted from life by Gilbert Stuart. This unique group of paintings was lent by Thomas Jefferson Coolidge, a young member of a distinguished Boston family, who had inherited them in recent years from his father. The paintings, understandably, were greatly admired, but like most private loans, were returned within a few months.

The second loan, of six portraits (though not an orderly progression of Presidents by a single artist), was equally spectacular. At this time there were only a few historic portraits of museum quality in the White House, and these six were offered, said Mrs. Kennedy, from "out of the blue and were so incredibly welcome." The paintings belonged to John J. Ryan of Virginia, a grandson of Thomas Fortune Ryan, the financier. "They were such wonderful paintings," the First Lady commented enthusiastically, "— they were the ones seen by every guest at State Dinners."

Mr. Ryan came to the White House to supervise the placement of his paintings. The twin portraits by Chester Harding of Bushrod Washington (the first President's favorite nephew who inherited Mount Vernon) and his wife, were hung in the East Room on the end panels flanking the famous portraits of George and Martha Washington. The remaining four were placed on the walls of the Cross Hall, which connected the East Room and the State Dining Room. They were George Washington by Charles Peale Polk; American Revolutionary hero General Starke painted by Samuel F. B. Morse, the talented inventor of the telegraph; Charles Carroll of Carrollton, a signer of the Declaration of Independence, by Chester Harding; and the dashing naval commander of American Revolutionary renown, John Barry, whose portrait is artistically one of the most exciting executed by the prolific Gilbert Stuart.

Occasionally, these superb portraits have been rehung in perhaps even more advantageous positions, but the great miracle was that Mr. Ryan permitted them to remain and be admired by the almost two million tourists who now file through the White House each year.

Great Americans Return to the White House

Above all, for the White House Collection, Mrs. Kennedy had wished to obtain museum-quality portraits of the early Presidents, painted from life. When she came to the Executive Mansion, the only life portraits of excellence in this early group were the Gilbert Stuarts of Washington. By the time the First Lady left, likenesses of the first seven Presidents hung in the Blue Room; and of these, five were fine life portraits. The missing pair, John Adams and James Madison, the second and fourth Presidents, were represented by paintings of a later date.

The first additions to this galaxy were a portrait of James Monroe, the fifth President, by that busy artist-inventor, Samuel F. B. Morse; and John Wesley Jarvis's version of the seventh President, an elegant Andrew Jackson in gold braid and epaulettes, with nose and cheeks crimson as a polished apple. The Morse, bought in the early 1900s from a Monroe descendant by Mr. Willard Straight, was a gift from Michael Straight, son of the purchaser. The Jarvis, originally intended as a legacy from the owner, Gerard Lambert, to his daughter, Mrs. Paul Mellon, was donated at her suggestion to the White House.

The life portrait of Thomas Jefferson, the third President, by Rembrandt Peale, was not only the most prized but the most romantic painting in the White House. Though it had never been farther away from Washington than Baltimore, the painting had been lost for half a century. During those fifty or so years it had hung in placid anonymity, on a library wall of the Peabody Institute, in Baltimore. In 1959, through research by the editors of the Jefferson papers at Princeton University, the portrait had been "rediscovered."

"It is one of the finest male portraits ever painted," Mrs. Kennedy said, "you can look at it for hours, because it is so alive.

His expression seems to be changing as if he were not only alive but actually looking at you. Everything Jefferson was is there: aristocrat, revolutionary, statesman, artist, sceptic and idealist. Compassionate but aloof. The Stuart portrait of Washington is so remote in comparison. Allegorical and not human. You can't feel what Washington was like from looking at it.

"The spirit of the eighteenth century is in Jefferson's face. I remember that Uncle Lefty [Wilmarth Lewis, Mrs. Kennedy's stepfather's brother-in-law] once said to me when I was at Farmington — that the eighteenth century had three geniuses and two of them were Americans: Jefferson, Franklin, and the third was Voltaire."

In 1800 Thomas Jefferson sat for the Rembrandt Peale portrait in Philadelphia, before the fledgling United States government had moved permanently to Washington. The likeness became his popular as well as official image both at home and in Europe. Throughout the nineteenth century innumerable engravings, lithographs and paintings were all based on the Peale portrait. Jefferson admired the picture so much that the following year he asked Peale to make him a copy, which the artist did.

The original Jefferson portrait was included in Rembrandt Peale's collection of paintings when he opened his celebrated museum in Baltimore. The museum subsequently changed hands several times. When the last pictures from the Peale Collection were dispersed privately in 1856, the Jefferson portrait became the property of Charles J. M. Eaton, afterwards president of the Peabody Institute of Music. When Eaton died, his paintings were willed to the Institute. After the "rediscovery," when the picture was appraised, it was considered too valuable for the Institute to keep. So, in a most discreet manner, it was offered for sale.

Neither Jim Fosburgh nor anyone else connected with the White House Restoration had mentioned the Peale to Mrs. Kennedy. She was unaware of its existence until one day quite casually Mrs. Mellon told the First Lady that she and her husband, Paul Mellon, intended to give a Jefferson portrait to the White House. Mrs. Mellon also mentioned, in an equally understated manner, that she had arranged for her father to donate the Jackson portrait.

Mrs. Mellon was well aware of the difficulties in finding suitable paintings for the White House. She knew that the acquisition of these two pictures would permit the portraits of the first seven Presidents to be hung together in the Blue Room. Yet she had given no hint of her intention. "I am sure that Bunny Mellon knew she was going to give the two portraits — which we so badly needed. But she wouldn't say anything about them until she had them 'right in her truck' ready to give," said Mrs. Kennedy.

Wilmarth Lewis, Mrs. Kennedy's courtesy "Uncle Lefty," had told her that, like Jefferson, Benjamin Franklin was one of the trio of eighteenth-century geniuses. He was also one of the first internationally known Americans, and the popular inventor-diplomat had posed for many artists. The original of the famous Franklin portrait, copied many times, had been owned for several generations by the Philadelphia Biddle family. Recently it had been offered for sale by a New York art gallery. The price, however, was prohibitive to most prospective buyers.

David Martin, a Scotch artist, executed the portrait in London in 1767, when Franklin was sixty. Martin had been commissioned by Robert Alexander, a London businessman for whom his American friend had refereed successfully a property claim dispute. This commemorative painting shows Franklin seated, holding one of the property deeds in his hands and, to represent his interest in physical sciences, a bust of Isaac Newton in the background. It is considered Martin's masterpiece.

The painting had passed to Jonathan Williams, a grandson of Franklin's sister, who, coincidentally, married a granddaughter of Robert Alexander. It was then bequeathed to successive elder sons. When two brothers died childless, the picture was inherited by a sister who married a Biddle.

The ultimate owner in the Biddle clan was the stylish and social Christine Biddle Cadwalader Scull, wife of R. Barclay Scull. Mrs. Scull, instead of selling her inheritance, exchanged it at a New York gallery for a number of French Impressionist paintings and a Brancusi sculpture. Immediately after this unusual transaction, Mrs. Wrightsman, well known to every New York art gallery owner, was shown the Franklin. She was determined that this important picture be added to the White House collection, and drew it to the attention of a friend, Walter Annenberg, then publisher of the Philadelphia *Enquirer,* who later would be appointed United States Ambassador to the Court of St. James. Appropriately, as Benjamin Franklin was a native of Philadelphia, Mr. and Mrs. Annenberg presented his most famous likeness to the White House.

When the Benjamin Franklin was, so to speak, safely in the White House, Mrs. Scull wrote a letter to Mrs. Kennedy. In her father's house, Mrs. Scull explained, she had "grown up under Benjamin Franklin." Through the years, his sober gaze had become oppressive. So, some time after the portrait had come into her possession, she had "traded it for some French Impressionist pictures which seemed more suitable to our way of life."

Some time after its first sessions, Vincent Price, the actor, was to be an active member of the Paintings Committee. In the early thirties, Price and Jim Fosburgh had studied Art History together at Yale, and they became very special friends. Price's acting career had begun by sheer chance when Helen Hayes, meeting him in Rome, had persuaded him to play Prince Albert to her Queen Victoria. He never wanted to be a star, never even considered himself a good actor, but he continued to act as a means of earning money to buy works of art.

When not in the theater he lectured on the arts, and, among his many affiliations, he was president of the University of California Art Council and a member of the United States Indians Arts and Crafts Board. Along the way, in his colorful life, Sears, Roebuck and Company, which had decided to "go in for art" in a suitably lavish way, engaged Price to act as both art adviser and purchaser for their organization. Equipped with these unusual contacts, Price was to make a double contribution of value to the White House.

There were five extremely rare portraits of Indian chiefs which Mrs. Kennedy longed to obtain. They were dated 1821 and were executed in the Washington studio of Charles Bird King, the first native-born artist to concentrate on our earliest Americans. These were the vanguard of many other portraits commissioned later by the Bureau of Indian Affairs, of which some 130 had been destroyed in a Smithsonian Institution fire in 1865.

In 1819 the Secretary of War had dispatched a scientific expedition to inquire into the habits and manners of the Plains Indians. The band of four chiefs and a squaw who were depicted in this group of King paintings, had accompanied the Indian agent, Major Ben O'Fallon, to Washington, where they were received by President Monroe.

Monroe staged a special council for them at the White House, and, as none of them had "ever before seen a white man's lodge," they dressed grandly for the occasion. They were made up with slashes of bright paint and wore feather headdresses or simpler buffalo horns; necklaces of blue beads or grizzly-bear claws, Each of the five proudly displayed a silver chain from which was suspended a medal embossed with Monroe's handsome features. They were wrapped against the Washington chill in fur wraps and fur throws, and their names were as delightfully complicated as their costumes — "Sharitarish" (Long Hair) Wicked Chief of the Great Pawnee Tribe; "Petalesharro" (Generous Chief) of the Pawnee Tribe; "Monchousia" (White Plume) of the Kanza Tribe; "Shaumonekusse," Oto Half Chief; "Hayne Hudjihini" (The Eagle of Delight), wife of the Oto Half Chief.

Through the good offices of Vincent Price, the likenesses of perhaps the most exotic guests ever to visit the White House were obtained. They were the joint gift of the employees of Sears, Roebuck and were presented to Mrs. Kennedy shortly before Christmas in 1962 by Mr. Crowdus Baker, president of the company.

The four chiefs and the lady, Eagle of Delight, were hung in the White House Library; and Caroline Kennedy, who was charmed by Indians, watched excitedly as her mother supervised their placement.

The Library, once so drab, was fast becoming a delightful room. Its restoration was undertaken by the American Institute of Interior Designers, who partially redesigned the room architecturally. The walls were paneled with woodwork in late eighteenth-century style; a mantelpiece attributed to Samuel McIntyre of Salem was added and random size boards replaced the incongruous tile floor. Among the furnishings was a remarkable suite of caned sofas, armchairs and side chairs, signed by Duncan

Phyfe and the gift of the Winthrop Rutherfurd family of New York. The festive Indian portraits seemed completely at home.

The more personal contribution which Vincent Price and his wife were to make gave President Kennedy great pleasure. It was a small cloudscape, circa 1880, by Albert Bierstadt. A study of storm clouds over the land, it was chosen for artistic merit rather than historic importance. President Kennedy often said it was his favorite painting.

In Memoriam

Among the gifts made to the White House in memory of President Kennedy were two extraordinary paintings — one donated by Whitney Warren, a member of the Paintings Committee, the other by the Kennedy family.

Whitney Warren was a New Yorker who had long since moved to San Francisco. The son and namesake of the famous architect, he concerned himself with the arts and was trustee of the California Palace of the Legion of Honor. Through the years Warren had assembled a true connoisseur's collection of unusual paintings.

On a visit to Washington, the First Lady had invited Whitney Warren to tea and afterwards personally conducted him through the White House. "He was absolutely charming," she remembered. But he made no gift to the White House.

To round out the White House collection, Fosburgh and his committee members had searched diligently, but in vain, for a John Singer Sargent canvas. The most popular among American painters, Sargent was practically impossible to acquire. The First Lady may or may not have mentioned this fact to Whitney Warren. But almost immediately after the death of her husband, Mrs. Kennedy received a touching letter from Mr. Warren. In it he offered to the White House his most incomparable painting, *The*

Mosquito Net by John Singer Sargent. There was a single stipu-
lation attached to the gift: the picture must bear a plaque with
the inscription that it was given "In Memory of President John
F. Kennedy."

The Mosquito Net was one of ten or so of his canvases which
Sargent had prized highly and refused to sell. At exhibitions it
had been hailed as a masterpiece. It had come on the market in
1925 when Sargent's personal collection was sold after his death.
The painting, which was hung in the Oval Room, centers on
Polly Barnard, daughter of artist Frederick Barnard. Polly appeared in many of Sargent's charming watercolors. Here, her
figure is reclining, her head cushioned by a mound of white
pillows, and a white comforter is thrown across her legs. Over her
head floats a transparent black mosquito net, which Sargent himself invented when his sister and a friend traveled to Majorca.
The painting was described in a recent exhibition catalogue:
"*The Mosquito Net* is a bewitching study in contrasts, where
sexual beauty and opulent material seem to polarize each other
and produce a kind of sensuous electricity."

Mrs. Kennedy had asked Jim Fosburgh to return to Washington the day after her husband's funeral. She received him in the
private living quarters and told him immediately that the Kennedy family wanted to give a painting to the White House in
memory of the late President. "They want to have it hung before
I leave," she added.

Fosburgh asked if an American painting was preferred. "Not
necessarily," Mrs. Kennedy replied. "Jack liked French paintings —"*

Fosburgh, back in New York, made the rounds of art dealers,
galleries and friends. He finally accumulated about twenty paintings. It had been agreed, because President Kennedy loved the
outdoors, that all should be landscapes, and the artists included
Corot, Whistler, Cézanne, and Monet. For the last time, paintings which Fosburgh had chosen traveled to Washington in a
White House truck.

In the upstairs hall, now crowded with packing cases, the
paintings were ranged against the walls. The Kennedys — Eunice

---

* "The only painting he bought," Mrs. Kennedy noted, "was a Boudin — He
loved paintings of water and sky."

Shriver, Pat Lawford, Joan and Teddy — perched on the wooden boxes and drank a great deal of coffee. They weeded out all but six of the twenty, then Mrs. Kennedy asked for a vote. Joan, not being Kennedy-born, refused to participate. Fosburgh eased off his perch. "I'm leaving," he said, "you'll have to decide this without me."

When he returned, the Kennedys had chosen a painting by Claude Monet, the French Impressionist, titled *Matinée sur la Seine — Beau Temps* (*Morning on the Seine — Beautiful Weather*). The picture combined the elements — water, air, light — which President Kennedy had so enjoyed. It was a breathtaking mixture of blues, greens, pinks and lavender with dark trees in the foreground, the dappled river all dissolving into distant, airy pastels.

Fosburgh hung the lovely landscape on the silk moiré walls of the Green Room. On it was a plaque which read: "In Memory of President John F. Kennedy, by His Family."

Beauty Shared

"The significance of the President's House goes beyond its historical meaning," John Walker, director of the National Gallery of Art, had written in his introduction to the first edition of the White House guidebook. "It suggests a way of life in which we all take pride. We want it to be an example of excellence. We are endeavouring to bring back the old and beautiful things which symbolize the dignity of the President's House. We wish to see here as many objects associated with past Presidents as it is possible to recover. This goal can never be completely realized, but the White House will continue to seek this unattainable perfection."

Mrs. Kennedy never ceased trying to attain unattainable perfection. Her friend Mrs. Wrightsman, herself a noted perfectionist, said, "Jackie had a terrific overall grasp, the idea of what the White House should be and a great sense of what was right for the State Rooms — whose proportions were so outlandish — she never stopped working for one second, nothing was too much trouble — it was a miracle what she did in three years." Though hard work is admittedly the basis of most successful endeavors, it was not only work but sure knowledge and the enthusiasm personally projected by Mrs. Kennedy which attracted a response to the restoration project from citizens of every origin and station.

"These improvements in the White House would be impossible without private donations," John Walker's guidebook Introduction had continued. "And this is right; it is typically American. Elsewhere in the past the great palaces were created by a King or Emperor who ordered his painters, sculptors and cabinet-makers to decorate the building in which he deigned to live. Here, the head of the government welcomes the generosity of private citizens who provide the works of art whose beauty he shares with his fellow Americans.

"The gifts from private individuals have been as varied as they have been touching — they have ranged from paintings and drawings costing many thousands of dollars to a piece of velvet of exactly the right period, color and design to cover two chairs which Lincoln once used —"

During the span of two years and eight months, from the organization of the Fine Arts Committee to the date on which Mrs. Kennedy wrote what was to be her last letter to Mr. du Pont, the generosity of private citizens had, to all practical purposes, completed the redecoration and refurnishing of the President's House. Presumably no stone had been left unturned in the search for objects which would enhance the White House heritage. Yet to Mrs. Kennedy, as well as to Mr. du Pont, the effort to attain unattainable perfection was still a strong, continuing force. The lengthy letter, which preceded what was also to be the last meeting of her Fine Arts Committee, mixed business, humor, a sense of history and love for the White House.

Dear Mr. du Pont: —

I will try to make this letter efficient.

I have the most marvelous idea for the Colonial Dames' present: the 11 lanterns and chandeliers in the ground floor hall. They cost

$5,200 — and have not been announced or photographed — and, to me, they do more than anything to give the feeling of an historic house — as it is here everyone comes in.

It would be wonderful if you, who was brilliant enough to find all those chandeliers, could persuade the Colonial Dames that nothing they could give would be more appreciated. Then we will announce it.

As you know most of our last year Guidebook profits will be used to pay back bills. If they could give that (we can pay $200, so their gift will be just $5,000) it would give us $5,000 of our precious money to pay for all the little things: chintz, lampshades, carpets etc. that we will never find donors for —

About the Queens' Room mantel: I find it was made in the White House carpentry shop under FDR. It was replaced by a molding after the Truman Renovation, then someone returned this one. For that reason, because it was lovingly made in the house (tho it may not be the most beautiful in the world) I think it has historic value and should not be removed. I don't really mind it, as it has that rather ugly charm that so many WH objects had (i.e. furniture in the Treaty Room). Anyway, before we rip it out, I should like to wait and think about it because it is the last piece of carving done in the WH carpentry shop. We always have to make concessions to history and I am sure you understand my reluctance to replace it with a period one.

Subjects to be discussed at the Fine Arts Committee meeting: Whatever you wish to say is fine with me. — I think a résumé of what has been done — Any exhorting you can do to raise money is, of course, always helpful though, I think, we probably need that for pictures more than for furniture now. If there is any special furniture you think we will need (I think some writing tables or small desks), it would always be useful in the third floor Guest Rooms, Children's Rooms, when we leave, and a suitable desk for second floor hall when we take our French bureau-plat [the Kennedys' own Louis XVI flat-topped desk] away.

I suppose that, besides showing the Committee what we have done, we could tell them what is still to do — and I leave that to you. —

I do look forward to our meeting. It is marvelous what we have accomplished and you should make a long speech, patting yourself on the back, and I am so glad you say there's still lots to do as I will be so sad when it is all over.

Sincerely —

347

Mrs. Kennedy could well have made a long speech and patted *herself* on the back. She had given permanency to the new White House beauty which she had planned and provided. For the first time in White House history, a curatorial staff had been organized to tend the treasures which the White House now contained and to supplement knowledge of their history. She had sought, through painstaking research, classic perfection in even the most minute details. With the unflagging support of so many, from the prominent members of important committees to the equally devoted though anonymous workers from every trade and profession, the achievement was superb.

Epilogue

On the morning of November 22, 1963, newspapers throughout the country headlined the Kennedy swing around Texas. A Washington newspaperwoman, known for her direct political approach, wrote in an unaccustomed lyrical tone. FIRST LADY INSTANT PRO was the headline. "She had been nothing less than sensational on her first, official domestic trip outside Washington as a political, campaigning wife. . . . She has become an instant political pro and may turn out to be the President's secret weapon in the 1964 campaign. From the moment she entered the drawing room, she stole the show from the President. She was stunning in a black cocktail suit of cut velvet . . ." Earlier, when the President and Mrs. Kennedy arrived in Texas, the same newswoman had written: "As Mrs. Kennedy smiled and smiled and shook hands and more hands, everyone could be heard saying how beautiful she looked. . . . And she did, in a simple, white wool bouclé suit with black accessories and a coneshaped black cloche. Her cheeks were rosy and she appeared to be glowing with health . . ."

A New York *Herald Tribune* correspondent agreed with his feminine colleague. "It was apparent from the time his plane landed that the big thing going for him is his wife. This was Mrs. Kennedy's first visit to Texas and she arrived wearing a black cloche hat on the back of her head, a two piece wool suit and a smile. The crowd smiled back. They applauded the President, but it was obvious they had eyes only for her."

In the morning, after the night spent in Texas, President Kennedy asked his henchman, Dave Powers, how the crowds looked. "Just about the same as they did the last time you were here," replied Powers with a grin, "only about a hundred thousand more have come to see Jackie!"

That day Mrs. Kennedy had spent five hours in a plane and four hours in motorcades; she had shaken hands with thousands,

PHOTO BY ELLIOTT ERWITT, COURTESY OF MAGNUM PHOTOS

November 25, 1963.

had been to a reception and had made a speech of just seventy-three words in Spanish to American citizens of Spanish heritage.

At ten o'clock the next morning after that terrible night, the family, half a dozen friends, and as many presidential aides and some members of the White House staff gathered in the White House for a private mass. A temporary altar and chairs were set up in the Family Dining Room. Those who had been invited stood stiff as statues, separately, eyes averted from each other, in the adjoining State Dining Room. The President's flag-draped coffin could be seen in the East Room, at the end of the long corridor. During the night William Walton and Nancy Tuckerman had arranged the swags of mourning crepe. The design was similar to that used at the funeral of Abraham Lincoln.

Suddenly, those in the State Dining Room were aware of Mrs. Kennedy's presence. A slim figure in stark black, she stood facing the coffin, holding her children by the hand. She turned and the three walked slowly along the red-carpeted hall toward those who were waiting. John, within a few days of being three, was asking his mother question after question in an insistent baby voice. Those gathered for the service could not bring themselves to look and stared down desperately at the complex design of the new Bessarabian rug.

Mrs. Kennedy glanced briefly into the Family Dining Room and walked away. Robert Kennedy returned and softly announced, "Mrs. Kennedy wishes the mass celebrated in the East Room." The altar and the rows of chairs were moved, and those waiting walked in misery through the three glowing State Rooms. There, near the coffin, they knelt on the hard oak floor. As the friends left Mrs. Kennedy stood in the hall and thanked each one for coming. She wore no makeup. Her pale features seemed luminous with a sustaining inner strength. It was this same hidden resource which carried her through the next days and gave her the power to thank personally each of the sixty-two heads-of-state who had come to President Kennedy's funeral.

On the final day of the two weeks Mrs. Kennedy was to remain in the White House, the United States Marine Band, in their cheerful red coats, were playing with unusual zeal to hide their sorrow. They were fiddling gaily because Caroline and John, whose birthdays had fallen in that terrible week, were being given a joint party. Their mother wanted them to leave the White House in gay remembrance.

Alone that final night, she sat up until four-thirty in the morning. On prayer cards bearing the likeness of President Kennedy, she wrote a personal note of thanks to every member of the White House staff.

Index